On Becoming a
Rock Musician

Legacy Editions

Legacy Editions

On Becoming a Rock Musician

H. Stith Bennett

Foreword by Howard S. Becker

Columbia University Press / New York

Columbia University Press
Publishers Since 1893
New York   Chichester, West Sussex
cup.columbia.edu

Copyright © 2017 Columbia University Press
All rights reserved

ISBN 978-0-231-18284-3 (cloth : alk. paper) |
ISBN 978-0-231-18285-0 (pbk. : alk. paper) |
ISBN 978-0-231-54440-5 (e-book)

Library of Congress Control Number: 2016956459

Columbia University Press books are printed on permanent
     and durable acid-free paper.
Printed in the United States of America

Cover design: Mary Ann Smith
Cover image: © New York City / Alamy Stock Photo

Contents

Part III. Mastering the Technological Component

Part IV. Performance: Aesthetics and the Technological Imperative

Foreword to the Legacy Edition

Howard S. Becker

Can a book published in 1980 still bring us news on the subject of contemporary pop music? Stith Bennett's pioneering study combines the skills and knowledge of a top-notch sociologist with the comparative and technologically informed perspective of an ethnomusicologist to do just that. For the most part, studies of pop music focus on the symbolic content of the words of recorded songs, the political and social attitudes those words convey, or the business arrangements that underlie the music and make the whole thing possible—they never get around to the notes the players play, the sounds they make, and how they make them.

Bennett, making just such matters central to his analysis, produces a startling, almost apocalyptic, conclusion: that the kind of pop music that began in the 1950s or 1960s, or whenever it began, inaugurated a distinctly new direction in Western music, and did so by bypassing the lengthy history of music stored, taught, and transmitted by written notation, replacing it with an aural "notation" derived from recorded studio music. This is a large claim, based surprisingly on the study of music made by a crowd of musically illiterate players. Is that how music history gets made?

Based on his long and intensive observation of a small population of such players in Colorado, Bennett makes a convincing argument that new ways of "reading" and "writing" music and, consequently, new ways of becoming and being a musician, came into being in the early 1970s (or thereabouts). In fact, he gives us a ringside seat at the birth of a new art world: new relations of interdependence clustered around new electronic technologies, new performance venues, and new systems of distribution, all of which totally changed what it meant to make and hear music. In so doing, Bennett shows interested readers how one can go about the study of any new social world.

Bennett learned by spending a lot of time associating with and participating in the activities of young local recruits to what he calls "The Music," the popular music on the air that kids everywhere were practicing in their parents' garages. He describes his two years of serious data gathering this way:

> My research technique was based on a willingness (and in most cases, ability) to present myself as a musician to other musicians who had indicated in some way that they were interested in form-ing a group.... I actively pursued some formation attempts and sev-eral times a performing group was the result. (xi)

He wrote extensive notes on all of it. Excerpts from his field notes show the depth of his involvement as a player and participant. His copious documentation displays the skilled observational techniques and interviewing tactics that produced his deep understanding of the path from inexperienced musician to working professional.

This relatively small book effortlessly and economically explains the small but revolutionary shift these boys (and his descriptions make clear that they *were* all boys) in garages were creating—not because they were inventive musical geniuses but because, given their lack of technical musical knowledge and skills, their methods were the only way they knew to reproduce the music they heard on the radio and records. They saved their money until they could buy one of the guitars (or basses, or drum sets) they lusted after in local music stores, and then taught themselves, the hard way, to play them— without a teacher or instruction book, without lessons or classes— by picking at the strings and playing along until they found a way to make one of the sounds they heard. After interminable hours of this, they could turn the three basic chords they had discovered—the backbone of the music they wanted to play—into a replica of the sounds on the records.

At that point, they found, one way or another, three or four others who had similarly acquired instruments and rudimentary knowledge of the variety of instruments they heard on the records they wanted to imitate. And then the new group taught themselves (just as they had initially individually learned to play their instruments) a song from one of the records that took the place of a written score they couldn't have read, spending days and weeks "getting the song" until they could approximate the original. And then it was on to the next song.

Mind you, this is the progression successful groups follow. Most can't manage to learn a whole set's worth of music before some inevitable difficulties arise. Complaining neighbors, internal conflicts, or sheer discouragement at how long it is all taking knock out most contenders.

Bennett follows the progression of the relatively few groups who first learn one song, and then enough to make up a complete "set." At that point they have enough repertoire to offer their services to potential employers: bar owners or groups of their age-mates looking for entertainment and music for their parties and ceremonial occasions.

For those who do find employment, the bar, dance venue, auditorium, or outdoor concert area presents new difficulties that require them to learn more new skills. The most important new challenges stem from the physics of sound, which Bennett explains elegantly and economically; and from the inevitable differences between live performance and music made in a technologically advanced studio by musicians who may not be in the same room and may not even be playing at the same time. In a studio, sound engineers individually "mix" this mélange of sounds, creating a complete track that no one, however skilled, can reproduce in live performance.

The newly formed band learns, if they want to get the jobs that will keep the band working and playing, to make approximations

that overcome not only the unavoidable physical difficulties of reproducing a recorded performance, but also the troubles added by the
socially created troubles of bar noise, dancers' inattention, and all the
rest of the clutter of ordinary life.

Bennett tells us, finally, how the most successful of these musicians learn to use and manipulate the new musical sounds that
electrified instruments make possible, the kind no one can produce
on an acoustic Spanish guitar or an acoustic bass, but that can be
made with an *electric* guitar or bass and its accompanying speakers,
amplifiers, and producers. Thus begins an exploration of the *recording consciousness*. When the groups Bennett started with in the first
chapters reach this stage, they have become musically and economically viable local musicians.

There's much more to Bennett's description and explanation,
whose outlines I've just quickly suggested. He includes, for example,
a comparative analysis of musical notation systems that is relevant
for twenty-first-century musicians. His analysis of group formation
and group integration into the larger commercial music landscape
suggests an area of inquiry that has yet to be fully explored by those
studying popular culture (except, of course, the ethnomusicologists,
whose work relatively few readers know). Bennett focuses on music,
music-making, and musician-making. In so doing, *On Becoming
a Rock Musician* lays out, explicitly and implicitly, a large research
agenda that remains less investigated than it ought to be. It's not too
late for other researchers in a variety of fields to follow the lead of this
prescient book.

Preface

This is a book about contemporary American popular music and the particular kind of musicianship that is appropriate to it. It is based on fieldwork that I did full-time for about two years (1970–72) in the state of Colorado and on about six years of sporadic fieldwork done in Illinois, Washington, California, Missouri, and southern France (Provence).

The bulk of the examples are taken from the period between 1970 and 1972. When I look at them now I occasionally notice that certain details appear dated. One example is the late popularity of cocaine as a drug of choice for musicians—something that was typically not encountered in Colorado before 1972. However, marijuana products have held their own with American popular musicians since their original (and legal) widespread use after World War I, and the same is true today. Such changes are interesting from a sociological perspective, but are not to be confused with my special interest in music. I have expended considerable energy over the last decade or so in various attempts at checking or ultimately disproving[1] my findings. I found that although cultural trappings change from time to time or from location to location the *musical* identities of "small-time" popular musicians as well as the kinds of resources that make those identities possible have remained the same.

My research technique was based on a willingness (and in most cases, ability) to present myself as a musician to other musicians who had indicated in some way that they were interested in forming a group. I answered ads in newspapers, responded to notices on bulletin boards, inquired at music stores, and used an ever widening circle of contacts for word-of-mouth information and introductions. I actively pursued some formation attempts and several times a performing group was the result. Sometimes I played the role of organizer but in most instances I presented myself as a "joiner." Sometimes I simply followed up on social contacts without attempting to get involved as a performer. I never hid the fact that I was involved in social research. On the other hand, I did not advertise the research aspect of what I was doing until an initial face-to-face meeting and playing session had transpired. Once I was accused of using the musicians with which I was performing as "guinea pigs." This came during an argument with the drummer in our more or less commercially successful group who correctly pointed out that I had "been through" five or six groups in as many months. My most typical experiences, however, were with musicians who did not understand or care about sociological fieldwork, but who were nevertheless willing to answer my endless questions. I often operated by showing (or reading) them notes or analytic statements and soliciting criticisms. I usually got what I asked for, and many of the words that follow represent the conscious collaboration of those whose activities are reported and studied in those same words.

The people I studied identified themselves as musicians and were recognized as musicians in their communities, yet it is safe to say that the names, faces, and performances of these people are not celebrated throughout the nation. Instead, they represent the phenomenon of the local group. A *local* group (1) plays to a regional market, (2) is self-producing, and (3) plays live performances. By a local market I mean a traditionally and demographically defined area of economic unity. For most urban areas this includes "the city" and "the suburbs," and in the case of Colorado it encompasses the concentrated population of the state, which forms a north-south strip just east of the Rocky Mountains. By self-producing I mean that production resources are wholly internal to the group, and not derived by contract with a production staff which is external to the group. Such resources include personnel, practice sites, transportation, instruments and equipment, gigs and commercially recorded music, and were found to be essential to group formation. By live performances I mean that services are defined by the group's appearance at an event where an audience is gathered, and not defined by the production of commercial recordings. According to the tone of most books about "the world of popular music," these musicians were not "making it." Which means, I suppose, that they were not under contract to large record companies—that they were not "stars." Engaged as they were in a regional market for their personal appearances, these local musicians caught my sociological eye precisely because their identities were not specialized and "successful." They allowed a look at how one begins to take on an identity as a cultural worker in situations where traditional training institutions are not at hand. And this leads to the recognition that this book is not so much an ethnography of American popular musicians (it is not complete enough to be that) as a focused study of how skills, ideas, and human identities manage to be created and transmitted in the context of industrialized culture.

My observations assume a relativistic approach to questions of cultural legitimacy. I assume that no cultural object or event is more legitimate than any other. On the other hand, it is of signal sociological importance that members of various collectivities feel compelled to rank cultural phenomena as to legitimacy (as in "*real* art") or, for that matter, to completely exclude certain creations from the ranking (as in "trash"). To me it is obvious that whether something is culturally legitimated or not depends *entirely* upon who is doing the assessing. In actual life, though, this is anything but obvious, and all manner of "natural aesthetic rules" and "objective canons of taste" are invoked to pass upon the legitimacy of things cultural. Within the implications of this line of thought are the keys to an understanding of cultural life that places it at the center of social organization and reaches far beyond conventional Western concerns with enrichment, aesthetic enjoyment, and art-for-art's-sake. But that will be saved for another book. Here the concern is with a kind of twentieth-century

American culture that has a history of being devalued and explained away in pejorative terms that rarely explain anything at all. Consider, for example, the empty negativity which it is possible to express with adjectives such as *popular, industrial, commercial, kitsch, mass,* or even *mickey-mouse.* This process of automatic devaluation is associated with most academic views of popular culture where descriptions taking the point of view of the producers and distributors tend to suppress the viewpoint of the recipients and participants. It is my intention to consider popular music and popular musicians as cultural manifestations which are as legitimate or, for that matter, as illegitimate as any other cultural form; and further to consider those who themselves participate in aspects of popular music to be legitimate commentators on the phenomenon. Since most things contaminated with popular culture end up being undermined in academic circles, my observations will be vulnerable to expert criticism for not distinguishing between "high" or "artistic" culture (Culture with a capital C) and the "lower" or "nonartistic" forms (such as rock music). If that is a fault, then the words which follow are certainly flawed in that way.

In addition, I assume that music is something that is created by the way in which people listen to sounds. This breaks with the prevailing definitions of music which assume that "musicality" is a quality of sound events themselves. To say that music is "organized sound" and that noise is "disorganized sound" belies certain habits of listening on the part of the perceiver rather than discernible features of vibrating objects. Most of us have been narrowly trained in our listening abilities, and as a consequence are able to approach only a small portion of our aural environment as music. The selectivity of sonic perception is a central aspect of the sociology of music. Members of elitist music cultures, for example, can easily become chauvinistic by finding performances from another music culture to be "noise" if they do not meet accepted standards of sonic organization. To say that music is the *score* or symbolic representation of a composition is also an unduly narrowed approach in at least the sense that unwritten music then goes unrecognized. To say that the general acoustic ambiance in a location is not music denies the possibility of considering the composed nature of sound environments.[2] Often so called background sound is rich with cues as to how to act, and clues as to the social and cultural makeup of one's surroundings. Furthermore, to say that sounds heard as unpleasant are not music denies the possibility that they may have been intentionally made by someone who considers them music. For example, the monotonous clatter of machinery *could* be music to the ears of an industrialist (who, we can safely assume, is not next to the machinery for eight hours each day), or the squeal of tires on the pavement outside the high school *could* be music to the ears of an attention-seeking adolescent. Instead of demoting objectionable sounds to the status of non-music it might bring more relief to find out who orchestrated them. In this matter I find that I agree with the description offered by John Cage: "Wherever we are, what we hear is mostly noise. When we ignore it, it disturbs us. When we listen to it, we find it fascinating. The sound of the truck at fifty miles per hour. Static between the stations. Rain. We want to capture and control these sounds to use them not as sound effects but as musical instruments."[3] To this description should be added the explicit case of recorded sound and, more generally, sound that arrives via electronic media. Perhaps at this very second someone is finding a playback device disturbing, perhaps because he or she has found it necessary to try to ignore it. On the other hand, there are people who are enmeshed in the sounds of paper cones which have been electrically excited. These people would find it disturbing *not* to hear electronic devices. Whatever the effects it has on people, recorded music is *encountered* in the same way that truck sounds and rain are encountered. Since both rain and radios are now distributed across the landscape, radios tend to be taken for granted as naturally occurring phenomena. This makes the producers of electronically mediated sound very influential people.

Another assumption I make is that labels for types of popular music represent sales categories for recordings to a far greater extent than they represent distinguishable music cultures or even styles within a single music culture. In this respect, my use of the term *rock* is intentionally imprecise. It certainly includes any usage of the term as a combining form: *country-rock, folk-rock, jazz-rock, progressive-rock,* and even *punk-rock*; and it overlaps a variety of other usages that might typify music, such as *middle-of-the-road, easy listening, old favorites, standards, party music,* and *bar music.* A precise definition is actually unattainable. Consider the parallel example of jazz. My best definition of jazz music is (1) simultaneous collective improvisation. To some people it means (2) *be-bop* and black musicians such as Charlie Parker. To others it could only be (3) the big bands of the 1930s and 1940s, composed primarily of white musicians. To still others it is (4) an "accepted" repertoire of compositions by John Coltrane, Charlie Parker, Thelonious Monk, Miles Davis, Duke Ellington, and A. C. Jobim (among many others) and includes pieces originally written for Broadway musicals. Lately it could mean (5) recorded performances and compositions by people as diverse as George Benson, Stevie Wonder, Grover Washington, John Klemmer, Chuck Mangione, and even Joni Mitchell. A variety of other definitions of *jazz* could be sketched out but it should be understood that the possibilities for confusion are enormous. Consider, for instance, that Herbie Hancock or The Jazz Crusaders (now—revealingly—simply The Crusaders) could belong to definition (4) or definition (5), depending on what recordings and performances were selected for attention. To those who heard him as the pianist with The Miles Davis Quintet, Herbie Hancock's more recent playing may not be heard as *jazz.* Similarly, The Crusaders' recent efforts might be called *rock* or *soul* music by someone who first heard them in the 1950s, but would be definitely referred to as jazz on the radio in the 1980s. Both *jazz* and *rock* tend to be applied to whatever the people from radio or television or newspapers or magazines want them to be associated with, and these usages change from month to month and year to year.

The truly important characteristic which underlies the categorization of popular music lies in the fact that music can be a money-making enterprise. Musicians who desire to make money from their playing allow currently popular labels to be placed on their playing.

And, of course, they tend to play what they think current audiences will want to hear. Often the same musician will operate under a wide range of music labels, and the studio musicians whose performances are attached to specific media music labels are often admired by other musicians for their ability to "play anything." All of this is included in the term *commercial*—which can clear up confusion when it is used without negative implications: commercial music is the music that makes musicians money. Commercial music could mean one style of playing for one audience, and a different style for a different audience, but it always centers on the audience attention which is currently being created through recordings and on radio and television. When I use the term *rock*, I am selecting the label I perceived to be most used in self-definitions by the musicians I studied. It is also the media category most appropriate to the commercial features of their performances. However, my continued fieldwork convinces me that the processes I describe here illustrate the initial steps in becoming a commercial musician of any description.

While on the topic of labels for music, notice that I follow a sensible ethnomusicological precedent by referring to "classical" music as *European* (or *Western European*) *art music*. *Classical* by itself is a vague term. Certainly there is "classical" Chinese music, and even "classics" in popular music. "Art" music (usually implying upper class sponsorship) comes a bit closer to precision, but still there are many kinds of art music. The most straightforward way of referring to music is to be specific, and what is known as "classical" music in everyday American language has been appropriated from the specific source of the European art tradition. In fact, this has been (and continues to be) the pattern in the industrialized countries of the world.

I should point out that some parts of what I have to say involve technical principles and technical language. I have tried both to simplify these descriptions and retain the popular language in which they are often encountered. The problem with this (and any kind of shop talk) is that it is endless. Details abound. In simplifying I have undoubtedly ignored the detailed truth which would take pages to explain. I suspect, then, that most musicians would want to elaborate on my explanations of how sounds are made and controlled. I have the same temptation. But the point of this book is sociological in substance, even where it makes use of technical evidence, and so I have purposely left the exacting detail out of my accounts. Finally, I should warn sensitive readers that vulgarities of everyday speech and some obviously sexist remarks have been retained in the examples as they were actually encountered.

A Guide for the Reader

European scholars laid the groundwork of theories that contemporary sociologists are still in the habit of citing, proving, disproving, debunking, resurrecting, and simply digging around in. Among the topics which were of interest to the "classical" social theorists was music. For example, Max Weber's unfinished and unpolished analysis of music and social life (*The Rational and Social Foundations of Music*, Weber 1958 [1918]) was written near the end of his life and discusses the historical and social significance of Western European art music as a manifestation of rationalized, "modern" social relationships. The theme of *rationalization* appears and reappears throughout works on music and popular culture, and if Weber had not supplied a language for its explication a new and very similar language would have to be invented. Georg Simmel, another "classical" sociologist who dealt at length with the sociology of music, anticipated the concerns of contemporary "interactionist" sociology. His *Psychological and Ethnological Studies on Music* (Simmel 1882, but see the translation in Etzkorn 1964a) raises many of the issues which are of interest in present-day investigations of music as part of his refutation of Charles Darwin's theory that music is a result of general organismic sexuality. For Simmel music is a more complex and more highly developed phenomenon than sex, and is implicated in the forms of interaction which have grown to be appropriate to collective life in particular parts of the world. The idea that social reality and musical reality are somehow interlocked, are isomorphic manifestations of one another, or are even identical appears frequently in historical, anthropological, sociological, and musicological writing. Simmel's early arguments for this position represent a theme that runs throughout modern German thought, and extends to contemporary American thinking on the subject.

Although known primarily as a cultural historian, rather than as a sociologist, Wilhelm Dilthey included music as an important aspect of his analysis of German culture, and promoted the theory that a nation's "character" becomes embedded in musical form (Dilthey 1933, or see Hodges 1944). It is interesting and ironic to note that the self-proclaimed intention of Richard Wagner—that his music embody the German national spirit—foreshadows Dilthey's later "scientific" theories. This same genre of musicological thinking also appears in other German works of the time (Buecher 1896, Bekker 1916), and in contemporary American scholarship (Finkelstein 1960 or Lawrence 1975, for example).

Most contemporary sociology of music takes its lead from yet another German, Theodor W. Adorno (see Adorno 1941, 1949, 1973). The central theme of Adorno's Marxist analysis of modern music concentrates on its increasingly commercial character as a *product*, which subordinates it to economic demands divorced from aesthetic considerations. But despite the admirable radical humanism which is displayed in the great bulk of his writings, Adorno's obvious attachment to upper-class art music and special disdain for African-based music erode the anticapitalist spirit of his biting and largely correct observations about "the music business." Even in the music section of the popularized introductory sociology talks for radio by the Frankfort Institute for Social Research (Horkeimer and Adorno 1972 [1956]) the discussion of jazz music remarkably parallels the tone of reactionary American right-wing treatments of African-based music (see Noebel 1966a and b). The reasonable approach for a reader, given Adorno's otherwise excellent insights into music, would be to "bracket" these rough spots in his work.

During the 1950s a small number of American sociologists published articles on music and musicians in scholarly journals. It is typical of these analyses to use musical life as an example of some other sociological interest, for example community studies (Merriam and Mack 1960) or deviance (Becker 1955). Of special interest was jazz, and it seems that music which was—and is—called "jazz" generated as much (if not more) criticism and turmoil than music which was—and is—called "rock" (see Kamin 1975). Social observers offered various illuminating accounts of this "new" musical phenomenon (Lastrucci 1941, Slotkin 1943, Becker 1955), while others focussed on the institution of the jam session as its socially unique feature (Cameron 1954, Lippincott 1958). Of course jazz attracted the attention of intellectuals of all stripes, and a prodigious amount of scholarly material exists to lend substance to its "intellectualization." For example, American jazz has had the distinct honor of being defined and elevated into intellectual discourse by a Frenchman (Hodeir 1956, 1962), just as America itself received the same treatment from Alexis de Tocqueville more than a century ago. (But see also Schueller 1968, Oliver 1970.) The reader should note that many kinds of music known as jazz maintain audiences and other direct forms of economic support by being identified with the intellectual classes (see Peterson 1972b).

Other topics connecting musical and social life have appeared. As the relationship between music and mass culture became obvious, popular song text analysis was instituted as a research technique (Horton 1957); for some it also seems to have been an excuse for professional moralizing (Hayakawa 1955). Early on, the profit-making character of popular music was recognized as sociologically significant (Meyerson, et al. 1953; Meyerson and Katz 1957), but this aspect of a quickly growing mass culture industry did not result in an integrated theoretical analysis for the American armchair researchers as it did for the more directly involved Germans. Some potentially valuable work dealt with the relationship of psychological variables to musical taste (Schuessler 1948, Cattel and Saunders 1954, Seeger 1957), but, again, this type of research did not flourish to the same degree in America as it did in Europe. Other sociological work gave evidence of both musical and social insight, but could not find even the minimal place in the conventional professional categories of thought that, say, a "jazz," or "mass culture" topic might muster (Mueller 1951, Kaplan 1955, Nash 1957, Wilhelm and Sjobert 1958, Schutz 1964). In retrospect, the 1950s do not represent a particularly vital period in the sociology of music, at least as far as American sociologists are concerned.

Working in the spirit of European social and musical research, K. Peter Etzkorn is a unique figure in recent American sociology of music. He has translated various important German works (Etzkorn 1964a, 1973b), brought developments in both West and East European sociomusical research (as well as little-known American research) to English readers (Etzkorn 1973b, including a large bibliographical section), and conducted original research on American popular song writers (Etzkorn 1963, 1966) and musicians (Etzkorn 1976). Most other social scientists who have made a specialty of music have lacked Etzkorn's basic musical competence and have, instead, focused on social and economic organization of American music industries. One of these is Serge Denisoff, whose early work on music and communism (Denisoff 1971) leads into historical and organizational analyses of the business of music (Denisoff 1972, 1973a and b, 1975). Richard Peterson has also contributed substantially to a sociological understanding of the American music business (Peterson 1971, 1972a, 1973) and it is not surprising that Peterson and Denisoff are the co-editors of a collection of articles on the sociology of music which represents their style of scholarship (Denisoff 1973b). One feature of this style is a reliance on the textual analysis of song lyrics whenever musical examples are discussed—an engaging and potentially creative method which is flawed only by its singularity. The lack of musical awareness in this style of work might lead one to believe that the only important aspect of popular music is its *poetry*, or that literary analysis is sufficient for the sociological analysis of music. Although they ignore sound-making, the historical and organizational research which is the essence of the Denisoff and Peterson style is carefully done and sensibly presented.

Two lesser-known but similarly oriented and competent researchers are Paul Hirsch and Peter Hesbacher. Hirsch's statistical-theoretical (i.e., "quantitative") approach to the organization of the American mass music industry is a cogent example of what an integrated theory of the American popular music business might look like (Hirsch, et al. 1969, 1970, and Hirsch 1971, 1972, 1973). To the extent that this work and some others of its genre (e.g., Basirico 1974, Peterson and DiMaggio 1975) use industry-supplied data there exists a methodological problem which is not unlike the problems involved in using officially supplied data for a sociological analysis of crime. Hesbacher's interests are more specifically oriented to the study of communication than of social life in general, but this has inevitably led to insightful studies of the nature of the business of American music (Hesbacher 1973, 1974, 1975). Fragments of sociological theories which could insightfully tie together work like that of Denisoff, Peterson, Hirsch, Hesbacher, and others interested in the social organization of mass culture are available (see McPhee 1966), but remain speculative "theories in progress" without a grounding in actual social life.

The idea that social and cultural structures are to be found in musical structures (and vice versa) is the basis for the few contemporary accounts of music and social life which have received an aura of authenticity from the established scientific community. Some fascinating comparative research which was sponsored by the American Academy for the Advancement of Science (Lomax 1968) used elaborate measurement techniques (*cantometrics, choreometrics, phonotactics*), complicated data displays, and statistical techniques to demonstrate that the folk songs of the world are "psycho-social indicators." The severity of people's sexual restrictions, for example, can be measured by the degree of tension which is found in singers' voices. By making similar assumptions *Tiv* songs have been analyzed (Keil 1979) to show that patterns of social organization and musical organization are *exactly* the same. A variety of less ambitious projects (e.g., Ridgeway 1973) also claim to demonstrate such results, yet their conclusions do not significantly expand upon Simmel's statements of one hundred years ago.

This way of thinking about music and social life is simply one manifestation of a more general and popular assumption—that art *reflects* society. As a metaphor much mileage can be wrung out of this viewpoint, and as an exercise in numerical coding and correlating (which is, after all, a metaphorical procedure) certain data patterns can be interpreted through it, but no causal explanations of how the sociocultural "mirror" does its reflecting have been advanced. Where, for example, can we expect to find unequivocal definitions of "musical structure" and "social structure"? And where do we find the tangible manifestations of these "structures" so that they may be empirically compared to one another? How, in short, are the apples of the world of sound phenomena to be shown to be identical to the oranges of the world of human interaction? Perhaps this *could* be shown. If the human condition would simply cooperate by requiring all human interaction to be played on an instrument or sung or danced, music could be thought to be *the same as* social life; or if melodic and rhythmic motives showed the same mathematical proportions as, say, income differentials in a stratification system, there might be some abstract logic to the statement that music and social life are "structured" in the *same* way. However, an actual testing procedure that makes direct comparisons between musical and social phenomena has yet to be put into operation. I think that until such a test shows otherwise it is safe to assume that organizing people and organizing sound are two different procedures. The sociology of music will begin to make more sense when the relationships between these two distinct phenomena are explored, and the simplistic claim that they are identical phenomena is dropped.

To the extent that there is a business of music there is a *law* of the music business. It may be the richest and most neglected source of social science research information on the music industry. It has undoubtedly been ignored because legal research is not a conventionally recognized method of social science scholarship, but also because it is time-consuming and often boring to do. A more or less authoritative treatise on the topic is available (Shemel and Krasilovsky 1977); yearly analyses and seminars are available (e.g., The Practicing Law Institute) in several areas of interest; a large volume of sample contract language can be most useful (e.g., Spiegel and Cooper 1972); and a quarterly journal might be consulted (e.g., *Performing Arts Review*); but the richest source of information would seem to be tracking down particular cases through the conventional case law publications.

Occasionally a historically oriented work will yield vital information about the state of music in contemporary life. One such work which is written from a fresh viewpoint is Murray Schafer's *The Tuning of the World* (Schafer 1977). Another is *The Music Merchants* (Goldin 1969) which documents the pattern of entrepreneurship in American music. A similar viewpoint is convincingly argued for Europe in *Music and the Middle Class* (Weber 1975). These works are well worth reading in conjunction with the works of Henry Raynor (e.g., Raynor 1976) or other more conventional histories of music. For the particular case of American music other sources of the historical and "popular" historical type illuminate specialized topics: Tin Pan Alley (Goldberg 1930, Ewen 1964), composers (Ewen 1966), matinee idols (Marks 1934), the musician's union (Leiter 1953), deejays (Passman 1971), payola (Karshner 1971), and record companies (Gillett 1974). Finally it should be noted that an understanding of contemporary music and musicians necessitates a familiarity with technological development, and a number of surprisingly detailed "media histories" are available (Read and Welch 1959, Gelatt 1966, Harris 1968, Barnauw 1966, 1968, 1970).

Sociological research which is not primarily oriented to the organizational aspects of American music continues to develop along the familiar lines of status and class analysis (Stebbins 1966, Bensman 1967, Aronowitz 1973), professionalism (Kadushin 1969, Kealy 1974), history (Lesure 1968, Braun 1969), and taste groups (Conyers 1963). Text analysis is still a viable method (see Carey 1969a and b), although it and other accepted approaches to the study of mass culture have received fundamental criticism (e.g., Denzin 1970). In fact, content analysis of lyrics has been extended to "country" music (Cohen 1970), and deserves even more sociological attention (see Freedman 1969) as the traditional pop-country "problem song" bears down on modernized rural American culture.

Another alternative to the strict organizational approach to the sociology of American music is the work of Robert R. Faulkner, which combines a methodology of participant observation with a theoretical orientation that is often associated with the sociology of occupations. This has resulted in a detailed study of Hollywood studio musicians (Faulkner 1971) and composers (Faulkner 1975) as well as symphony musicians (Faulkner 1974). In a less elaborate project Charles Keil has produced a similarly straightforward fieldwork account of blues musicians in Chicago (Keil 1966). The interesting aspect of this type of work is its ability to provide a sociological analysis of the economics of music—usually described in an abstracted and quantified way—in terms of human actors and their orientations. Charles Nanry's collection of articles (Nanry 1972) continues this approach through what might be called "update sociology," which places a sociological and historical frame around the last generations' jazz music and this generation's rock music. This is a scholarly version of a recurrent style in contemporary analyses of twentieth-century music, where the music and musicians in question, even if they are part of the present, are treated as historical entities.

The more commercial "instant histories" of the recent American music scene deal in some way with rock music, but are usually deficient in terms of accuracy and literacy. There are several exceptions to this. One is Charlie Gillett's *The Sound of the City* (Gillett 1970) which mixes knowledgeable historical research with sensible journalistic research on contemporary music. Another is Ian Whitcomb's *After the Ball* (Whitcomb 1972). The sheer number of "instant histories" available attests to the marketability of information (and misinformation—or even noninformation) about popular music, and points to the durability of a twentieth-century pattern which makes literary culture out of what was originally distributed as nonliterary culture. One way of recycling popular culture, then, is simply to *celebrate* its existence.

Another discipline of social and musical interest is ethnomusicology, which, ironically, is separated from academic musicology in the prevailing scheme of things musical at most colleges and universities. While a musicologist might continue to mine the treasures of the European tradition (largely *literary* research), an ethnomusicologist professes to study all the musics of the world on their own merit (which could easily include *unwritten* music), and to understand music as a culturally integrated phenomenon worthy of anthropological (as well as purely musical) attention. The intellectual roots of ethnomusicology are, not surprisingly, nourished from European (especially German) soil where the names of Erich von Hornbostel, George Herzog, Carl Stumpf, and Curt Sachs (all with technical support from A. J. Ellis) carry pioneer overtones. Through the lineage of Jaap Kunst (see Kunst 1960) an eclectic style of American ethnomusicology has developed (see Hood 1971), but there are other viewpoints (e.g., Merriam 1964, Nettl 1964). Even with this diversity of approach few ethnomusicologists collect sociologically relevant data, and therefore direct use of their analytic material for sociological purposes is limited. On the other hand their global and naturally comparative approaches to music are a necessary beginning for sociological music research, while their archival material in the form of field recordings and films is invaluable. Finally it should be noted that ethnomusicologists tend to act as facilitators of contact between musicians of different cultures—a situation which has already had an effect on new music, and has sown the seeds of an international "world music" culture.

One last area of intellectual support for the sociologist of music is academic philosophy, and its branch of interest in these matters is aesthetics. This is another intellectual arena with a large literature but it can be approached by reading a straightforward introduction (e.g., Dickie 1964) and a history (e.g., Beardsley 1966). Of special worth in this regard is John Dewey's *Art as Experience* (Dewey 1934), which can serve as an illuminating link between "classical" aesthetics and the aesthetic implications of modern perceptual philosophy. Phenomenology appears to be having some effect on contemporary sociology, although just what substantial changes will result remain to be seen. A familiarity with the works of Husserl, Merleau-Ponty, and other phenomenological writers might be a source of theoretical insight, and combining the experiential emphasis of phenomenology with the social and economic emphasis of critical (often Marxist) sociology might result in an integrated theory of the sociology of culture. The potential student of the sociology of music would do well to imagine an understanding of social life in which art and music and other cultural endeavors are considered as seriously as, say, income differentials. Such promising areas mark points where new researchers might start exploring.

Acknowledgments

At Lake Forest College I was encouraged in my sociological pursuits by Mihaly Csikzentmihalyi and inspired by Franz Schultz's vision of art.

At Northwestern University I was taught well by my dissertation chairman Howard S. Becker (who remains my most professional critic) and got much needed help from John Kitsuse and Remi Clignet, the other members of my committee. Sparks of support and insight also came from Bernard Beck, Scott Greer, and Paul Bohannon.

At the University of Washington the doors of ethnomusicology were opened to me by Robert Garfias, Frederick Lieberman and Philip Schuyler gave excellent and patient advice.

At the Center for World Music Robert Brown continued my ethnomusicological journey along with the numerous master musicians, dancers, and students from all parts of the world.

Long discussions with Edward Kealy have helped considerably and comments by John Hall, Rob Faulkner, Arthur Paris, and others have been the basis for the revision of several points.

Special thanks go to Arlan Lazere, who typed the first draft of the manuscript some years ago, and to Edie DeWeese who typed the second draft last year.

Thanks are also due to Richard Martin, editor of the University of Massachusetts Press, and to Deborah Murphy, Deborah Robson, and all the others who were involved in the final production of this book.

On Becoming a Rock Musician

Part I
Group Dynamics

1

Introduction

GROUPS AND GOOD MUSIC

Becoming a rock musician is not a process which is steeped in the history, theory, and pedagogy of prestigious academies; nor is it a learning experience which is guided by an informal tradition of teachers and teachings. Becoming a rock musician is not even a process of apprenticeship. In fact, rock music is *learned* to a much greater extent than it is ever *taught* by teachers. Where Western European art musicians are created through a formal academic (and by this time "classical") educational system, and jazz musicians can rely on either the art music process or an apprenticeship in an informal "school" of players, the potential rock musician meets no externally formulated educational institution and relies instead upon resources which are internal to local groups for the experiences of recruitment and learning. Although the spontaneous institution of the local rock band is the typical career route from non-musician to rock musician, it is not conceptualized as an *educational* form, but as an economically legitimated *musical* form. In a few words, the career of *becoming a rock musician* is simply *being* in a local rock group.

To a great extent this is what is meant by calling something *popular*. Popular things are widely distributed, things that anyone can come in contact with, things that are shared by entire communities, and things that require no prior training to appreciate. While elite musicians are required to train and pass tests, the status passage to *rock musician* is easy—anyone who can manage to play in a rock group can claim the identity. In this sense there are no students taking notes in the classrooms of rock, there are simply inexperienced groups. Likewise, nobody "flunks out" of rock music—a situation which is aided by the existence of a highly differentiated set of categories for *musician*. Rock musicians "bootstrap" themselves into existence, instantaneously invoking an identity which is perhaps only a claim, but a claim which has its own legitimating principle in the form of group and community *membership*. It is thought, perhaps not completely incorrectly, that social identity is the source of musical skill and creativity. In any event it should be understood that the learning processes which I delineate take place *after* a person has initiated a self-definition by becoming a member of a rock group.

It is striking, in an age in which much sociological knowledge has become common knowledge, to observe the degree to which initial attempts at group formation by would-be rock musicians ignore the prevailing cultural concerns with the interpersonal problems that groups of any kind are now known to create. This is not to say that such problems do not exist, but rather that the conscious focus of group interaction in this case is *sound*. And, for those who are just beginning, ideas about sound and ways of making particular sounds are absorbing problems. At first a pool of potential rock musicians is intermingled with a great many non-musicians, and there is no set of experiences upon which to draw for integrating the group in such a way that collective performance is possible. Instead, there are single musicians, musicians with non-musician friends, non-musician "managers" with and without musicians to manage, musicians in twos and threes, some the remnants of previously unsuccessful group formation attempts, most from the immediate region but also some who have moved from other parts of the country. The thread which holds together the interaction of this seemingly disintegrated, usually disenfranchised, and inexperienced pool of musicians is the exchange of ideas about listening to and playing music. The attempt to establish a specialized identity produces the integrative conversational phenomenon of *shop talk.* It is a consuming interest in elaborate exploratory conversations about how recorded sounds are made that separates beginning rock musicians from their non-musician cohorts—who appreciate listening to music but whose interest is not sustained by the endless ramifications of musical shop talk. Undoubtedly this process is contextualized by the continuing attempts of various media operators to promote sales of recordings and instruments by promoting talk about their latest product, but the specificity and detail of aspiring musician talk goes beyond the anticipations of businessmen. Sometimes it reveals confusion and ignorance, at others hyperbole and heightened expectations of musical success, and at others precise descriptions and demonstrations of musical possibilities. But always it is a revelation of ways to control sound.

This leads to a set of specialized questions: What kinds of sound control knowledge could beginning musicians possibly possess? Where could that knowledge come from? What are the connections between claiming specialized knowledge about sound and the ways in which performances are actually presented? Apparently the musical expertise which is created during the period of transition from *non-musician* to *rock performer* cannot be explained through conventional patterns of teaching and pedagogy. Although some enterprising schools of popular music have sprung up in large urban areas,[1] and some longstanding colleges and universities have admitted the study of popular music through "appreciation" and history courses, rock musicians typically combine the availability of instrumental lessons from a private instructor (usually at a music store) and some formal art music instruction (perhaps in high school or at a local college) with the more important resource of a group relationship as the source of skills. Without someone to show them how, rock musicians learn to make music together by talking about "getting a group together," by finding places to practice, by talking about instruments and equipment and acquiring what materials they consider necessary, by getting gigs, by gaining access to compositions and learning how to play them, and, most importantly, by ceaselessly assessing who and what "sounds good." The interaction which accompanies the grouping and regrouping of rock bands is itself the critical factor in producing the initial expertise of rock performers.

In this sense, the conduct of rock musicians, like any other form of human conduct, cannot be understood unless some general features of human group life are recognized and respected. Perhaps the most crucial feature of any group is that the definitions and interpretations which comprise its collective knowledge are impelled by and shaped through interactional events. Acts and objects are not endowed with intrinsic meanings; they are, instead, only as meaningful as groups care to make them. The situations in which their music is created and performed and the meanings which come to be attached to the innumerable immediate events of their musical endeavors are, then, the fundamental elements of knowledge that rock musicians share with one another. In the phraseology of W. I. Thomas, rock musicians negotiate a collective "definition of the situation"[2] in that the things they *treat as real* are therefore made "real in their consequences."[3] This includes not only interactional events, but "things" such as electronic equipment, ways of transporting personnel and equipment, practice sites, and places to play for money. And it also invests with a special group reality a class of "things" which are usually thought to be exclusively musical in their genesis: notational systems, instruments, and techniques of practice and performance. While these are, indeed, of immense musical importance, they also fall well within the sociological domain, since they comprise the primary interactional form among rock musicians. In contrast to academic music worlds, these objectively real components of the rock music world are subject to renegotiation by all participants at all times. A respect for the intricate and subtle process which makes musical matters real for aspiring rock groups recognizes the existence of an even more complex musical phenomenon: There is more than one way to listen to sounds and, therefore, more than one way to hear them. In actuality, numerous socially produced ways of listening—musical aesthetics—coexist, and even compete as approaches to the perception of any particular musical performance.

This idea combines traditional sociological concerns with *human* definitions and a new sociological concern with *musical* definitions. It admits the existence of interactionally created aural aesthetics and recognizes that collectivities act as the influences which shape individuals' styles of sonic attention.

Aesthetic is not a term which is usually associated with popular music, since its most familiar association is with evaluations of "the fine arts" or with philosophical principles dealing with "the beautiful."[4] Given this shade of meaning, *aesthetic* means "good"—but "good" in the special sense of "formally correct" or "proper." The term has a more generic meaning, however, and, in that sense, is appropriate to the discussion of any type of music, including popular music. This is the sense in which the social appropriateness of music—its "fit" with its audience—is the standard of its "goodness." In this area sociological insight can provide a corrective to the kinds of cultural understanding (or misunderstanding) which may prevail at any given historical period: The distinction can always be made between an audience's collective assimilation of a "good" performance (the listeners' aesthetic) and the musicians' collective creation of a "good" performance (the musicians' aesthetic). This dynamic, which in its general form is important in all professions, is certainly operating with respect to musical "standards" and points to the existence, sequencing, and shaping of social change.

Musicians' aesthetics can often endure social change; listeners' aesthetics rarely do. For example, the Western European art music tradition supplies its contemporary personnel with the information and skills necessary to perform a huge number of compositions in a variety of styles, yet only a very few of these can be successfully presented to a general audience. However enduring musicians' aesthetics may be, non-musicians cannot always share them, for, with social change—the disintegration and reintegration of social groups and social identities—comes the reinterpretation and redefinition of innumerable existing objects, among which are the audiences' rules for "what sounds good." The possibilities for a lack of "fit" between musician and non-musician aesthetics are more common than established academic musicians care to recognize, even though experienced performers in all genres are resigned to playing for audiences in which only a minority is actually following their artistic intentions—or those of the composer. The majority of the typical contemporary audience is present for reasons other than the activation of careful musical attention, yet this alienated presence in the audience is rarely recognized in polite conversation. Even upon such recognition, it is important to note that, in contrast to the perennial possibilities for feuding among artists, the relationship between musicians and non-musicians is seldom antagonistic. Rather, when the compositions of a music culture become so differentiated from their human origins that they are no longer associated with a living aesthetic, the "goodness" of new materials—a new way of listening—is invited by musicians and non-musicians alike.

Those who perceive the weakening of ties between musicians and their audiences have the opportunity to make an enterprise out of their perceptions by attempting to define new audiences or new music or both. To the extent that there are new found ways of fitting audiences, compositions, and performances together, there is evidence for the existence of *cultural entrepreneurs* who sense the historical circumstances of potential audiences and convert them into markets for specific musical products.[5] The case of rock music, like popular music in general, exhibits one of the most recent entrepreneurial efforts at perpetrating a fit between musical performances and the life conditions of contemporary audiences. Significantly, it incorporates comparatively recent technical possibilities for making and distributing sound events in ways that the established music cultures do not utilize. Throughout the history of music new audience attention has been facilitated by technical innovation in sound-making (like putting metal strings on violins), in composing (like the mensural notation system), and in distribution (like the printing press). Music traditions *could* have survived—that is, new musicians could have been trained to perform—without technical innovation. But the vitality of the fit between musicians and the living, breathing people who might come to hear their music has always been negotiated in the company of technical changes. How the latest manifestations of audience enthusiasm have been managed—how a fit could possibly be negotiated between hundreds of thousands of musicians and many millions of listeners—is, therefore, intertwined with an analysis of sound control techniques and the enterprising people that make use of them.

The concept of greatest importance to this kind of analysis is the idea of a socially negotiated musical reality system. Howard Becker (among many others) has used the idea of *convention* to refer to the socially constructed aspects of any art form.

> People who cooperate to produce a work usually do not decide things afresh. Instead, they rely on earlier agreements now become customary, agreements that have become part of the conventional way of doing things in that art.
>
> Conventions place strong constraints on the artist. They are particularly constraining because they do not exist in isolation, but come in complexly interdependent systems, so that making one small change may require a variety of other changes. A system of conventions gets embodied in equipment, materials, training, available facilities and sites, systems of notation and the like, all of which must be changed if any one component is.[6]

Stressing the interdependence of conventions, I have decided to clarify my use of the term *aesthetic* by letting it describe *sets* of conventionally created ways of making sense that exist for any artistic endeavor. Since an aesthetic is a collective invention it is subject to change, but since it is derived from technical possibilities and agreements as to the use of those possibilities, it attains a distinguishable coherence over time. It is not by accident that I have chosen a word which sometimes means "goodness" to describe patterns of technical practice. I hope to be able to show the various forces which make *good* rock music *conventional* rock music. It is also no accident that I have chosen to conceptualize *multiple* aesthetics—as many systems for integrating conventions as there are roles for controlling

artistic resources. This idea breaks with much of the existing literature, which is based on the idea of convention in the arts in that it
is not exclusively focussed on artists and artists' agreements. In this
way more than one aesthetic of rock music can be conceptualized,
as different economic and cultural interests in that music are discovered. In the same sense that people who share a social identity are
said to share a particular viewpoint, people with identical musical
interests can be understood to share a particular "hear-point." In
this way I hope to be able to describe the *live performance aesthetic*
of rock groups as they develop and show how that way of listening
is both linked to and distinguishable from the aesthetics invoked by
audiences, employers, and especially the producers of recorded rock
performances.

By now it should be obvious that my view of the sociology of art
places what is beautiful in a negotiated reality system, and that in a
social universe of multiple realities there can be multiple versions of
beauty. As a sociological concept the general category of aesthetics
becomes a gigantic set of role-specific experiences of the good which
are inherent in a somewhat less gigantic set of separate art realities.
The film-maker's aesthetic, for example, is necessarily different from
the theater director's aesthetic since the materials which each uses
to produce the experience of a film or a play are part of a uniquely
constructed reality system, and therefore what is "good" on film
may be "horrible" on stage. It is only the socially derived specification of what experiences are "good" and what experiences are "not
good" that allows an artistic endeavor an identity, and it is obvious that there are a multitude of such identities. It is quite correct
to infer, then, that aesthetics have the opportunity of colliding with
one another, and that not simply the use of this or that convention,
but the invocation of entire schemes of conventionality are subject
to negotiation while only one "work" is being created. This makes
the problem of a sociology of art as complicated as the number of
experiences which are defined as "good" by the number of parties
who have an interest in the production of that art. Only the finding
that aesthetics are shared ways of making sense saves the sociology of

art from the doom of overwhelming complexity. Accounts of *what* is good and *how* it is good recur in different reality systems. The strictly logical idea of an aesthetic as an individual's category is unworkable, and the generally understood philosophic category is invisible in any specific social setting, yet the interactional negotiation of aesthetics is an observable sociological phenomenon among artists. It is in the spontaneous specification of the experience of beauty that the sociology of art finds its data, and it is in the comparative case that those specifications find a unity which is neither psychological nor philosophical, but uniquely social.

What is good for the local rock group's performance would not be determinable if each group did not go through the process of that determination as it comes into existence. It does happen, however, that musicians talk about what they are doing while they are doing it, asking and answering questions among themselves about "the way things sound." For each group there is a unique way of talking about the sounds they can make together which has been developed from the aural experiences they have, in fact, performed, and is therefore a universe of discourse which represents the experience of the aesthetic. What sounds good—what is beautiful—is initially an experience which the group shares without sharing a descriptive vocabulary, and it is only the attempt to account for the "goodness" of certain performances which brings about the group's musical knowledge. This way of establishing a musical aesthetic certainly has no primacy. The rules of "good" sound can be learned as a vocabulary to be matched to sounds which the learner has not himself made, and the music will still sound "good" or "bad." The primacy of a shared experience is only a performer's way of establishing a *performance* aesthetic, for it is only the performer who actualizes and assesses the same sounds; therefore, it is only for the performer that an aesthetic need be related to a set of actions. The point is that a performance aesthetic must necessarily involve a set of movements—the coordination of mind and musculature— which are not a part of a *listening* aesthetic (the interactional situation which defines an audience).

An aesthetic emerges as the group's shared specifications of the musical experiences which have been communally determined as "good," and the performance of those experiences for others is an assumption that the group knows what is "good." It is the professional expertise of the group that it assumes correctly, and it is the sociological insight that a performance aesthetic presumes a knowledge of the audience's expectations. In short, the local rock group's way of performing has been internally negotiated by accounting for good musical experiences which have occurred in the presence of an audience.

All of this seems to show that the socially constructed nature of an aesthetic of performance is an enigma—founded on a conceptualization of the audience's position, yet never actually negotiated with it, and constructed as a specification of the beauty of an experience which did not need that specification to exist originally. The disentanglement of these complications is to be found in the link between resources and aesthetics. If the musicians and the audience can share a definition of the performance as "good," even if their formulations of its "goodness" are separate entities, it may be because the means of production (i.e., the resources) of the performance are assumed by both parties to be identical. Similarly, the specification of an originally unspecified performance as "good" may only be motivated by the group's attempt to repeatedly perform for many audiences the experience which "worked" with one audience, so that a mutual aesthetic is not necessarily shared at all—even when the audience's response to the original performance has provided standards for future performances. The aesthetic of performance may remain within the arcane knowledge of the musician as a bundle of movements and still provide the audience with an aural reception system (the basis of a listening aesthetic), since the musicians' aesthetic of, say, "free-flowing moves" is created from a set of resources (like compositions and instruments) which can be assimilated by the audience in a much more general and passive manner. Therefore, it is possible for the audience and the musicians to hear the same rock event in different ways. This is neither a dogmatic nor an enigmatic assertion, but an indication that the audience/musician interaction need not be founded on a shared aesthetic as long as there is a shared definition of the resources which the musicians use to produce the music.

To account for any musical form is to account for the knowledge that its specialists must have in order to perform it. As with any artistic endeavor, this knowledge includes an extensive methodology for assessing, procuring, and manipulating the events, meanings, and things (i.e., resources) with which the artist has to deal. Questions of essential importance for the sociological exploration of music seek connections between instrument design, construction techniques, modifications, methods of acquisition, playing techniques, and the like, along with the form of the musical ideas which emerge from an interplay of these various factors. We know, for example, that the gut-string violin is associated with different music than the metal-string violin. Similar questions promote accounts of relationships between other resources and other musical forms. It is important to know, for example, the physical and social characteristics of the performance situation, the means by which personnel are recruited and trained, and the contractual relationship between musicians and their audiences—including the role of the ever-present musical entrepreneur. Of utmost sociological import is a system of notation by which purely experiential sonic phenomena are categorized (i.e., noted) for musician/musician communication. Relationships between such paradigmatic formulations of sound and the actual aural environment which excites eardrums exemplify the incisive social dynamic of music—the nature of the commitment between musicians and audiences in performance. The questions which arise from this are: What are the conditions which the musical event draws upon for its success? And, on the other hand, what are the conditions of an unsuccessful musical event?

The wealth of information that may be collected about what I have termed resources is of little interest in and of itself. Ultimately, one must account for *changes* in the interpretation, definition, and manipulation of resources in order to render a sociological account of changes in music or the emergence of new kinds of music. In other words, insights into the construction of musical realities require sequential analyses of resource modifications on the one hand, and of music modifications on the other.

Resources are the artifacts that make the enterprise of rock music possible—the physically and culturally constructed *objects* which define a rock event. In a Marxist vocabulary resources would be considered "means of production." In the words of Georg Simmel: "The motive (of 'pure sociology') derives from two propositions. One is that in any human society one can distinguish between its content and its form. The other is that society itself, in general, refers to the interaction among individuals."[7] From this viewpoint, and in a parallel vocabulary, resources are the *content of* social phenomena; they are "the *material*, as it were, of sociation."[8] In contrast, aesthetics are the ideas that make one's engagement with rock music possible—the subjective realities which allow multiple, selective, sometimes conflicting, and sometimes mutually exclusive perceptual systemizations of the same basic materials. From Simmel's viewpoint, aesthetics would be the *forms* of social phenomena: ". . . (realized in innumerable, different ways) in which individuals grow together into units that satisfy their interests."[9] Forms, then, are abstract patterns in the tangible content through which ideas are actually presented to others. For performances, the content of the musician/listener interaction is ultimately manifested in an elusive artifact—intense compressions and rarefactions in air—while the form of that interaction is the temporal patterning which is selectively perceived by ears and minds: a *re*-cognition of the pattern which the musician has placed in the air by making moves in a musical way.

Of course these analytic distinctions are of little use while rock music is actually being played. A group performance involves a state of merged awareness where dualistic (i.e., analytic) distinctions are collapsed into a monistic, momentous category: the *vivid present*. It is an episode of coherent coordination of mind and musculature, individual and instrument, form and content, and, in the present terminology, aesthetic and resource—an interactional resonance which goes beyond analytic distinctions. In Simmel's words: "This complete turnover, from the determination of the forms by the materials of life to the determination of its materials by forms that have become supreme values, is perhaps most extensively at work in the numerous phenomena that we lump together under the category of *play*."[10] Although I am presenting them in terms of *aesthetics* and *resources*, live rock events are actually a synthesis of the two into a third phenomenon: the *play* state of awareness (which in this case is brought to collective attention by music). Often analysts of cultural endeavors get so involved in understanding the conditions which make something possible that they fail to understand the *experience* of the thing itself. From my point of view there would be no need to perceive things as good (the realm of aesthetics) or to figure out ways to make good things (the realm of resources) if the experience of goodness itself—as an end-in-itself, or an *autotelic* activity—did not come to pass. The "goal" of cultural work is not simply to shape perceptions and environments but to share experiences of "the good" which are intrinsically rewarding and therefore break with patterns of "goal-oriented" activity. In this sense when suitable material environments are combined with developed cognitive and perceptual skills *play* becomes possible. To the extent that it is actualized, then, play transcends both mentality and physicality by combining them into movement. It is not simply a single move, but a series of moves that unfolds. The graphic representation in figure 1 may help in explaining this. When a large number of options are made available to someone who has only a small number of skills (or possible actions), a state of anxiety ensues. One way to reduce that anxiety would be to reduce one's field of awareness to match one's field of ability. Another might be to increase skills until they matched one's complex perceptions. When a large number of actions have been made possible in someone who has only a small number of options upon which to act, he or she quickly runs out of things to do and boredom ensues. One way to reduce that boredom would be to reduce one's possible moves and become, in effect, less skilled. Another might be to increase one's options. Most play is not a "straight line" activity, but involves weaving in and out of situations that threaten to promote anxiety

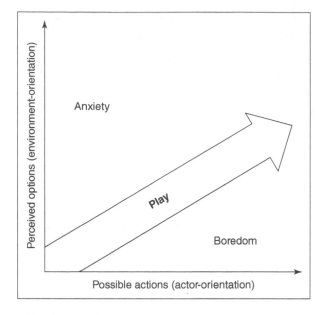

Figure 1 The play state of awareness.

or boredom. Those who cannot recover from immanent anxiety or boredom risk putting an end to the play episode's continuous time consciousness and reverting to a divided (or discontinuous) form of attention to life. Thus, to "keep on going" is playful, and it defines a special kind of attention; a flexible attention that might very well overwhelm initially overwhelming environmental conditions. This is the aspect that Simmel (in the passage I quoted above) seems to have noticed about the development of play: Values can eventually determine materials; although in the beginning it is always the other way around. Most materialist explanations of culture and aesthetics fail to recognize such a "turnover." On the other hand most normative explanations of culture fail to respect the concrete world which is the basis of norms or symbols or ideas. I have introduced the concept of play as a way of overcoming the narrowness of thought which tends to pervade these contemporary interpretations of culture and art. I see play at work where aesthetics and resources (in Simmel's terms: values and materials) have an approximately equal chance at determining one another. An autotelic state of consciousness is the feature of life which makes this possible: It places *subjective* human experiences at the center of *objective* cultural processes.[11] Even the case of local rock musicians displays this kind of development; as beginners, musicians' aesthetics are determined by certain environmentally provided resources, and then, as musical skills are attained, aesthetics determine new resource choices—or even create completely new resources.

2

Group Definition and Redefinition

SOMEONE TO PLAY WITH

Since there is no established institutional form to recruit, educate, and certify a rock musician's identity, the spontaneous institution of the local musical group provides these same anchors between individual aspirations and collective recognition. When he or she is not playing with a group the "musician" has only the remembrance of past groups to support a musical identity, and if the period of "not playing" is extensive—if there is no interactional reinvocation of that identity— a self-presentation as "rock musician" is practically impossible to maintain. This situational boundedness of the musician's career is the source of continual identity crises, since the phenomenon of rock music appears in quanta of spontaneous associations. The grouping and regrouping of rock musicians in a particular locality entails an alternating integration and disintegration of an individual's actual music career (the practice and performance of the group) and places a measure of insecurity at the foundation of one's musical self-image.

It is significant that the pool of people from which any rock group recruits its personnel can only tentatively be called rock musicians, since it is the absence of the situation of group membership that defines the category *personnel*. An exception might be said to exist in the case where someone is "stolen" from an existing group, but even in that situation a renouncement of membership in one group must precede membership in the next. It is the curious condition of rock group formation that human resources are drawn from a personnel pool consisting of individuals whose musician identity is more or less disintegrated. This is not just a semantic problem. Those who are called upon to staff a rock band are also those who are in the least advantageous position to play well since they may be out of practice, disoriented by strange surroundings, uneasy in the presence of new musicians, and unable to rely upon a familiar repertoire.

By considering the situation of being out of a group the uniqueness of being in a group is brought into focus. Each group's manner of operation—even much of the language used in coordinating activities—is constructed from the unique interactional history of its membership, and that knowledge is not necessarily transferable to another set of people who call themselves a rock band. Even if the world of rock music is virtually unstandardized—even if there is no universally recognized "core knowledge"—musicians do manage to move from group to group. This is possible because the formation of any rock enterprise is the initiation of a new and unique way of knowing how to make music together. That way of knowing is based on the amalgamated resources of its individual members, and that is why the category of personnel is critical. The group can make music together only if the "right" musicians are found, yet the criteria which define personnel needs are the spontaneous assessments derived from interaction with the pool of "available." At least in regard to processes of recruitment, local rock musicians and couples have similar fortunes: There is a lot of waiting and frustration; although some relationships are idyllic, the majority break up, and it is universally easier the second time around. The apparently static category of personnel is actually the dynamic situation of a search for someone to play with.

All of this recognizes that rock musicians are made, not born; that they have careers. Yet it also shows that the way in which rock musicians are made does not correspond to the traditional institutional careers which are typical of other kinds of musicians. Rock music is exemplified by the processes of *self-recruitment* and *learning without pedagogy* which are not possibilities in other forms of music in

America. What exists for a person who is trying to move out of the general population and into the population of rock musicians is an amorphous amalgam of knowledge about instruments and equipment, recordings of rock performances, experiences of live rock performances, and a group of like-minded contemporaries. What does *not* exist for such a person is a pedagogically routinized musical discipline. This state of affairs tends to bring about either floundering confusion or uninhibited innovation—or the inability to differentiate the two.

INSTRUMENT ACQUISITION

An individual's rock career begins with gaining access to an instrument. Both public and private schools are equipped with band instruments to be loaned to children at the first stages of their musical training, and this would, at first inspection, seem to be a logical means of access to an instrument for any young musician. The school pool of instruments, however, is geared for a style of music that largely excludes rock music. Even progressive school music programs intended to take the conventional "stuffiness" out of a beginner's educational experiences are not yet ready to be subjected to public scrutiny for promoting popular music. Guitars, for example, are typically provided by these innovative programs (at long last recognizing the immense popularity of the instrument), but they are acoustic instruments which cannot be converted to use in a rock band. Although an occasional saxophone, trumpet, flute, or trombone of school origin may show up in a local group, the essential instrumentation is not to be found so easily. Very early in his or her career an aspiring rock star is faced with the task of coming into the possession of a *rock* instrument, and in the situation of being young and hence more or less disenfranchised, the alternatives are to "beg, borrow, or steal" for an instrument. Surely all these methods have been used. However, the most common account of how one obtains an instrument seems to be direct parental funding.

HSB: How did you get your first instrument?

M: I guess there were two or three things going on. For one thing I had been listening to the radio, you know, and hearing all those old guitar instrumentals . . . like maybe the Ventures or even the Fireballs . . . and then my sister knew this guy that played in a band, and she was older and cooler, you know what I mean? . . . and I just got hung-up about playing electric guitar, and I would go down to the music store and just look and look, and get catalogs and take 'em home and read 'em over and over. I guess I just nagged my parents so much that they gave in and bought me a guitar for my birthday.

HSB: How old were you?

M: Fourteen.

HSB: Was it a good guitar?

M: I guess. It was a Melody-Maker. [*Guitar player*]

At the very first step in the rock musician's career the aspiring musician becomes aware of the subtle economic boundaries of the new endeavor. One cannot learn to play, practice with a group, or make money by playing until an instrument has been procured. On the other hand, the position of being a full-time student limits the economic resources which are available. This is an elementary case of the musician's universal economic dilemma, which, stated in very general terms, is that "if you are devoting your time to music, you are not devoting your time to other sources of income." In short, the chances of entrance into the rock musician identity are determined by the chances of access to equipment and instruments, and those chances are practically nil without sponsorship of some kind.

HSB: How did you get hold of your instrument?

D: Oh sure, my daddy bought me my drums [*sarcastic tone*]. I sold out, and you would too. I've still got two years of high school left, and I couldn't earn the money to buy that set working part-time for *four* years . . . besides I need that time to learn how to play. [*Drummer at his fourth gig*]

It is apparent that, for the most part, families are funding the entrance of their offspring into rock music. The complexities of the relationship between American families and popular music are a topic unto themselves, and all I can hope to show here is the style of economic sponsorship, leaving a psychological analysis of vicarious parental participation in group careers (a true form of the groupie urge) for another time and place. Family funding is an understandable phenomenon when it is recognized that the age of first-instrument acquisition is the age of the living-at-home situation (before age eighteen), and in this light the issue has a precedent in existing styles of allocating resources for "legitimate" instruments (e.g., piano, violin) and accompanying lessons. It is enlightening to see how easily the "classical" music career has crumbled as a parental expectation of success for the offspring, leaving open the argument that a family's rewards from investing in a piano, lessons, and a new dress for the recital were more along the lines of Veblen's conspicuous consumption than pure music appreciation.[12] The cost of investment in a "classical" or "rock" career is, however, roughly equivalent: A spinet piano is economically comparable to a good electric guitar and amplifier. Actually, the rock career with *no lessons* probably represents a discount from the traditional family commitment which typically included outlays for years of private instruction.

The investment in "real estate" which even a fledgling rock band finds necessary is considerable. Figure 2 gives some estimated prices for various categories of instruments and equipment. It can be seen that a four-piece group (guitar, bass, keyboard, drums, and sound system) would be hard to outfit for less than $5,000, and could easily represent a $10,000 investment. Just at this level of analysis it becomes obvious that most American families cannot afford to buy their children into rock music (although that does not stop them from trying). There is a consequent threshold effect on the supply of rock musicians due to family income, and, at least in terms of the tangible reality of the musical enterprise, the rights of access to the performance of live rock music are middle-class rights.

Type of instrument	Average price of used instrument (when available)	Average price of quality instrument	Maximum price of quality instrument
Drum kit with cymbals	$500–1000	$1500–2000	$3000*
Electric guitar with case	200–400	600–800	1500*
Electric bass with case	250–300	500–600	1200*
Keyboard instrument or synthesizer	750–1000	2500–7500	10,000*
Guitar, bass, or keyboard amplifier	300–500	600–1000	2000*
Effects devices	–	100–200	1000*
Sound system with microphones	1000–2000	3000–5000	20,000*

*Indicates the existence of custom-made instruments and equipment

Figure 2 Estimated prices of rock instruments and equipment.

If the aspiring musician was not born into a family with an economic surplus (or if he does not have a family), his or her entrance into the world of rock music is hampered considerably. Theft of instruments and equipment is a recurrent phenomenon, and although it may initially represent a way for anyone (musician or non-musician) to get money, the market for "hot" musical instruments represents the existence of musicians' needs that are not being met by legitimate means. The difference between the legal retail price of an instrument and its black market price represents a sponsorship in the same sense as family investment: In both cases, the musician does not completely provide his or her own initial economic resources. There are cases, of course, where instruments are purchased from job earnings, but these cases are special in nature when the principle of the "musicians' economic dilemma" is applied. To make enough money for an investment of the order of magnitude shown in figure 2, the student-youth would have to work, for example, a full-time (no music) summer job for adult wages, i.e., a "good," or "middle-class," job. Although it is possible for a young musician to provide his or her own initial investment in instruments and equipment, American economic systems make it an enterprise of relative hardship. The lack of family sponsorship, the unavailability of employment, or the unwillingness to participate in illegal activities leaves only the possibility of a more general sponsorship from some non-family source. For experienced musicians this can often be brought about by a contractual arrangement with a manager, agent, producer, or some other entrepreneur of music. For the beginner, however, such options are not available, and if there are no resources from one's legal guardians, an unrelated sponsor's benevolence might resemble the family relationship.

HSB: Where'd all this equipment come from?
T: The organ and the Leslies and the RMI and the Kustom Amp all came from Dr. ———. You know Bobby? . . . Well, that's his old man. He's bought most of the equipment I've ever played with.
HSB: Does he just give it away?
T: Oh no, you have to pay him back when you can . . . if you're not his son.
HSB: You mean that anybody can get instruments from him?
T: Well, no. I guess not anybody. But most of the bands in the ——— area have gotten equipment from him. He likes music . . . all his kids have played in bands. [*Guitar player*]

THE IMPETUS TOWARD GROUP FORMATION

At some point after the aspirant has come into the possession of an instrument there is the recognition that it is not a solo instrument. There were few means of conceptualizing this situation previously. The original desire for an instrument was based on a relationship with the world of commercial music and musicians, and simply *having* an instrument seemed to be a way to participate in that world.

HSB: What did you do with your guitar after you got it?

D: What do you think? ... I played it, or at least I tried to play it.

HSB: By yourself?

D: Yeah, at first. I would sit around for hours listening to records and trying to play along. Then I got smart and got this book that had pictures of chords. I could play "Mary Had a Little Lamb" real good ... but I still couldn't play along with the record.

HSB: Then what happened?

D: Then I met this guy at school ... he used to come over in the afternoons and on the weekends and we would try to play together. He wasn't too hot either, but I learned a lot from him. We figured out a few songs from the record ... like that Sly song—"Got to Take You Higher." Those were the first times I ever got off playing music. ...

HSB: And the first time you had ever played with somebody else. ...

D: Yeah, that's true, and after that was when I started looking for a group to play with. It was past the point where it was just a thing to do; I just *had* to play. [*Guitar player*]

The design of rock instruments and equipment points to a group music-making enterprise. It would be hard to argue that the various electric instruments and amplifiers or even the highly refined set of percussion instruments known as *drums* are designed for home use. It is, rather, the assault of a high school gymnasium, church basement coffee house, teen club, bar, or country club party which is the aim of anyone who has played with such instruments long enough to understand their possibilities.

The instrument owner's problem at this point is unique. The physical equipment for making rock music is at hand, but other musicians are not. Having an instrument represents passing an economic barrier, while having musicians to play with represents passing a more complex *social* barrier. Although it is true that no musical institution exists to guide the first rock group, there is no way that it can come about without some kind of institutional context. The aspiring band member finds it necessary to use his or her existing participation in a non-musical grouping to establish a connection with other musicians, and although this could be a church, camp, or club of some kind, the most typical example is the secondary school system which (even with the advent of bussing) draws its students from relatively definable geographic areas, and therefore is practically synonymous with the idea of a neighborhood or "part of town." The attempt at organizing a first group immediately develops a concept of *personnel* for the young rock musician. Experiences with school and neighborhood contemporaries allow a sorting-out process (by virtue of instrument ownership) during which a pool of potential group members is defined.

HSB: How did you meet the guys who were in your first group?

E: We were all friends before there was a group. Maybe not close friends, but we all went to the same school, and Jim and Wayne lived really close to me . . . I can remember playing with them when we were kids . . . oh yeah, and my parents and Jim's parents played bridge every once in a while.

HSB: How did you get the idea to have a group?

E: It just sort of evolved . . . it's hard to know exactly. It wasn't any one person's idea. We all really dug listening to music and sometimes we'd sit around together and play records . . . but everybody did that.

HSB: Can you remember the first time you ever played together?

E: Oh sure, we were in Wayne's basement. It was like there was this Christmas conspiracy or something, because I had gotten this set of used drums, and Jim had a guitar, and Wayne had a guitar. We had gotten tired of screwing around by ourselves I guess, and so we started screwing around together.

HSB: Was that the first group then—two guitars and drums?

E: No. We didn't really think of it as a group until we found Rob. He played bass and we all thought he was really good, and he had a really big amp and was really into music.

HSB: How did you meet him?

E: He went to our high school. None of us had ever really known him. He had moved from somewhere else, and he had played in this group wherever it was he lived before. He just happened to mention it one day that he played bass. [*Drummer*]

As fast as rock instruments are distributed through the general population according to individual desire and family economics, they are redistributed into groups which are the physical evidence of the social grouping of their possessors. For the purpose of first groups, the pool of instruments and the pool of personnel are practically identical.

GROUPING AND RE-GROUPING

It is inconceivable that any present-day locality in the United States has avoided the formation of its first rock group, and therefore the existence of a local rock musician culture—exemplified by an ongoing set of contacts between musicians. First groups which form in the context of a local culture have the example of their older siblings to emulate, but, because of their youth and amateurishness, still cannot participate in established musician/musician contact networks in order to assemble personnel. Therefore, the effect of existing musician/musician contacts, although it is the logical orienting institution, is negligible for the musician with no group experience. The personnel for first groups must somehow assemble themselves out of a much larger non-musician population before they can attain the legitimacy necessary for interaction with more established musicians.

Anybody in the world can have a rock and roll band. All you have to do is get a copy of "Louie, Louie" and play it over about a zillion times until your fingers automatically play those three chords. During that time you can learn a lot about rock and roll if you try to figure out the words, go crazy, and end up making up your own words. I'll bet there's a hundred bands playing "Louie, Louie" in fraternity house basements this weekend, and those poor suckers are sucking it down just as fast as beer and motorcycles. That's the real secret of rock and roll, man . . . "Louie, Louie"—guitar solo and all. [*Wine-drinking guitar player*]

By copying recorded performances and studying live performances a first group can usually pool its musical resources to the extent that it can play at least one song. At that point what was once an assemblage of high school friends turns into a musical group which is capable of performing its services for an audience. What needs to be seen now is that it is possible, indeed likely, that an assemblage of non-musicians can convert itself into a rock group (no matter how poor the quality of their performance) without any recognizable human guidance. Individual histories of private or school lessons and learning by listening provide whatever virtuosity that individuals bring to a group. Once the group is formed, the enterprise of copying recordings becomes the shared form of musical organization which, since it is accomplished by ear, does not require the ability to read music. Initially, then, the things that separate first groups from their non-musician contemporaries are the possession of instruments, the existence of group meetings, and the collective attempt to copy a currently popular recorded performance.

Because of the way in which they are assembled first groups usually have short lifetimes. The best musicians re-group into more lasting relationships, and the others lose interest in the enterprise altogether. Accounts of individual music careers end up being descriptions of the grouping and re-grouping in which one has been involved.

HSB: How many groups have you been in?

J: Wow, that's hard to say. I guess my first group was sort of a mickey-mouse group, we played Herb Alpert and all that lonely bullshit. That was my junior high group. Then when I got to high school I started a rock and roll group, and we were really good for about one summer until the bass player moved away and the guitar player quit. Then I heard of this group that needed a drummer and I went and auditioned and I got the

job. We played together for about three years, went on the road
and everything, but then that fell apart. The next two were only
about a month each. They never really went anywhere. And then
I moved to Colorado and played with my last group for about
nine months before the big bust. Since that broke up I haven't
done anything but jam, and occasionally sit in for somebody.
[*Drummer*]

Through this set of changes the musicians learn to differentiate
abstract categories for other musicians, since after a group breakup
there is an awareness of the fact that there are some people who have
trouble playing music together, yet the existence of viable groups
shows that such a thing is possible for some kinds of people. Similarly, there is an awareness that very different playing styles, abilities,
tastes, and presentations of self exist in what was once naively conceived as the monolithic category of a rock music *scene*. This consciousness of "more than one way to play" and the need for a group to
play together create the criteria for the personnel of the next group.

Someday everybody has to decide who he wants to play with—what
he wants out of his music. Just fucking around with some friends is
one thing, but if you really want to get into it, just because you're
friends with a guy doesn't mean you should get into a group with
him. To have a good group you've got to have guys that can really
play . . . and play each other's music, too. [*Philosopher/guitar player*]

The essence of these criteria is not some standardized technique of
assessing musical competence, but, quite to the contrary, an indi-
vidualized assessment of "who can play with whom." Belonging to a
group requires musical competence, but that competence is a spontaneous and localized assessment of the *fit* with the particular group
in question and holds little power outside of that bounded context.
What is *good* for the group is an entirely different way of assessing
musicianship than an objective assessment of virtuosity. It is often
said that someone is "a fantastic musician, but I could never play in a

group with him." In this sense, the most important thing for a group's success is that the members' assessments of each other's playing abilities match.

> The main thing is you gotta *respect* the other guys you're playing with. You can't play good together if you think the guy next to you doesn't know his ass from a hole in the ground, or if he's down on you for something. If you don't have respect for the way the other guy plays, you haven't got a group. [*Drummer*]

Each group is a separate musical reality in a system of multiple realities, and it makes the criteria for who fits and who does not fit. Someone who does not fit in one group may be exactly the player another group is looking for, and a group that is properly assembled can be recognized as fitting, even if the quality of the individual musicians or the style of performance is considered poor in that same recognition.

The phenomenon of grouping and re-grouping is attributable to a process which Simmel calls *levelling*.

> It is thus quite misleading to designate the level of a society that considers itself a unit and practically operates as a unit, as an "average" level. The "average" would result from adding up the levels of the individuals and dividing the sum by their number. This procedure would involve a raising of the lowest individuals, which actually is impossible. In reality the level of a society is very *close* to that of its lowest components, since it must be possible for all to participate in it with identical valuation and effectiveness.[13]

Whether or not the level of an individual is a relevant concept for the analysis of large, complexly organized groups, it is easily observable in local rock groups. Where there is the lack of an institutionalized educational form and the relative lack of experience with an established population of musicians, even an educated guess of an individual's musicianship is impossible by any objective criteria.

A *spontaneous* standard system which is wholly confined to each group's reality is constructed on the basis of the minimal level of virtuosity which the group has in common. This amounts to no more than an assessment of playing ability which is constructed around an individual by the uniquely formulated concept of musicianship which the group invokes. The same individual may not be "good enough" to play with one group and may be "too good" to play with another. This creates a nine-way set of situations which structure the grouping and re-grouping phenomenon. (See figure 3.) Out of the nine possibilities which account for the change in musical expertise of individuals in groups, six (4, 5, 6, 7, 8, 9) are conditions of imminent disintegration. Out of the three "stable" configurations only one (1) is an integrative condition which can be considered a "good" group. The condition of "normalcy" (2) is the integrative condition's

		Group skills		
		Decrease	Same	Increase
Individual skills	Decrease	3	4	5
	Same	9	2	6
	Increase	8	7	1

Situations 1, 2, and 3 are stable group configurations:

1 = a "good" group: the beginning of steady gigs
2 = a transitional stage: the end of steady gigs
3 = a disintegrative stage: "natural death"

Situations 4, 5, and 6 are unstable group configurations which result in "firing and hiring"—the individual is displaced by the group: an individual status degradation ceremony or a group status enhancement ceremony.

Situations 7, 8, and 9 are unstable group configurations which result in "quitting and looking"—the group is displaced by the individual: an individual status enhancement ceremony or a group status degradation ceremony.

Figure 3 The levelling process of attributed musical skills in rock groups.

next stage—usually brought on by the economics of "steady gigs" with little time to practice. During conditions of continued integration (1) the existence of jam sessions with new musicians and the discovery of more challenging material to play can prolong the transition to the condition of musical equivocality (2). The disintegrative condition (3) is one of internal group stability, but is the stage of economic "death" of the group, and accounts for the ultimate end of a local group's career. This is the most unusual way for a group to dissolve, but it occasionally occurs after a successful and musically balanced group which has developed a following over a number of years is eclipsed by an even more popular group which plays on new musical expectations (that is, new audiences) which have been created through electronic media.

When it is recognized that this nine-fold set of conditions may be assessed for each group member, the possibilities for unstable group configurations expand considerably. When dissolutions involve unmatched group and individual skills, ceremonial events of *status passage*[14] and/or *status degradation*[15] will occur. In general, status passage could mean any change in personal esteem or value as defined by a particular reference group. Here the sense of "going on" is read into the term *passage* and means upward status mobility or status enhancement. From the individual's viewpoint this could occur if a record producer or even the "best group in town" offered employment. From the group viewpoint, recording work or a big concert date or even a "steady gig" at a respected local hangout might mean a step up. In the individual case this might mean leaving the group behind. When dissolutions are defined as status enhancement on the part of one or more parties, the door is opened for a smooth resolution of the break-up in that no reason for leaving need be proffered or elaborated. Instead, the group's situation is defined by a ceremony of giving reasons for *going* somewhere else. Even those who are left behind can successfully manage their identities with this definition of the situation since their existing esteem is not subject to criticism or attack. On the other hand, dissolutions can sometimes be expected to involve degrading the status of an individual or a group. Without necessarily having a better offer, the upwardly mobile individual might "put down" the musical skills of the group he or she is leaving, or the group might "fire" a member. Tension and overt ceremonial displays of anger often accompany such decisions. Nowhere is the inability to differentiate musical and social identities more devastating than when a group member is ousted. That a group finds someone to be musically incompetent is invariably taken as social rejection no matter how profuse the claims of continued friendship. And where there is interpersonal conflict, attacking the rejected party's playing abilities is an expectable aspect of escalating that conflict. The crossover between music and community that makes local rock groups possible also sets the stage for the pain, anger, and continued feuding that makes them impossible. Needless to say, the dissolution and reformation of groups is a continuing phenomenon.

What I have called a decrease in musical skills is accounted for by both groups and individuals as an interactional form. One manifestation of this form is the failure to appear for a group event—a practice or performance.

We had been playing this one bar for about a week or so and it was getting to be the usual grind. Tommy and I were staying at my old lady's place, and the rest of the band was crashing around in different places. One night Tommy and I showed up about fifteen minutes before we were supposed to play, and we waited and waited . . . and no band. The manager was getting really hot, but we couldn't do anything about it—just the two of us. I started making phone calls to various places where they might be, and I finally found all three of 'em at this chick's place . . . stoned out of their heads and balling each other. . . . Christ, I don't know what they were doing. I was really pissed off and told 'em to get their asses over to the gig, but it was already too late—the manager told us to pack up our things and split. That ripped it with me . . . if they didn't care enough about playing that they didn't even show up for the gig, then they just weren't into playing music any more. They were, at one time—we had a really tight group—but then the three of them started making it into a twenty-four-hour-a-day party trip and the music went straight downhill. [*Drummer*]

The same kind of musical status degradation ceremony can exist by virtue of a group account directed toward an individual.

> We had picked up Mike in Denver where he was sorta hanging out after his group in Texas broke up. For a while there everything was cool and we were playing steady, but we were progressing too . . . you know what I mean? . . . playing new songs and doing originals and getting our sets really together. Then you'd start hearing these mistakes in the bass, it was really ragged . . . just sorta falling apart. The thing is Mike was getting hung up on speed. First he was just popping and finally he was shooting up every morning. And he just looked like shit warmed over. Finally we just had to get rid of him; he was bringing the whole group down. [*Piano player*]

In this case the presentation of self generated by amphetamine abuse accounted for an inability to play with the rest of the group—a literal case of the decrease in musical skills.

What I have called an increase in musical skills is accounted for as an interactional form as well. As an individual's account of the group's musicianship it may be described euphemistically as a change in musical taste.

> After a while with a group there's a certain groove established—the kind of material you do, the way the sets are arranged, the kind of introductions and solos . . . and after a while with these guys I felt that groove sorta drifting towards the same old formula, sort of soft, commercial rock. Every time I'd want to get it on, these guys would be dragging me down with the same old riffs. I guess it's just a question of taste, but I just had to get out of that and find some cats that wanted to blow. [*Drummer*]

A group constructs a similar account of an individual when his musical skills have not changed as rapidly as those of the rest of the group.

There was a while there when we got really good really fast. Johnny was writing at least a song a week and sometimes two or three, and we were starting to really get off on playing hour sets straight through without stopping. We were even working enough to buy food and pay the rent, amazing as that might seem. All of us had this gnawing feeling though . . . something was wrong and nobody wanted to be the one to bring it up. I don't know who it was, but finally one night . . . I think it was Johnny . . . well, the shit sorta hit the fan about Dave's piano playing. He just sorta stuck out like a sore thumb, and everybody agreed that he should leave. That must have been a real bring-down for Dave—in one night he went from rock and roll star to nothing. The shitty thing was that he was a really nice cat, everybody really dug him, but we just outgrew him musically. [*Bass player*]

The levelling effect which allows a stable group configuration is in constant conflict with the social, psychological, and musical presentation of the individuals that must construct that level. The result is that as individuals learn how to play rock music through the experience of the local group there are accounts of relative increases and decreases of musical abilities constructed by both individuals and subpopulations of groups. It is these accounts of lack of fit that instigate group break-ups and subsequent re-groupings.

A PATHOLOGY OF GROUPS

As many cases of grouping and re-grouping are observed, a general sociological unity appears out of what is treated by each group as an individual case. When someone has played with a first group and then that group has broken up, that musician has established an associative history. In the general case that history is the product of all the group formations and dissolutions the individual has participated in. To the extent that his previous groups performed to audiences, that history is a public history, and is a method of assessing the kind of musician he is; i.e., his potential as personnel from the viewpoint of some particular organizer. Previous group experience is used as a sample of personnel qualifications in much the same way as a visual artist's qualifications are shown by a portfolio. Entering a local band culture, then, is being associated with a particular group lineage, and hence a kind of music. Treatment as personnel depends to a great extent on the opinion these associations conjure up in an organizer's mind.

R: Do you know any drummers?

HSB: Yes, there's this guy up in Fort Collins by the name of Eric. I jammed with him one night.

R: Didn't he play with those cats from Estes? . . . the ones who played that night when we saw you in Fort Collins?

HSB: That's the guy.

R: Naw, I don't think so. They were just some dudes that were hangin' around school with nothing else to do but copy Crosby, Stills, and Nash bullshit. They never really played anything that was together. [*Guitar player*]

A group's presentation to audiences is impossible to erase from the regional collective memory (although it naturally drifts away), and to the extent that a musician is known by associations with previous companions, public credentials are constructed. What saves this from being a do-or-die system is the existence of different criteria for assessing personnel (representing different styles of rock groups) in the musician population. According to the organizer of an original group (one that plays only its own material), a musician who has only played with a copy group may be considered to have inadequate experience to be considered as personnel for the new group, yet that same musician may be considered perfectly experienced for playing in a group that is, say, recording commercials. To be treated as personnel is thus to be contextualized by some sort of musical history. This history is considered to be apparent in the musician's playing style, and is the origin of accounts as to the kind of music he or she plays. It should be remembered that this kind of account is not formulated in terms of non-musician categories such as folk-rock, jazz-rock, soft-rock, and the like, but in associations with known local musicians and groups whose performances have been experienced. A musician's career of treatment as personnel by an organizer of a new group (or the members of an established group in which there is an opening) is ultimately dependent on this history of performances. Even when *joiners* and *organizers* meet for the very first time, the *first session* establishes an experiential performance history through which treatment as personnel is grounded.

Those who have established themselves as a particular kind of musician form a specialized pool of recruits who can assemble enough of an audience to maintain steady gigs. In this sense, any good local group is a *supergroup*, made up of performers from previous groups, who carry with them an expertise that does not have to be completely developed as a part of the new enterprise. Being recruited into the company of known local musicians is the consolidation of various histories of public performance into one unit of expertise, and therefore a consolidation of experientially derived performance aesthetics.

> It's just not worth getting into it for me unless you can find guys that have had a lot of experience. Every one of the guys we've auditioned so far has just been mediocre—they could never play good enough to have a really good group. It gets so frustrating after awhile, but you've got to keep looking until you turn up somebody that can really play and has got equipment and everything, and knows what playing in a band is all about. [*Drummer*]

The previously stable group may break up for a number of reasons. For example, recruitment by an outside organizer or members of a competing group with the promise of more money and the other trappings of status enhancement and better jobs is frequent. This might be described as promotion and can only occur if there is something to be promoted *from*—a chance to compare economic rewards within the context of steady gigs and therefore a steady identity as rock musician. Only when there is an offer of increased economic rewards is the idea of a lifetime career as a rock musician entertained. This is the situation in which the musician's own view of himself as personnel is solidified, for he finds that his performance history is a reality which can bring offers of money. The outside recruiter's interaction with his prospect is based on the flattering assumption that he has outgrown the local group in musical skills. A typical case is that the sought-after musician is the "star of the show" (it is said in some idioms that he *fronts* the group), and that the absence of his services disintegrates the group's act to the extent that it cannot continue to play on the audience presentation it had built up.

> That's the real pisser about being into the music business . . . you work for about a year getting material together and learning how to play together and then, right when you're getting good, the guys that know all the material split, and the whole thing falls apart and you've got to start all over again . . . not completely from scratch maybe, but it's just all that time wasted. [*Vocalist*]

Good groups are the logical target of personnel raiders, and this is just one of the dangers inherent in "getting good." Through the steady practice and performance of rock an individual proficiency comes to exist in each group member, and it is ironic that the experience derived from the group is the construction of an opportunity to leave the group.

Like any group setting, the enterprise of rock music often exhibits a form of interaction which suppresses personal animosities "for the good of the group."

> I guess you could say we had a professional relationship. I couldn't stand his guts, and he couldn't stand mine, and we never saw each other except to play jobs or practice. But I had to respect him as a musician—he could really play drums—and when there was a gig, we played together just fine. [*Piano player*]

But when personal conflict boils to the surface it may result in the decision to quit a group in which anger interferes with the maintenance of the performance reality.

> I guess this business is just full of hotheads. I've had guys just walk offstage right in the middle of a gig because they were pissed off at somebody. I'll admit that things have a way of building up, but I don't know why they always seem to break wide open right in front of an audience. That's what happened to the last group I was in . . . we were playing this concert with three other bands . . . big deal, you know, outdoors in the summer, radio ads and everything, and about an hour before we were supposed to play the bass player just decides to split. He got everybody so mad at each other that the whole group just fell apart right there on the spot. The way it turned out we lost about $1,500 by not playing that gig. [*Guitar player/ leader*]

Organizational conflict may also prompt the disintegration of a group. This involves not the perception of the persona of any member as objectionable, but objection to the manner in which group decisions are being made, for example, the kind of music which is played, the kind of jobs which are being taken, or the amount of travel time which the band requires.

> When we were playing steady I was always tired from being on the road so much, and I got into speed and got really messed up. One night we'd play in some bar and the next night at some high school gig and the next night at some Air Force base which would be a five hours' drive. By the time you figured expenses we weren't making all that much money, and I was getting more and more strung out and finally I just had to quit. [*Bass player*]

There are certain inherent rigors to the band business which are overpowering enough that the decision is often made to "get out of music." Drugs, constant travel, and a consequent tenuous economic status can make continued membership in the group difficult for any individual.

Even if a group can avoid these possibilities for losing personnel, the economic resources of the locality may ultimately be milked dry, and without an offer of a recording contract or some other economic reality, the group may die what might be called a natural death.

> We were really big for a while, especially that one summer and fall—we must have played every boogie there was. But then we started getting fewer and fewer jobs, and the audiences weren't as big, and . . . well it was just *over*. There were two new groups that started taking the gigs we'd had to ourselves, and we didn't practice as much either. I guess we all started to think of it as a business. Then there was a two-month stretch after the first of the year when we didn't get any jobs, and that just did the whole thing in. [*Former guitar player*]

Steady gigging, although economically successful, has the tendency to overexpose the group to the local audience. Opportunities to hear a new group will be taken by the audience when they present themselves, and the excitement of a following dwindles to a mild roar, and then to nothing. What the group that has worked its way into the position of getting steady gigs often realizes is that steady market demand is simply a product of their novelty, and is therefore a transitory phenomenon.

THE SPONTANEITY OF RECRUITMENT

The processes of individual musician careers and group careers feed the local personnel pool with members for the formation of new groups or the re-formation of existing groups. One of the determinants of the supply of personnel at any moment is the timing of the formation and dissolution of all the locality's musical organizations, which creates a finite set of musicians that are available as personnel. Other variables include the emergence of young musicians from the obscurity of a first group, the reappearance of previously "retired" musicians, and the arrival of new musicians from outside the locality.

Any organizational attempt, then, is invisibly constrained by the luck of the draw which defines the personnel pool at the time it is tapped.

The processes of communication between musicians who are not known to each other through the local band culture further complicate recruitment. Such means of contact are traditionally the musician's union directory or perhaps a bulletin board at the union office (the days of the hiring hall seem to be over in all but the largest cities), or the network of contacts which surround another musician's economic institution—for example, an agency or recording studio. In some localities a rationalized service exists for (initially) impersonal musician/musician contacts in the form of a musicians' switchboard.[16] In the localities I studied none of these contact media were in operation for self-producing musicians. What was not handled by the friendship network and the occasional chance meeting (at a party, for example) became evident periodically in nationally distributed publications (*Rolling Stone*, for example), a college or local newspaper, and continually in the notices that appeared on bulletin boards and in music stores. The bulletin boards were unexpectedly important—probably due to the fact that they were free media and had no more attractive competitors. Located in the student centers of colleges, universities, and private businesses (a book store, for example), they were seen and used by the general public. They reflected the situations of musicians who did not have an entrance into a local friendship network or who had exhausted that possibility. For example:

Wanted. Experienced bass player for rock group. Must have own equipment. Wanting to play Rolling Stones, etc. We can have a good time and get it on.

Good rhythm guitar. Six years experience, some vocals. Have good guitar and amp.

We are two guitars and drums, and we would like to meet a bass player and an organ player and possibly a female vocalist who would be interested in forming a group that plays only *original material*.

This means of contact constantly provides new input to the local personnel pool by yielding the names and addresses of those who would be otherwise unknown as musicians due to their social obscurity (for example, a recently arrived student or traveller).

Not infrequently the question "How did you meet?" would elicit the story of a purely chance meeting of musicians. For example, a bass player who was looking for a group was picked up as a hitchhiker by a drummer. The encounter eventually led to the organization of a band. One group told the story of meeting their guitar player when he moved into the mountain cabin next to them. These uncontrived events of contact are worth mentioning, for although they were considered chance meetings by the participants, the number of actual occurrences of this situation gives rise to the idea that rock musicians are prone to cross each other's paths. This evidence points to the relatively large proportion of rock musicians to the general population for certain ages—roughly 15 to 30—so that the statistical chances of musician/musician contact for those ages are raised to an empirically significant level. It is hard to find a high school student, a college student, or marijuana smoker who does not know a rock musician.

The primary event of the recruitment process is the first meeting, where those who have been ferreted out of the personnel pool through some means of contact are assembled for the first time in a playing situation. The excitement (and sometimes tension) that these events can create is evidence of the imminence of group formation. Those who are present are seeking a change in their musical activities (or they would not be present), and the logistical feat of assembling musicians and instruments in the same place at a certain time is a tangible sign that such a change is occurring. The organizer's special entrance into the situation is based on a willingness to handle the logistical hassles of communication, transportation, and a playing site. By these actions the organizer is demonstrating his or her abilities as a leader/decision-maker, and that the outcome of this organization will be, in some sense, "his" or "her" group.

> Yeah, I think that's right. If a guy says he's getting a group together, then I would assume that he'd be the leader, and you would work for him. Maybe that would change later, but that's how you'd have to think of it at the beginning. [*Bass player*]

First contact situations show that there is at least a two-fold differentiation of personnel which can be thought of as joiners and organizers. Organizers initiate musician/musician interactions and handle logistical problems; joiners respond to calls for personnel and expect "just to play music." Both are necessary to the rock enterprise—they are less social types and more interactional presentations by which a group may be talked into existence. They have little to do with musicianship and recognize only the non-musical aspects of having a group. The organizer who has an idea for a group is dependent on some initially unknown musicians to give actuality to his idea, and the joiner who has no idea for a group is dependent on some unknown organization to give idea to his actuality.

The main consideration of a first meeting is that it is impossible to tell whether those present can play together unless they do, in fact, play. Playing in a strange and possibly disorienting environment, though, may not be easy. Consequently there is a great amount of attention to the management of comfort and rapport. This is usually handled with domestic accommodation—the offering of food, drink, and marijuana (or more). Equipment and instruments that are to be moved and arranged get an attention that is never in evidence after the Saturday night job. Even when there is a mutuality of good feeling between the musicians, first sessions are often frustrating.

> Whew. Let's stop and smoke a joint and get ourselves together. That was really ragged . . . but it's good that we got it out of our systems. . . . [*Guitar player after a first jam of thirty minutes*]

Knowing that their companions have not heard them play, musicians at a first session are quick to point out a situation in which they are dissatisfied with their music. The example above is illustrative in this respect, for although the musical assessment does not mince words, it is defined as a positive sign which is in keeping with the spirit of rapport and flow. Sometimes very understandable material circumstances promote a dissatisfaction with the music.

> I'm havin' a hard time gettin' it together . . . I really feel tight and I'm not playin' for shit. It would really help if I could play my own guitar. [*Guitar player at first meeting turned first session*]

The tension which the new playing situation brings about can boil over into a disruption of the continuity of the event.

> I picked up the bass and we just started playing. He was obviously nervous—missing notes, dropping beats—and after about ten minutes he just stood up and put his guitar in his case and split. It happened so fast—I wasn't expecting that. He mumbled something about "not getting it together" and just split. [*Guitar player describing a first session*]

Leaving the group as a response to perceived tension may also appear as retaliation.

> Now this cat was just too much. The first time we played he turned his blown-speaker Sunn amp to ten—louder than anyone else— and he kept playing continually for twenty minutes, at least, and when he saw that we just couldn't follow him he leaned his guitar up against the amp—so it would feed back—and just walked away. [*Bass player describing a first session*]

The feel of a first session may not be a describable sensation, but the assessment of a good or bad feeling is a recurrent theme of post-session conversation, and is a matter of consensus.

> You don't have to analyze it man . . . when it feels good everybody can tell, and when it feels bad, it's even more obvious. Getting it

together is always a chance you take—sometimes it works, sometimes it doesn't—and with new people there's bound to be tension.
Overcoming that tension, man, that's the best high there is—it just
happens by itself. [*Drummer*]

The tension which is present at any first session is an indication of
some of the most important knowledge that a musician acts upon.
There can be no assumption that any particular assemblage of people calling themselves musicians can play together until it is demonstrated, and so in the situation of the first session a performance
which is, to some degree, mutually acceptable needs to be forthcoming for the possibility of a group to exist. The first session is truly an
audition; a time when the spontaneously produced music is listened
to with a special ear to decide whether it is possible to have a group
or not, and yet it is well known that for many reasons the first session
is the least conducive circumstance to good playing. Through the
music, however, the fate of the potential group is divined. The single
musician has no way of knowing his companions' musical abilities or
tastes—the music of the first session "just appears," and his ability to
play with it, the feeling that he belongs in the company of the sounds
that are around him, is his way of assessing the potential for turning the first assembly into a group. "Getting it together" as a musical
stranger is the necessary experiential prelude to a musician's commitment to the group enterprise. It shows that the necessary common
ground for performance exists prior to the constructed communality of the practice reality—that the *talk* of organization is linked to a
spontaneous *experience* of organization.

Whenever a set of musical strangers are able to "get it together"
in the first playing situation, a *group organizational event* takes place.
This is not to say that every "good jam" produces a group, but that
every group is founded in a "good jam." The recruitment process
appears as a spontaneous *good session* (in the consensual assessment
of the performers) which is brought about logistically by an organizer, but which is dependent on the spontaneous, and therefore
unexpectable, music of a particular episode and a particular set of

musicians. The quality of a local rock musician culture is in the ratio of good sessions (group invocational events) to total sessions, for, whether in private or public, rock music only exists in resonant performance. Strangers who "get it on" invoke a group, and friends who "get it on" re-invoke a group.

An interactional concept of a rock group has its primary definition in a particular kind of experience which musicians are able to identify. It is not necessary to understand the technique of assessing a good session (i.e., the experience of "getting it on" or "getting off")[17] to recognize that such assessments exist, nor is it necessary for the participants to make their assessments in the same way. What is necessary is that each musician becomes so totally involved in music-making that no attention is given to any other reality system—including the non-musical events taking place in the room around the musicians. It is at the essence of the idea of play that a player maintains a boundary system on sensory input—some things are included, and some things are excluded from the player's operational world. The good or playful quality which is associated with making music together is reported in these terms.

D: I really got off on that.

HSB: What do you mean when you say you "got off"?

D: Aw, come on man . . . I got *off.* I was no longer here, I was *there.* [*Drummer*]

Playing good music, for the musician, is the occurrence of a *wholly other* experience[18]—something for which an entire spatial and temporal vocabulary exists (e.g., "getting off"); and playing good music, for the group, is the positive experience that "everybody is getting off." Players of rock music have learned to recognize each other by providing that experience for one another.

Part II
Rock Ecology

3

Instruments and "the Outside World"

INSTRUMENTS

Traditional musical instruments are constructed according to a design principle by which a part of the human anatomy is brought into contact with an object by the body's musculature, causing the object to vibrate. Ears are set up to receive vibrations in air, and so a musical instrument is not complete until it can turn its object-vibrations into audible air-vibrations. When allowed to vibrate continuously, objects typically create resonant or standing wave patterns in the air around them. A simple example of this is banging a pan lid: The impact of the lid sets up vibrations which are audible as a continuous sound until the vibrations are damped by coming in contact with another object (say, putting the lid on the pan) or by gradual dissipation in the air. Of course standing wave patterns may tend to decay quickly in the case of items that are not specifically designed to be instruments, yet it is the specific quality of a *musical* pan lid to have some resonant properties, and an auditory selection process could undoubtedly isolate a few excellent gongs from a collection of cookware. For wind instruments, the vibrating object is a particular volume of air which is pressurized by contact with the lungs, and vibrates by virtue of its enclosure in a somewhat closed container which is the physical manifestation of the instrument. For stringed instruments, the vibrating object is the string itself, yet the amount of air that a string alone can move is so small that some sort of resonant material is placed in contact with the string so that its sympathetic vibrations will move enough air to make an audible sound. Traditional musical instruments are designed to operate, that is, to be audible, with energy which is derived from human muscular manipulation. They are human-scale instruments.

The simplest human-scale instruments, like the pan lid, put muscular energy through two transformations—from *impact* to *vibrating metal* to *vibrating air*. Generally, the number of objects which exist between the musician's body and the listener's ear is the number of transformations or energy changes by which the musical device modifies its human input energy (see example 1, figure 4). In the case of the traditional acoustic guitar, muscular energy is transformed into string motion which is then transformed into movement within the bridge and shell of the instrument which then moves air and listeners' eardrums (see example 2, figure 4). The sonic uniqueness of various instruments has to do with the way in which media (objects) are placed in between human movement and air movement. The history of the development of musical instruments is a history of the quantity and quality of vibrational energy transformations and the media that produce them. Plucking a guitar with a pick (plectrum) instead of a finger, for example (example 3, figure 4), alters the sound quality and quantity of the instrument. Throughout this same history, the sound quality of an instrument has also been determined by the way in which *reverse* transformations are made to influence the original vibrating object. The analysis of this kind of vibrational interaction turns out to be a tremendously complicated physics problem, but musicians hear it and talk about it in terms of *resonance* (as a property of an instrument).

An instrument which operates on a single human's energy is necessarily limited as to the volume of air it can move, however ingenious the design of the instrument, and is therefore limited as to the intensity of air pressure it can produce at the ear. Those metal-string violins I mentioned before were obviously an attempt to maximize sound output as the instrument encountered larger audiences.

Type of instrument	Transformations from body of musician to body of listener
Pan-lid	Hand – Lid – Air – .... Ear
"Classical" guitar (nylon strings)	Finger – String – Bridge – Shell (of instrument) – Air – Ear
"Popular" acoustic guitar (steel strings)	Finger – Pick – String – Bridge – Shell – Air – Ear
Solid-body electric guitar	Finger – Pick – String – Bridge – Solid body (of instrument) – (Air) .... ↳ Magnetic pick-up – Amplifier – Speaker – Air – Ear
"Acoustic-electric" guitar	Finger – Pick – String – Bridge – Shell – (Air) .... ↳ Pick-up – Amplifier – Speaker – Air – Ear
Non-magnetic "acoustic-electric" guitar	Finger – Pick – String – Bridge – Shell – Air .... ↳ Pressure-sensitive transducer – Amplifier – Speaker – Air – Ear
Electric guitar with signal processing	Finger – Pick – String – Bridge – Shell – Air .... ↳ Pick-up – Preamplifier – Amplifier – Speaker – Air – ↳ Signal processing ↱ Ear
Analog synthesizer	Finger – Keyboard – Oscillator Amplifier – Speaker – Air – Ear ↳ Preamplifier–Signal processing ↰
Digital synthesizer	Finger – Keyboard – Digital computer – Oscillator – Amplifier – Speaker – Air – Ear

Figure 4 A transformational analysis of selected musical instruments.

Even when they are technically souped-up, though, the ability to hear human-scale instruments depends on the distance of the ear from the instrument (the moving air's energy dissipates exponentially with increased distance from the sound source) and the presence or absence of competing sound sources in the proximity of the instrument and listener. With human-scale instruments, the distance factor places a limit on audience size and the competition factor places conventionally enforced constraints on site design and audience conduct at performances. At distances of several feet from the musician even a whispered close-range conversation can effectively mask many traditionally designed instruments. When we have a listening focus in mind, such competing sounds tend to be considered as noise. Perhaps in the individual case this noise is insignificant, but an assemblage of thousands of humans coughing, sneezing, breathing, squirming, and rustling, plus the sounds of heating and cooling systems and outside traffic, is the noise which is conventionally understood to be *silence* in concert. The point is that any performance situation comes complete with noise, and some provision must be made to make the performance site's signal-to-noise ratio[1] considerably greater than one before the audience can even be expected to hear the music.

The existence of electric instruments, electronic amplification devices, and electromechanical transducers (speakers) allows the rock musician a control over sound which is larger than human scale, and changes the experience of a performance drastically. Consider the case of the solid-body electric guitar (example 4, figure 4), in which the instrument's metal strings move in a magnetic field and produce an electric signal which can then be amplified to ear-splitting volumes. At human scale (without electric power) the instrument relies only on its strings and the mass of its solid body to move air, and is so weak as to be nearly inaudible, even at close range.[2] Electrically powered devices very obviously dominate the transformational path from musician's muscle to listener's ear, and are necessarily an integral part of the instruments to which they are umbilically attached. When an acoustic shell or a non-magnetic pick-up device is used (examples 5 and 6, figure 4) the sound quality of an electric guitar is altered, but is still dominated by amplifier and speaker systems. Notice that the remaining human-scale resonance aspects of the guitar can be easily overwhelmed by the amount of air that a speaker can move, resulting in power-driven or runaway resonance which is often referred to as feedback. Finally, consider that the waveform[3] of the guitar's electric signal may be drastically altered by using all manner of filters, oscillators, envelopes, and the like (in general: signal processing) before being amplified and sent to speakers to move air (example 7, figure 4). The implications of these technical innovations are vast, and my introductory discussion of electric guitars is just the tip of the iceberg. Perhaps the first point to make about all this is that electronic possibilities have added a thick last chapter to the long history of design changes intended to make musical instruments louder. Now even a moderately powerful assortment of electric instruments and amplifiers can completely overpower ambient audience and site noise. Aural competition, then, is simply eliminated from the musician's definition of the situation because it is impossible for the audience (or, for that matter, anything else) to compete with him.

J: ---.
HSB: Your lips are moving but I can't hear a thing.
J: ---.
HSB: What?
J: ---.
HSB: [*Waving arms in frustration*] To hell with it . . . can't talk . . . can't
           talk. . . . [*Conversation at rock concert*]

This scene is familiar enough to be a cliché of new American music. In general, the electronic medium of rock music (1) assures the musician that his sounds will be heard by the audience, no matter how large, (2) allows the musical event to be presented in rooms wholly unsuited to human-scale sound, and (3) removes the need for restrictive rules of audience behavior.

The ability to make extra-human-scale sound has been packaged and distributed to Americans in the form of amplifiers. What is conventionally called an amplifier includes (1) loudness or volume control circuitry, (2) waveform or tone control circuitry, often using electronic filtering devices referred to as equalizers, (3) other signal-processing effects such as tremelo, reverberation, compression, and the like, and (4) a complement of speakers. In rock musician shop talk, distinctions between brands and models of amplifiers are made with these categories in mind.

HSB: What kind of amp do you use?

T: I have a Twin Reverb and an extra Bassman bottom.

HSB: What kind of amp would you get if you could have anything you wanted?

T: Maybe another Twin, for when we play big places . . . otherwise I'm satisfied.

HSB: Did you ever play through another kind of amp?

T: Yeah, I had an Acoustic guitar amp. It was a motherfucker for sure, but it didn't have the sound my Twin does. You know this really sounds funny, but it was too loud. I'd always catch myself turning it up a notch trying to get a different sound. [*Guitar player*]

The phenomenon of product loyalty is as prevalent in the rock musician's reality as it is in any world of specialized consumerism. Especially important is the religious quest for a unique combination of the right components—which match the amplifier's sound control capabilities to the musician's expectations.

HSB: What kind of amp do you use?

B: Right now I've got an Ampeg V4B top with two cabinets I made myself . . . two twelve-inch speakers in each one.

HSB: What kind of speakers?

B: I've got SROs in one of them and Altecs in the other.

HSB: Are you satisfied with it?

B: Not really, the amp's great but I think I'll get rid of all those speakers and get Lansings. It sounds good, but not as good as I want. [*Guitar player*]

Whether or not there are audible differences between amplifier and speaker brands and models is a moot point. Obviously, a tiny practice amplifier cannot be compared to a huge, concert sized amplifier, but every musician has an opinion about which electronic equipment should be used. Arguments supporting those opinions are diverse, contradictory, and often invidious. Ultimately, amplifier choices are symbolic of a personally constructed myth of quality which musicians develop in order to enter into a knowledgeable relationship with the last stage of their instruments, but about which (in most cases) little is actually known.

The electric guitars used in rock music are predominantly of thin-acoustic or solid-body design. Two manufacturers (Fender and Gibson) have tended to dominate the market, which is less diversified than the amplifier market.

I'd say about 95 percent of all the guitar players I've known or seen use either a Gibson or a Fender. Occasionally you'll see a Gretsch or a Guild or a Travis Bean or a Japanese copy of a Gibson or a Fender, and there are a lot of other brands that kids buy to learn on, but if they keep on playing they switch to something better. [*Guitar player*]

In particular, the Fender Telecaster and the Gibson Les Paul models are the most popular electric guitars among rock performers. Lately there is an antique collector's consciousness invoked to gauge the quality of a guitar.

It's really true, man, the new stuff they're putting out is just shit compared to the old stuff. It's really true for guitars, that's for sure. An old Les Paul is worth two or three new ones, no matter what they look like—it plays better and sounds better. [*Guitar player*]

Old in this case refers to the late 1940s and 1950s (before which the instruments didn't exist). The interest in old Les Paul guitars became so intense at one time that Gibson resurrected its discontinued model and began making new ones in the style of the old. The phenomenon of recycling not-so-ancient popular culture deserves sociological attention on its own, but there is more at work in this matter than profitable market manipulation. A guitar that was made in the early 1950s and which could be found in reasonable supply five years ago for a few hundred dollars is now a rarity and prices have risen 500 to 1,000 percent and more. Getting the "right" guitar means being able to distinguish new "shit" from both old and new "quality" and having the money to pay for it.

Electric basses are known in virtually the same manner as guitars. They are all solid-body instruments with four strings tuned an octave lower than the lowest-pitched four strings on a guitar. Fender has tended to dominate the market and Gibson is of secondary popularity. When electric basses first appeared *Fender bass* was a synonym for *electric bass* just as Frigidaire and Kleenex were provided as general names by fashionable American consumerism.

The complex set of percussion instruments which is known as *drums* (or less often *trap set* or *drum kit*) in the rock idiom consists of a snare drum, usually of metal construction, from two to five tom-toms (which are mounted on stands or stand on the floor), one or two bass drums with foot pedals and beaters, occasional specialty drums (such as *tymbales)*, a high-hat (a pedal-operated two-cymbal closure device), several lathe-machined brass cymbals of assorted diameters and thicknesses, plus a variety of other percussion devices: wood blocks, cow bells, sleigh bells, gourds with serrated edges, and the like. The pedal devices provide each foot with a percussive voice while the hands can manipulate many sound generators with tapered foot-long wooden sticks. Interestingly, the profession of drumming is split in two in popular music with the second player (called a *percussionist* when there is one) playing a variety of shakers, bells, tambourines and the like but always having conga drums available. (All tom-toms and bass drums are cylindrical shells made of wood, plastic, or metal.) There are numerous drum manufacturers whose products appear in rock groups: Ludwig, Rogers, Gretsch, Slinger-land, Premier, Yamaha, and others. Their construction techniques are essentially the same, although Ludwig and Rogers have often been associated with popular notions of quality. Cymbals manufactured by Avedis Zildjin have tended to be a rare universal standard.

Rock keyboard instruments fall into three general categories: the pianos, the organs, and the purely electronic keyboard devices including synthesizers of all sorts. The original electric piano was developed and marketed by Wurlitzer in the late 1950s. Its distinctive sound is derived from metal bars or *reeds* which are struck by the keys and amplified. Since that time the similar Fender-Rhodes instrument—actually a set of gongs with a keyboard—has become the standard portable electric "piano." The quest for an electric piano which derives its initial vibrations from strings is underway, and a few models of this sort—often excellent and expensive—have appeared. The organs (mimicking pipe-organ design) usually depend entirely upon electronic oscillators for their sound generation and include pre-set *stops* to select signal-processing possibilities. An exception to this is the Hammond organ, the original, and to most musicians "best," electric organ. Its original vibrations are keyed to a mechanical tone wheel device and allow some degree of *analog* control over signal processing. It is an old design, expensive, and a heavy, cumbersome instrument to transport, yet it is a familiar feature at rock events. Other organ manufacturers provide a wide range of styles, sizes, and prices, including a number of small, compact, easily portable instruments. Associated with the sound of electric organs for most audiences is the unique speaker system known as the Leslie. Although the Leslie is usually used with organs, it has no particular primacy of sound source and has been used by electric guitarists, vocalists, and the like. Its two-speed rotating speakers (and/or sound-dispersing rotor for low frequencies) provide a unique and readily identifiable sound. Synthesizers are an elaborate development of the signal-processing concept. Operated by a keyboard and using purely electronic primary vibrations, they allow their controller to perform major electronic surgery on unsuspecting signals by using arrays of triggers, filters, envelopers, auxiliary oscillators, and signal analyzers (and other items which shall remain nameless) which are connected at will by switches and patch bays. In contrast to organs, synthesizers allow a musician to set the parameters of signal processing rather than depending on pre-set parameters which are switched either in or out. Furthermore, sound events of all kinds can be programmed into a synthesizer and enacted in fairly long sequences on command. This has added a previously unheard-of set of effects to the more conventional performances of popular music keyboardists.[4] Of equal impact is the use of synthesizers to process signals which originate in acoustic vibrations. Guitars, saxophones, voices, and anything else that vibrates can be synthesized into an amplified sound that might bear only a minimal relationship to the original sound. Unique signal-processing *effects boxes*, intended to deliver one particular sound parameter (for example, those marketed by MXR),[5] have long been a part of the rock scene, although recently these have been challenged by devices which combine many effects and allow a performer some parameter-setting control. Actually, these are simplified mini-synthesizers especially intended for use by non-keyboardists. It is even possible to carry around a device which will synthesize harmonic intervals (like a fifth above, a fourth or an octave below) to any pitch the musician is sounding.

The pattern of basic rock instrumentation is well known:

HSB: How do you decide whether a group of musicians is a rock group?

D: The most obvious thing is what instruments they're playing. If they're not playing rock and roll instruments they're not a rock and roll group.

HSB: What are you calling rock and roll instruments?

D: The usual. Bass, drums, guitars, and vocals.

HSB: What about keyboards?

D: Sure. Almost anything really, as long as you've got a bass player, a drummer, a guitar player, and somebody shouting. [*Bass player*]

The aspiring musician meets the definition of his instrument resources as an unalterable condition of the rock enterprise. "Everybody" knows what instruments a rock group is expected to have—even those who do not play themselves. What is more amazing is that within this fairly narrowly bounded set of basic instrument designs there are a few acknowledged *right* instruments and manufacturers: Fender and Gibson guitars, Fender basses, Rhodes pianos, Hammond organs, Avedis Zildjin cymbals, and so forth. These particular instruments certainly do not account for the profusion of instruments which find their way to rock events, but they do account for the vast majority of musicians' assessments of *good* instruments.

The need to acquire instruments ties musicians to the locations of instrument entrepreneurs: music stores. Most rock musician careers begin "in the store" where the tools of the trade attract an inordinate amount of attention.

I can still remember my first days of hanging around the music store . . . looking at all the guitars and amplifiers and getting the salesman to let you try them out. Oh, yeah . . . and getting all the catalogs and advertising hype to read over and over again at home . . . the music store is an expensive toy shop—it's got everything in the world a musician could possibly want, right there in one place. Music stores are musician-magnets. [*Drummer*]

Musicians initially get involved with instruments that are simply *found* in their environment. They do not have to construct their instruments, nor even know of their design principles, to be able to acquire and learn to play them. People who distribute instruments are inevitably in the situation of starting musician careers by providing a selection of sound-control possibilities for the new recruits of the resonant air-moving business. It is not surprising, therefore, that music stores are centers of musician/musician interactions, that the employees and owners are themselves musicians, and that they serve as institutions of contact for musicians' continual grouping and re-grouping experiences. The instrument is the musician's artifactual communality with a culture, since it ultimately places limits on how music can be made, and defines it among culturally expectable sounds. The instrument store, therefore, is the universe from which one selects a somewhat pre-arranged sound and an already socially reified musical identity. Lately electronic supplies have been stocked, and new musician identities created.

PRACTICE SITE

Practicing rock music is a major sonic and social event. As such, the rules of its existence or nonexistence are well defined. From the musician's viewpoint a place to practice is any space large enough to accommodate the group's equipment, in surroundings which will tolerate the playing of rock music. From the viewpoint of most of the place-owning population, the majority of American architecture is not available for the "noise" and "disturbance" which accompanies band practice. For friends, groupies, and passers-by the event of band practice is worthy of attention, and in its normal existence, band practice is a *scene*. From the audience's viewpoint practice is not seen, yet it is the invisible context of the more or less coherent performance which is witnessed. This *backstage* reality is when the social and musical organization of the *onstage* reality is negotiated. Each of these viewpoints makes gaining and maintaining access to a practice site a bundle of problems and each problem shapes the quality of local rock group rehearsals.

The musician's requirements for a practice site (besides the obvious necessity of electric power) are primarily defined in terms of floor space. When a group is looking for a place to practice, the need for architecture with a specified minimal floor space complicates the search, since the space requirements of a group are considerable. The attempt to find a suitable practice site uncovers an interesting fact about the configuration of the American interior environment: The vast majority of private structures are designed so that their rooms are too small for a rock band.

By knowing the approximate measurements of the customary rock equipment, a group's minimal floor space may be computed. Consider this somewhat typical five-person group: guitar, bass, drums, keyboards, saxophone, and/or vocalist. The guitar amplifier (3 square feet), the bass amplifier (3 square feet), keyboards or organ (10 square feet), drums (30 square feet), and sound system (15 square feet) account for more than 60 square feet of floor space just for the equipment. An absolute minimum of human space in between the equipment space allows a one-to-one equipment-to-human ratio, and generates an estimate of the group's absolute minimum floor space at 120 square feet. This estimate has not accounted for space for the storage of cases, covers, tool kits, and the ever-present extra equipment; space for friends, lovers, clients, and managers; furniture or walkways; or building services of any kind. The addition of all these factors brings about an interesting rule of popular music space definition: The set-up expands to completely fill the space provided for it.

> Did you see how much shit those guys had in there? . . . an extra Leslie over in the corner and a couple of old amps—looked like a really funky Fender Concert—and then there were those home-made enclosures. I wonder how many home-made enclosures there are just sitting in corners all over the country . . . and besides all the stuff they were playing with there must have been ten other people in there . . . just sardine-packed with people and things—band practice always looks the same. [*Bass player after visiting another group's practice*]

Finding a practice site can be problematic simply because of the physical size of the band's portable environment.

The predominant architectural structure in America is the single-family dwelling, and, as we have seen, rock groups begin forming at an age when the musicians are "living at home with the family." When these factors converge, a bid for space use occurs, and the family ends up providing a practice site for fledgling groups. The minimal

floor space requirement excludes most of the family's available space
so that, depending on family income, the group can usually be found
practicing in the basement or the rec-room. An occasional garage
also undergoes a change in space definition. The only other rooms
which could possibly be large enough for practice would be the living
room and dining room. Never have I seen these spaces given over to
rock music, and the remaining parts of most single-family dwellings
are designed on such a small scale as to be unusable for anything but
bedrooms.

Musicians who are not "living at home" are confronted with
the dual problem of finding living space as well as practice space. In
a housing market which has been tightened by population growth
and individual space habits, the rock group's space requirements are
esoteric. One solution is to consolidate the group's space needs into
the rental of a living/practice site—typically affordable for the local
group in the American housing market only by an economics of
communism. Whether or not the group desires a communal lifestyle,
existing costs of access to architecture in which both practicing and
living are possible often make "family living" an economic necessity.
The structures which are procured by pooling resources are defined
by what the housing market makes available: single-family dwellings.
The only major change in space definition from the parent's family house in comparison to the band's "family house" is that the living room/dining room area is invoked as practice space. What was
designed-in by the paradigms of residential architecture as space for
family socializing and was, in the "living at home" situation, unavailable for rock becomes the space of the band family's main form of
sociation: playing music.

Musicians who neither live at home nor find the resources to rent
a "home" find unique solutions to the practice-site problem. For one
thing, the physical plants of colleges and universities support music
practice, since they abound with large structures, large rooms, and
students who are rock musicians. The fraternity house is an example
of this kind of space invocation.

It seems like there used to be more fraternity bands than there are now, but there's still a couple here at CU. Maybe only one guy in the group will be in the fraternity, but they'll still practice there—probably in exchange for playing for a party or two. For most groups it's worth it to find a place to practice where you don't get hassled. [*Student guitar player*]

Students who are not affiliated with "Greek" organizations manage access to large dormitory lounges and basements or other special access space.

We've got this really nice place to practice. The acoustics are really good because it's carpeted and there are drapes on three walls. It's actually a room in the basement of the student activities building, which is a rip-off because it's right across the street from the new gym, and all they ever use it for is alumni receptions and shit like that. Most of the time it just sits there, but since Arnie is on the student activities committee—dig it—he's got a key. [*Student bass player*]

Non-student musicians use family and friendship networks to procure privileged entrance into desirable practice space.

The place where we usually practice is in the basement of this club. Jerry has known the manager for years . . . he ought to, he's played there enough . . . and besides, the guy that owns the place is a friend of Jerry's old man. The only thing about it is that you've got to practice in the afternoon, but that's when we like to do it anyway. It's really good because you can leave the stuff set up and not worry about anybody screwing around with it or stealing it. [*Bass player*]

The rarest practice site is space that has been rented with the sole and expressed intent of using it for rock practice. In urban areas there are rehearsal studios which are rented by the hour, and the additional service of access to recording equipment is available. This is an expense in time, money, and logistics that local groups can rarely afford, yet the existence of the enterprise shows that there is a market in pre-defined popular music practice sites, and therefore a scarcity of such space. The option of a rehearsal studio did not exist for the musicians I studied.

THE NOISE

Quite apart from the problematic aspects of the group's physical space requirements, the greatest problem is to find a place where acoustic phenomena of intensities on the order of one hundred decibels (or more) may be regularly created. This is something akin to the problem of finding a needle in a haystack. From the viewpoint of the owners and operators of American real estate, the noise of a rock band destroys the norms of space definition. The cultural expectation is that for purposes of access to real estate, the American citizenry will "keep quiet." This conflict between tightly-packed population patterns and a musical form that relies on an innovative technology of loud sound is an ever-present part of playing rock music. It sorts the places which are available as practice sites in any locality into a very small stack.

> Where are you going to find a place where you can really have a good practice? In your average subdivision or apartment building you could maybe do it for twenty minutes before the cops showed up. All the places where nobody is around to hear, like warehouses and storerooms, are owned by old farts that would just as soon shoot you as look at you. Sometimes you can find a place like that, but most of the places that would work are out in the sticks someplace, an old farmhouse or a place in the mountains, something like that. When you go looking for a place like that you start finding out a few things—like it's gonna cost you an arm and a leg, or else the guy just don't like the way you look. [*Manager*]

In addition, the requirements of access to a site promote the imposition of a practice schedule on the group from outside sources.

HSB: Can I give you a hand?

T: Yeah, we need to get these mattresses up against the windows.

HSB: Neighbors complaining about the noise?

T: Well, actually the nearest neighbor is a half-a-mile away, but he started complaining to the landlord, and so now we're not supposed to practice past ten at night.

HSB: [*Struggling with a mattress*] It's pretty close to ten now isn't it?

T: Well, that's why we've got these mattresses. It seems to work. We haven't had any complaints. [*Bass player*]

An additional problem is the presence and consumption of drugs which accompanies the practice event, and to which many real estate entrepreneurs object.

HSB: Would you guys like to smoke a number?

B: We'd like to but we can't. This is my mother's house and that's one of her rules—"no dope smoking in the house." I know it's really a drag, but this is about the only place where we can practice and leave the stuff set up where it's fairly safe, so I guess we'll have to go along with her. [*Guitar player*]

The obstacles to procuring a practice site would be insurmountable were it not for the privileges resulting from families and friendships, or the discovery of rare sites where the usual "no noise" norms are not a factor. The noise norm has always been invoked against "undesirables in the neighborhood" who have had loud parties, loud arguments, or loud electronic devices—all of which could not begin to put out the sound energy of a rock group. Many community governments now enforce anti-noise legislation with patrol car officers armed with decibel meters and ticket books. What is being witnessed, as rock musicians mix with the general population, is an obvious flaunting of a previously unquestioned and untested norm which was pushed to the limit by loud radios and squealing automobile tires, and has now been completely destroyed by the two-hundred-watt guitar amplifier.

In the case of the group that practices at "the parents' house" it is the privilege of family membership that makes practice possible.

> We could never get to practice here if it wasn't for my father. The neighbors have complained a couple of times and the cops have come by and he's the one who's talked to them. If it was us they'd probably fuck us over, but my father's a straight, law-abiding citizen, and he gives them the "my home is my castle" rap and cools 'em out. All we really have to do is quit playing by nine or ten, which is really no hassle at all. [*Drummer*]

Externally imposed scheduling and sound level rules must be tolerated in exchange for the otherwise free space. Family house practice sites operate in this way only as a transitory phenomenon in an atmosphere of negotiated tolerance, until the group either breaks up or moves out to its own quarters.

> It would have been hard for us to get together if we hadn't had my parents' house to use for practice. When we were just starting out we didn't have any money or anything—we were just juniors in high school—it must have been a real drag for them to listen to all that racket day after day. But they put up with it until we got out of school and started making money enough to get a place of our own. [*Bass player*]

The rented band house is a similar situation in which the landlord takes the place of the parental figures in the negotiation of the way in which the group organizes its practices. Occasionally a site is found which matches the group's needs without externally imposed restrictions. In Colorado this was relatively easy to achieve since isolated farmhouses and mountain cabins existed. It is a sign of social and economic stability if a group has complete environmental control over its practice site. Even in the urban context a "good place to practice" is a possibility.

> The only thing about it is that it's pretty small, but besides that it's perfect. We don't have to pay any rent because Jimmy's father owns the place, and it's right here in the downtown area. We still call it "the shop" because it used to be the shop for his father's business. We've got it pretty well soundproofed, and when you shut the door you can't hear anything outside. We've been here almost every weekday afternoon for three years . . . it's sort of like the band's home. [*Guitar player*]

All of these situations are indicative of the way that constraints are placed on the practice of rock music by people and things that are not connected to the music itself. It would be shortsighted to claim that these constraints do not affect the group's playing, for they actually determine the scheduling and total amount of practice time, the ability to chemically alter the consciousness, and most importantly the sound power which is available during practice.

MAINTAINING THE BACKSTAGE REALITY

Access to the practice site of a group is always selective, and sometimes amazingly restrictive. Sometimes the attraction of "free live music" can develop a sizable audience, and although devotees are usually appreciated by musicians, their sheer presence can so redefine the practice session as to render it useless to the group.

> There's barely enough room in there for the band and all the equipment, and when it's hot outside you sweat your ass off inside. We can't open the door because of the noise. Any more than a few visitors makes the place impossible, and you can't get anything done. [*Manager re "the shop"*]

Visitors often redefine the situation in a non-musical way as well.

> We finally had to make it a rule that no chicks could hang out at
> band practice. . . . Wow, did that go down hard! It was getting so the
> drummer would go outside with his chick, and then maybe go for a
> ride with her, and everybody else would be waiting for him to show.
> Then somebody else would say "fuck it," and that would just hang
> up practice for a whole day. [*Guitar player/leader*]

Often the tension that surrounds the presence of outsiders at practice
sessions is rooted in the musician's dislike of being watched in the
practice of his craft. In order to develop the ability to play a particular
piece together, a lengthy interaction including criticisms, rearrange-
ments, shaky run-throughs, and many mistakes (literally, mis-takes)
may occur. It is always necessary for the group to "play bad" in order
to "play good," and the essence of the practice reality is, after all, the
provision of a place for recognizing what does not work and correcting it by mutual consent. If there is any embarrassment on the part of
the musicians at being criticized in front of "outsiders," or a distaste
for playing poorly while being scrutinized by a gallery, the visitors
turn into intruders. Practice sessions are the *backstage* episodes in
which a group's musical competence and mutual confidence are created. Due to the fact that it is a uniquely constructed system of discovering, demonstrating, and talking about music, a beginning rock
group reveals an imprecision and an ignorance of traditional musical
knowledge which is, at times, too fragile to withstand the superim-
position of other realities.

> Man, I know I'm playing shitty anyway, but having all those peo-
> ple around—people I don't even know—just gets me tighter and
> tighter. In the group I used to play in we didn't let just anybody come
> to practice. I think we ought to do that too. [*Drummer after practice*]

> When you're having trouble with a song, or things are just not
> sounding too good in general—that's the time you need to relax

and help each other out. When there are a lot of people around that's hard to do, because . . . well, it's a personal thing, you know . . . that stuff's not part of the show. [*Guitar player*]

Even with these restrictions, band practice is the scene of meetings and sessions between musicians, since it is the only institution of stable music activity which is not a performance reality. Musicians who are considered friends and even friends-of-friends may be allowed or asked to "drop by practice and jam for a while." This is an act of pure sociability—to play just to play—and reinforces the musician identity of all participants. Practice sessions are ideal settings for spontaneous musician/musician interaction—the equipment is at hand, plenty of personnel are in attendance, and the group's established control of the environment promotes a relaxed, unscrutinized atmosphere.

The ability of band practice to become defined as a performance simply by the presence of non-musicians leads to a conceptualization of the practice site as a *club room*, i.e., where there are literally "insiders" and "outsiders." The principle at work in this situation is succinctly stated by Simmel: ". . . occasionally one can make the interesting observation that an intimate circle of a few persons attains the character of a 'party' if only one more person is added to it."[6] If the pure musician/musician interaction of the performance reality (*play*) is to be maintained onstage, the rules of that interaction must be invoked in a reality where there is no stage, that is, where the entirety of the assembled individuals are insiders. The practice of rock is the explicit negotiation of concerted actions which are implicitly and automatically assumed by the group in the performance.

J: How're we gonna end this?

D: How about ending with that riff that comes after the second verse?

J: O.K., but maybe we should do it more times . . . how about four times?

D: Let's try it. From the beginning of the last verse . . . one, two, three. . . .

J: [*After the ending*] It's good, but it won't work right unless we cut
         it off *clean:* da-da-da-*dum.* And that's it.

D: We'll just have to run through it a few times until it's auto-
         matic . . . ready? One, two, three. . . . [*Group practicing a clean
         ending*]

If the effect of endings or any other pre-arranged elements of the performance are to be experienced by the audience in the *onstage* reality,
they must exist as the arcane knowledge of the group. To be able to
negotiate those elements, however, there must be a time and place
where the group can treat them as non-magical, discussible, and
changeable—the mundane antithesis of a group's onstage presentation. Maintaining the practice place as a *backstage* reality eliminates
the presence of an audience (in Simmel's terms, the character of a
"party") so that the essentially mundane (literally *profane)* definition
of the practice reality may exist.

G: I don't really see any use in practicing if the whole goddamned
         world shows up for it. . . .

M: Aw, George, what difference does it make?

G: Man, look . . . there was about four or five people just sitting over
         in the corner today, smoking dope and having a good time and
         all, and I've never seen 'em before. And if *they* can come, *any-
         body* can come . . . and if anybody can come and hear us work
         on the same fucking song for three hours, it's not exactly gonna
         knock 'em out on a gig.

M: I don't know who they were either, but what difference does it
         make? They were just some people that came over with Jim to
         hear some music . . . they weren't hurting you.

G: Music—that's the point—*music.* When we stop and fuck up
         and play really shitty when we're working up a song—that's not
         music. Nobody ought to be hearing that but us. When we get
         the thing down and everybody knows what he's supposed to
         do—that's when we should be playing music for the people to
         hear. [*Bass player vs. his manager after practice*]

Whether or not "the people" can hear the sounds of practice depends on the environmental control the group has over its practice site. When the practice site is the parent's basement or the dormitory lounge, the group has no way to maintain the exclusivity of a backstage reality, and the ability to profess arcane skills is threatened by the presence of an audience for the negotiation of those skills. When the practice environment is under the group's complete control, criteria for the labelling of insiders and outsiders—the creation of the club room—are forthcoming. The instigation of a club room reality was an established resource of the groups which stayed together for more than a few weeks. The possibility for that definition ultimately came from procuring a practice site that allowed group-controlled access.

All of this shows that practicing rock music is constructing the group's secret foreknowledge of the performance episode—the specialized knowledge that a rock performer professes. Given the insight that there is no formal or informal training institution, and therefore no paradigm of rock practice, the practice site becomes the focus for the experience which replaces pedagogy. Musically, local rock band practice is a case of the blind leading the blind, and wherever that leads is the shared presentation of the group. Socially, however, practice is an elitist event which produces and maintains the sounds that audiences follow. Maintaining the isolation of the practice reality preserves the uniqueness of the performance reality—and that isolation allows the group to sequence its presentation and surprise its audiences with newly unveiled material.

4

Equipment and the Band Van

AUTO-MOBILITY

Musicians have always been travellers, and road musicians have always been auto-mobile. The economic expectation which is placed on a local group is that it produces itself. When that production consists of thousands of pounds of equipment, transportation requires a major investment in time, energy, and money. It is a fair estimate of a group's schedule that as much time is spent in transit and preparation as is spent performing; it is a fair estimate of the group's expenditure of physical energy that more is consumed by transportation than by performing. And it is a fair wage that is inevitably depleted in the rental, purchase, repair, and operating costs of a suitable vehicle.

> The thing a lot of people don't understand about the band business is that you've gotta get yourself there and back, and that starts eating into the profits. . . . We had a weekend gig down in Vail and we didn't trust the old van so we rented a new one. It ended up costing us about $100 by the time we got through. That didn't leave very much after we bought about a zillion burgers and paid for the motel room. [*Guitar player*]

No analysis of the local rock group's resources can be complete without a consideration of the complexities of going and coming.

Since the rock group's instruments and equipment are heavier and more voluminous than the members themselves, the group's vehicle must provide for the enterprise of trucking in some way. The most common vehicle type is therefore a van, since it combines the features of human comfort and specialized cargo space.

> I made a big mistake when I bought that Ranchero. I got a really good deal on it but I forgot about the weather out here. When it rains or snows I have to put a tarp or something over the equipment, but that's not good . . . I really don't like to do it. What I should have gotten was a van of some kind so everything could be locked up and out of the weather. [*Bass player*]

The acquisition of a suitable vehicle is often a part of an individual musician's career of identification. The economic resources of a family can often be directly tapped for a band vehicle, and, if not, the direct advantages of the living-at-home situation allow the successful young musician to earn enough money for his or her own mobility. Later this access to transportation becomes as much of an asset as the resources of instruments and sound equipment.

> D: [*Standing at window.*] You see that guy coming up the steps . . . that's the best bass player in Colorado.
>
> HSB: Oh, yeah, how do you know that?
>
> D: Well I played with him for about two years and we're really tight . . . besides, if we are going to get a group together, he's the only one with a van. [*Drummer*]

During times of group formation it becomes obvious that criteria other than musicianship are applied to personnel. Someone who can supply the group's transportation is often more of an asset than a musician of superior quality who is without wheels.

> HSB: Did you find your bass player?

J: Well, we've got to decide between two guys. They're both okay I guess, but one of them has this really nice van and right now nobody else in the group has a car that can carry anything, so I guess we're going to get transportation and a bass player at the same time. [*Guitar player*]

When this kind of extra-musical decision-making is in evidence, it makes sense to observe that the sound of a local group does not necessarily depend on a purely musical recruitment process.

Musician careers are often thought of as "easy" in the sense that they are devoid of manual labor. This image is patently false with respect to rock groups. Each engagement means tearing down the existing practice set-up, packing it into a vehicle, unpacking it at the performance site, setting it up, playing, tearing it down, repacking it in a vehicle, and unpacking it at home. In that process a lot of sweat ensues.

HSB: [*Watching a Hammond organ disappear into its trailer.*] I thought you guys were musicians, not lackeys.

T: [*Grunting and gasping for breath.*] Man, let me tell you, this is what it's *really* about. We spend more time fucking with the equipment than we do fucking our old ladies! [*Bass player*]

It is a critical point in the group's career when the physical work involved becomes an area of conflict.

T: Man, I thought we were in this thing together, hauling shit and everything . . . but Jerry never seems to be around when there's stuff to be loaded.

P: He was helping just now wasn't he?

C: [*T's "old lady."*] A couple of mike stands. . . .

R: . . . and the snare and one of the small toms.

T: Where was he when we were getting hernias off that bass amp? I don't mind doing my part, but things are just getting out of hand, man.

P: I've seen you disappear a few times yourself. Maybe that's why you know so much about it.

T: Now goddamn it, that pisses me off. I've been carrying my load and you know it [*and on and on*]. [*Group conversation after a performance*]

The actualities of hard work are special problems for beginning groups, not only because the members are inexperienced in logistical techniques, but because the prevailing musician identities are sometimes too fragile to tolerate the demonstration of ignorance and the intrusion of frustration. When equipment handling is the source of group friction, the conflict inevitably reveals itself as grounded in the more meaningful issue of the style of the group's mutual identity construction.

> The thing I want to know is: Are we gonna be musicians or are we gonna be diddly-shit laborers? Every other band I've ever seen has guys to haul their shit around for them, and I don't see why we can't do that either. What we're supposed to do is play music, man, and when my hands are tense and cramped from hauling equipment I just couldn't play a decent lick if my life depended on it. [*Guitar player*]

The origin of support personnel (sometimes called *roadies*, after the terminology in use by touring concert groups) in local rock groups is the creation of a permanent staff that can reinvoke the musician's special identity through the equipment-handler/musician form of interaction. Whenever there are preparations for a performance the support personnel are in evidence, and the musician's privileged identity is visible. Acquiring an equipment manager's services, then, is a common solution to the frustrations of physical work. Not only does it relieve the musicians of part of the physical labor of performing, it instills a mark of financial success (and therefore, status-upgrading by conspicuous consumption) into an otherwise unlegitimated social grouping.

The first thing I'm gonna do when we start making a little bread is hire a cat to haul my amps around. I know this guy that said he'd do it for $ 10 a night. That may be a cut of my pay, but it's worth it not to kill myself. Besides, when you're playing steady gigs you owe it to yourself to act like a rock and roll star. [*Bass player*]

THE BAND VAN

At the performance site the band vehicle becomes the group's backstage reality.

The cops and the musicians really have that one figured out. Wherever they go they've got a base of operations on four wheels. Their presence at an event is more powerful because they have a familiar environment to hide in. [*Equipment manager*]

The uses of the group's vehicle in unfamiliar surroundings provide a private and familiar space definition which is, in some ways, superior to an employer-provided dressing room.

Like when we were up at Fort Collins waiting to play, all we could do was hang out in the van and smoke dope. You couldn't do any dope outside or the cops would bust you, and besides we didn't want to be out there with all those drunk loonies. It was good too because Rita had a place to nurse the baby. [*Guitar player*]

Band vans have symbolic values attached to them. Often they are decorated, and therefore designated as unique.

HSB: That's a hell of a paint job.

W: Yeah, that took us a long time. Whenever somebody would get an idea they'd run out and start painting. The big rainbow was an all-day acid test—it's my favorite.

HSB: How do you feel when you're going to a gig in a truck like this?

W: About the same as I usually do.

HSB: Come on, man.

W: Well, I guess you do feel kind of special, and one thing's for
sure ... they know you're coming. [*Guitar player*]

Nothing is more logical, American, and traditional to the band business than painting the name of the group on the vehicle. For a local
group the advertising power of an identifiable name and a telephone
number is considerable.

> When we park the van outside of the place we're playing, anybody
> that's passing by can see what's going on. It's like a theater mar-
> quee ... the people that are coming to hear you catch part of the
> excitement while they're still on the street, and even the people that
> are passing by can still associate your name with the general brou-
> haha. [*Organ player*]

For others, anonymity is more desirable.

> I've thought about painting the van some weird colors and putting
> our name on the side, but it's so conspicuous. Every cop in the world
> knows there's some guys smoking dope inside a band van. . . . All
> I've got is a little peace symbol on the rear window. [*Guitar player*]

The unique assortment of meanings which a band vehicle symbolizes
for a group is inherent in the association of performing and travelling. Actually, the group goes on tour every time it assembles for a
performance. In the sense that its aggregate performance experiences
are a history of trips (in every sense of the word), a group's vehicle is
an appropriate mark of the rock enterprise.

> Man, I nearly died when that van finally died. It was like the band had
> died, too. We had gone so many places, gotten so stoned, loaded and
> reloaded so much equipment in that thing ... every time you looked at
> it you got a flash. It was like another member of the group. [*Bass player*]

EPISODIC INVOCATION OF ONSTAGE AND OFFSTAGE

Whether roadies are members or non-members of the group, the division of equipment-hauling labor is the demarcation of the episodic boundaries of the musician identity. When there are support personnel, those boundaries are more or less permanently established, and when the group "hauls its own" a boundary invocation ceremony tends to separate *working* from *playing*. There is always a time before a performance when the musicians are engaged in a mutual tuning-in episode. The disintegration which accompanies travelling and preparing for a performance is reintegrated by a group gathering. In sports this form would be a *pep talk*, in political maneuvering the form would be a *caucus*, in scientific warfare the form would be a *briefing*, and in the band business the form is *getting up for the gig*.

Onstage and *offstage* are normally poorly defined for self-producing acts. For example, carrying the equipment into a crowded bar where you are a stranger provides the prior visibility which prevents a spontaneous onstage appearance. For local groups a ready room, acoustically acceptable architecture, a theatre-type stage and lighting, and an introduction are all rare experiences. The existence of these things represents a privilege of musicians of a higher class, whose economic bargaining position is such that the provision for the onstage-offstage consciousness shift is an assumption of any performance situation. In situations where one cannot expect these privileges a local group operates in such a way as to provide their effect in any environment through socially constructed resources. Whatever the unique customs of the group or the particular contingencies of the situation, the performance is separated from the physical production of the band environment by an interlude of group integration. The ritual of leaving the audience behind is the ceremonial event which changes equipment manipulators into rock performers.

The interactional form of this interlude often incorporates drugs. Without delving into a long discussion of the socio-pharmacological relationship between drugs and music, it can be seen that the sequential relationship of drugs before playing provides a sacrament which symbolizes the edge between *offstage* and *onstage*.

[*Equipment set-up is essentially complete at the first night of a bar gig.*]

B: Mike . . . you in tune with the organ?

M: Yep.

B: P.A. workin' okay?

M: Most we're gonna get out of it in this place.

B: Then why don't we take a walk?

The "walk" in this case winds up at the band van where in about a minute's time three or four large marijuana cigarettes are being passed around. The group arrived at the site in three different vehicles, the bass player was late—there was concern as to whether he would show up at all—and the commotion of the bar plus the "hassle" of moving and setting up the equipment has promoted anything but group integration. The communal "dope-smoking" activity provides a private (privileged) meeting of the group. There is plenty of eye contact, a circle of bodily closeness, considerable touching between players and wives and lovers, the passing of a communally shared object from each to the other, and (because of cannabis carburetion) an episode of concerted deep breathing.

[*Sitting in the band vehicle.*]

B: Sure are a lotta people in there.

M: Sure is a lotta dope in here.

B: The thing is, we gotta be *here* in *there*.

J: Right now?

B: Yeah, I think the natives are gettin' restless.

C: I guess I'm as ready as I'll ever be.

J: [*Getting up*] . . . long as we're at it, we might as well do some mind-blowing.

M: Well, let's get *on* with it then.

The band van has conspired with the band itself by providing an off-stage reality in which the assumptions of the performance reality are reinvoked. The musical characteristics of this sequence are subtle, for the conversation seems to be concerned with anything but music, yet it is wholly concerned with the social aspects of playing. Each member of the group gets in an invocational word signifying a commitment to playing. Participating in an offstage reality is any performer's temporal division between *everyday consciousness* and *performance consciousness.* In the case of local groups the offstage reality depends solely on portable props and social ceremony.

It should be emphasized that the socially constructed backstage need not be concerned with a chemical alteration of consciousness. Surprising as it may seem, not all rock musicians are drug users. The essentials of the pre-performance episode are a space which is physically isolated from the performance site and a humorous (in the sense of *liquid* or *flow*) definition of the situation.

> [*A mountain near Boulder, Colorado.*]
> Last night we played this gig at ——— [a 3.2 bar].[7] There was another act going on first, so after we set up we decided to climb up Flagstaff. We just sat there and grooved for a long time on the lights from Boulder, and the glow from Denver, and even the hazy air which would have been chocolate milk in the daytime. We almost didn't make it back in time, but we were so relaxed, you know, we played a really good set. [*Guitar player*]

The understanding, evident in this kind of example, that a change of consciousness is expected from the temporal separation of setting-up and actual playing is an element of a rock performer's (in fact, any performer's) aesthetic. The separation is a consolidating pause between the mundane world of practical logistics and the sacred world of rock heuristics. If any group of humans is to synchronize its actions it must necessarily start from the same place—meaning both a site and a state of mind. Given the phenomenology of any self-producing group's performance situation—their place on the mid-point of a trip, which brings with it the identity of strangers in a strange environment—there is a need to call a meeting to reify those meanings which have so recently been countered by unexpectable "foreign" experiences. If a rock group is to contribute to the same flow of performance it must first construct a situation of readiness to start the performance ("one, two, ready, play"), and that situation will be dependent not on the permanent environment, but on the portable environment of a vehicle, instruments, and equipment, and, most importantly, a socially invoked and shared state of mind. A local group's aesthetic includes a way of sensing performance events with a detachment which is derived from its ability to negotiate the abstract transformation from production staff to musical group. In this way, *starting* to play music as a group is immediately preceded by an episode of ceremonial *stopping*.

EQUIPMENT MANAGEMENT

Whether an equipment manager is present as a specialist or the responsibilities of the position are simply shared by the performers, the job of handling equipment is necessary to any travelling musical enterprise. Managing equipment means that a transportation system, a running inventory, and spare parts are provided for the group's portable environment. Someone has to know "where it is" and "where it goes."

> You really learn fast about equipment. In the first group I was in we just piled stuff into the car any old way . . . nothing had a case or a box—jesus, what a mess. We got to this one gig and we were short a microphone . . . and another time we didn't have any cords that worked. All of that sounds stupid to me now. I mean, how can you expect to play if you can't even plug in? [*Guitar player*]

The ability to "plug in" is the ability to assemble the group's portable environment at the performance site. In order to transport the environment it must be dismantled, and for reassembly to be an actuality, no parts can be missing or damaged. Negotiating the transformation from packaged environment to performance environment and back again requires an ordering of the operations of "setting up" and "breaking down" into a routine. Learning the most efficient ways of manipulating equipment is essential to the rock musician's career. Newcomers to the band enterprise can be separated from those with logistical experience by their understanding of containers and packaging systems.

> If you want to keep equipment from hassling you, you've gotta have your equipment organized. Everything that can possibly be damaged or lost needs a case or box, and each piece needs a specific place in its box. You've got to learn how to roll up cable without mutilating it, and how to carry speaker boxes without killing yourself or the speaker . . . and you've got to know what spare parts and tools you're likely to need. If you want to do it right it's a full-time job. [*Equipment manager*]

The systemized and contained equipment must be packed in the vehicle in such a way as to maximize space use and minimize damage. During the course of my observations I witnessed many packing systems, some poorly executed and detrimental to the equipment (these tended to coincide with the least experienced musicians), some of compulsive rigidity, and some of creative ingenuity. There was always a recognition of the problem, however, and unique solutions consisted of custom-made, foam-filled cases for microphones and amplifiers, special reels for long cords, and even verbally described techniques for the placement of particular pieces in the vehicle. Consider, for example, this explanation of how to carry an entire drum set in the back seat of a Volkswagen.

HSB: Where does the snare go?

T: Oh, just put it down anywhere . . . I'll get it. I have to pack these in a certain way or they won't go.

HSB: Why don't you show me how you do it?

T: Well, the bass goes in first—see how it just clears the seat if you hold it like this? . . . Then you just stack the floor tom, the small tom, the snare, and the cymbals on top of one another. The stands go on the floor and the cymbals ride up against the seat if you push it all the way back . . . it's really not hard once you know how it's done.

HSB: Did somebody show you?

T: No, I was tying them up on the roof, and filling the passenger seat, and I just got sick of that. One day it just occurred to me that the difference between making it inside was the cases. Once I eliminated them it just sort of evolved. [*Drummer*]

As is the case with most human endeavors, innovation in the face of unprecedented problems sometimes means the questioning of existing precedents for related problems. In this case, eliminating the container and conceptualizing the car as "one big case" sparked an innovation in packaging.

Final delivery of all rock equipment takes place by the use of human muscle power. Well-systemized groups are supplied not only with motorized vehicles but with human energy-saving devices as well. Amplifier manufacturers, for example, sometimes supply their heavy and bulky products with wheels or special wheeled racks. Some groups have the foresight to carry a hand truck. All of this requires a considerable investment in "real estate." In general, the poorer the group, the more sweat is expended in human transportation.

HSB: [*Looking at a Hammond organ in a Volkswagen bus.*] How do you move this thing?

L: Well, you have to pick it up at each side, sorta like a casket, okay?

HSB: [*At door of building after considerable groin strain.*] Shit, it's not going through the door.

L: Wait—I'll take off the Leslie switch. You got a phillips screwdriver?

HSB: Yeah, sure. [*There is a pause while part of the instrument is dismantled.*] . . . Now, how in hell are we going to grab it to get it through the door?

L: We'll just have to inch it through, man. I sure wish I had a rack for this thing. They're so good, the handles are in just the right places and they're perfectly balanced. It's got big wheels and it rolls really nice.

HSB: That's what we need right now.

L: Yeah, but they want a fortune for the damn thing. [*Organ player*]

Instrument and equipment manufacturers long ago realized the necessity of transportation and packing accessories for their products and have priced them with a seller's market in mind. The hidden costs of investment in an instrument are revealed when its constant transportation is a known phenomenon. Either the equipment is subject to damage, and the show does not go on, or the price is paid for adequate packaging and transportation systems.

The perennial project of transportation, for all its headaches and expense, is the essential element of a local group's self-production. No rock group depends on the *house sound system* or expects to have a tuned piano waiting for it. All the elements of the musical production of the rock event are provided by the group, and production costs are absorbed by musicians, not their employers. Although this promotes an amazing investment and requires considerable experience on the part of the group, it also allows the group almost complete control over its presentation.

> It's like a travelling medicine show, man. We can go anywhere there's power and have just the set-up we need. We've even been places out in the woods where they've had portable generators. It takes a lot of time and trouble to do a rock and roll band, you know—it's not like picking up your acoustic guitar and that's it. But when you get there and you get set up—you've got the audience . . . they know there's something really *happening*, and when they get off on it, that's all that matters. [*Drummer*]

5

Gigs

M ost recent meanings of the word *gig* derive from its use by earlier twentieth-century popular musicians as a term for performance events where social dancing might be expected to take place. The fascinating thing about the term is its long and revealing historical association with popular music and dance, apparently beginning as a medieval European term for a type of stringed instrument used by Islamic musicians.[8] This, in turn, became a word for instruments of the *viol* family, an Irish or English popular dance form of the sixteenth century (jig) often associated with vulgar comedy and most likely introduced into America, and a movement in seventeenth- and eighteenth-century European art music suites (for example, by J. S. Bach). Even the term's non-musical associations with spinning tops, vehicles such as carriages or small boats, or spears or snares for fish or frogs can be understood as images of risk and movement which are not incompatible with its musical meanings. Although derivative terms like *gigolo* have been associated with popular music and dance culture since the mid-nineteenth century, the recently generalized American use of the word to mean any *job* points to a revelation and acceptance of musicians' ways of seeing the world. Perhaps this is because musicians are now popularly recognized as cultural leaders whose styles of living are presumed to be worth emulating. In any event, the musicians

I observed used gig to mean a piece of musical work, as in the following examples:

> We've got a gig Friday and Saturday night at Clancy's, and it takes about an hour to get there from here, and allowing an hour to set up, we should leave here before seven to get there by nine. [*Band leader*]

> Yeah, I'm really good friends with Chuck, and we can play a gig there any time we want. [*Musician recruiting a group*]

HSB: Why don't you come over and have a little dinner with us tonight?

A: Can't man, we're gigging tonight. [*Musician identity prevailing*]

I use the word gig, as do musicians themselves, to distinguish the special nature of individually contracted events of employment from the more common notion of job, which connotes an economic permanence which is absent from most musicians' lives.

The continued existence of the specific idea of a gig shows that social situations exist which call for the services of live popular musicians, and further, that those situations are important and numerous enough to carry with them certain conventionalized forms of interaction. For local rock groups these situations can be sorted into four categories: social gigs, ceremonial gigs, bar gigs, and concert gigs. For the musician each of these categories represents an identifiably different set of expectations on the part of an employer and audience, and therefore a distinct way of dealing with each situation. This is akin to the recurrent anthropological discoveries of seemingly monolithic categories being broken down into finely graded categories. The ability to differentiate numerous kinds of snow, or the recognition of many kinds of soil, or colors, or corn plants where English speakers tend to know only one category are examples of this. For local rock bands, such differentiations reflect only minor differences in the group's performance per se, but, rather, refer to the physical and social environment which surrounds the performance. Different kinds of gigs exist because different kinds of markets exist for essentially the same service, and it is the ability of the group to play to many audiences that determines its monetary return.

It is in this kind of economic diversification that the local band's quest for steady gigs can be recognized as the development of a kind of *ad hoc* anthropological knowledge by which the responses of various employers and audiences are known. A musician is always able to assess whether the audience liked or disliked the performance, and much time is spent discussing audience reactions after a performance. Since they travel from place to place, musicians eventually learn to recognize that distinguishable audiences have similarly distinguishable expectations about performances, and further, that those expectations are indicative of particular musical aesthetics and interactional settings in which music is experienced for that audience. Ultimately *audience* means *cultural grouping* and playing for a variety of audiences means knowing how to satisfy a variety of cultural expectations.

SOCIAL GIGS

The social category refers to situations which are concerned with pure sociation events, gatherings, which are primarily ends in themselves. For local rock musicians this includes events which are called both dances and parties; both refer to a similar performance reality and both include employers like social clubs, fraternities, sororities, student organizations, and assorted private individuals.

It is useful to note that dances split into three economic categories: (1) sponsored funding with free admission, (2) break even, and (3) fund-raising. The sponsored-funding type prevails where institutional funds are allotted for the provision of a rock event.

HSB: [*Walking into a university auditorium.*] What's happening?

D: It's a boogie—a free boogie, tonight at eight.

HSB: Who's playing?

D: There's ———, that's those guys over there, and then there's some acoustic group, I can't remember their name, and then there's ———, that's *our* group.

HSB: And it's free?

D: Yeah, sure, everybody's getting paid out of the student activity funds from the university. [*Conversation at local "boogie"*]

One argument for providing funds for dances in a college or university setting is that there is no social event which is common to the entire student body, and that some provision should be made for such an event. It seems common, however, that a sizable proportion of the audience at such events are non-students. The continuing provision of funds seems to be a gesture in the face of the university's anonymity; clearly though, this gesture provides a periodic source of employment for local rock groups in any number of university areas.

The break-even type is promoted largely by community organizations and specially motivated individuals, where there is only a small charge for admission.

HSB: How can you only charge 75¢ at the door?

R: Well, I get this place free because my parents own it. I get a hundred dollar band, and I pay a couple of guys five dollars to sweep up in the morning, and so I only need about 150 people to break even. It's turned into a good thing—people can come hear some music and even dance if they want without feeling like they're being ripped off. [*Young rock entrepreneur at a local dude ranch*]

The problems inherent in break-even attempts were made obvious in this particular case. The operation was eventually closed down by local police who were called to the site on many occasions when fights broke out, and who, in the process, developed a number of narcotics arrests from the wide open dope-smoking and dope-dealing scene inside. A more important problem, from the musician's point of view, was that when attendance was sparse there was no monetary guarantee, and the gig could not always be expected to provide "enough" money.

The prevailing form of dance is the fund-raising event sponsored by a club, fraternal organization, or school. These are the public events *par excellence* of the local group, for there is payment of the asking price for the group's services and, what amounts to the same thing, a large audience in a large room.

HSB: What kinds of jobs do you like best?

B: Got to be high school dances, man—they are the least hassle, everybody treats you O.K., and there's thousands of screaming kids who are really digging it. That's where I heard my first rock and roll band—in the high school gym. [*Drummer*]

The original economic relationship of the local rock group and its audience is based on dancing. In the undefinable seventies there were simply *parties* or *dances*, in the specific sixties there were *boogies*, ten years before that there were *hops* (updated from *sock hops*), and in elite social circles there have been (and, anachronistically, still are) *balls*. Any social gig (that is, music/dance event) involves a recognition of the music of the time: "the kind of music people can dance to." The fact that an organization can hold dances where it is assumed that the music will be *rock* music means that this particular kind of musician has assumed a necessary place in the socializing of the audience. It is not surprising that the audience at a high school club's dance is composed of that club's members and the locality's high school cohort, nor that the musicians are of the same age and live in the same locality. It is more surprising that this kind of locally self-sufficient music and youth culture has recently been overshadowed by nationally distributed recordings of disco music played at the local dance by a DJ over a portable sound system.

The conventions which surround dance gigs define a cultural event of *pure sociation* (the phrase is Georg Simmel's) where the almost sole control which an employer has over the musicians is the choice of group. The relationship with the employer is that the group has been scouted and found to meet the criterion of being a good group, and therefore can be counted on to manage the performance event in the expected way. Groups who have learned to be good groups for dance gigs perform a selected repertoire which has been shown by past experience to be "good music to dance to."

HSB: What kind of stuff do you play for high school gigs?

R: Well, you can play anything you want really . . . as long as it's got a good beat and you can dance to it.

HSB: Give me a break, man. . . .

R: O.K. Rolling Stones, Led Zeppelin, the latest top-40 song or something . . . but you gotta get on a real simple rhythm and beat it to death. You know what I mean, man, everybody wants to boogie. [*Guitar player*]

The conventions of dance events are simple: The music must be recognizable and the rhythm unmistakable. Groups that play high school and college dances have assimilated a performance aesthetic of "good and loud" since the social event of the rock dance requires it.

Parties differ from dances only in the sense that they are meant for an exclusive rather than an inclusive (i.e., public) audience. The public which appears at dances in some way or other shares the social reality of the organization which is sponsoring the dance, but there is a rationalized payment-for-entrance system, and, at least theoretically, anyone who wanted to buy his or her way into the event could do so. The party, on the other hand, is an in-group gathering usually much smaller than the dance and is a form of pure sociation for a known circle of friends. In this situation the employer/musician interaction is more authoritarian in form. The group can expect to be told where to set up, how loud to play, what to play, when to play, and when not to play. In addition, there is the possibility that some party-goers will try to usurp the stage for an expression of in-group identities. It is assumed that such intruders cannot be rebuffed (as could strangers at a public event) since they are "at home" with their circle of friends and virtually any act on their part will find group support. Fraternity parties are notorious for their conventions of usurpation.

> Man, it just never fails, if you've got a fraternity party you've got at least one drunk that wants to get up and sing. It used to really piss me off. . . . I can remember this one really sharp-looking dude grabbing the microphone away from me in the middle of a song and he sorta holds onto the mike stand for support and screams these incoherent words . . . jesus, was I pissed off. After a while, though, you sort of expect that kinda stuff, and it doesn't get to you so much. When somebody says something to you just don't respond to it, and when the party's over you get your fucking check and get the fuck out of there. [*Bass player*]

The party is inherently an alien scene to the musicians and their presence there is strictly economic. Included in that economics is the conventionalized (even if resented) acquiescence to the rigid expectations of the employer. If the musicians take it upon themselves to control the reality, then they remove the in-group definition of the party reality and threaten the identity of their employers. It is therefore a technique of playing parties to manage the impression that the employer's every wishes are being met.

> Requests, man, requests . . . that about sums up where it's at at those parties. Play this, play that . . . they'll shout out from halfway across the room. We finally got into this thing of saying "We've had a request for this song, and so we're gonna play it," and then go ahead and play whatever we wanted. Most of 'em are so fucked-up they don't know the difference. [*Piano player*]

Private parties are a steady source of income for local groups. A large university campus may provide ten or twenty gigs a weekend and even a medium-sized community might provide a similar number of non-student party gigs of various types, whereas less frequent high school or college dances might provide four or five gigs a month in the same-sized community. If the conventions of the party reality can be conceptualized by the group to the extent that they relinquish control of the onstage reality (the sound system, for example, or the choice of material to play) to the audience members when there is pressure to do so, they show that they have learned the cultural expectations for this kind of event and will be recommended as a good group to future employers.

CEREMONIAL GIGS

Aside from events of pure sociation, there are ceremonial events which demand the service of rock musicians. These are weddings, debutante parties, birthdays, graduations, bar mitzvahs, and the like. For this kind of gig even more control of the group's conduct by the employer is required as part of the economic agreement.

> The thing about weddings is that you gotta let whoever is running the thing to tell you when to start and stop playing. They've got this wedding thing going down, and you're supposed to be ready to play at the exact moment when everybody shows up at the reception, and then stop while somebody makes a toast, and then play "something slow" while some old fart dances with the bride. They're putting you through so many changes and everybody's so uptight about whether everything's going all right that it's hard to get into the music. [*Bass player*]

Ceremonies are marked by a culturally ordered sequence of events, and the ability of the musicians to understand and respect that order is essential to their ceremonial presence. The ceremonial reality can therefore place the group in some of its most compromising situations.

> We used to play a lot of bar mitzvahs, and somehow the word got around to the parents that a bar mitzvah was not complete unless there was a "freeze dance"—dig it—where you stop playing

suddenly, and all the little bastards have to stop in their tracks or be eliminated. Sort of a game. Man you just can't imagine this scene where some old lady who's had a few too many is giving us hand signals for when to stop and start, which, aside from being the most degrading thing I can think of, is almost impossible to do. But we did it, 'cause she was writing the check that night. [*Drummer*]

Playing a ceremonial gig is almost entirely a mercenary enterprise for it is inherent in the definition of the situation that the audience has been assembled for a reason other than listening to music.

BAR GIGS

The economic mainstay of local groups is the local bar. A bar gig is a more complex economic event for the group than either the social or ceremonial one-nighter—it could mean "Friday and Saturday nights" or "six nights a week" depending upon the clientele the bar services, but it always means a performance reality which is purchased as entertainment in the same way as mixed drinks and bar chatter. Bar owners and managers consider the group an economic investment which draws customers to the site; from their viewpoint they are paying the group for the number of bodies it pulls through the door.

The door is an important economic parameter of bar gigs. It refers to the cover charge, entertainment charge or admission fee, which the customer pays to gain entrance to the bar environment. It is most advantageous to the management to pay the band the money collected at the door when the bar has not established a capacity clientele. With this arrangement it is impossible for the management to lose its expenditure for entertainment on a bad night, since the band absorbs the loss.

The rap they always give you about playing for the door is that if you get popular, you get rich . . . the first few nights are usually a bust, but you hang on anyway, hoping you'll build up a reputation . . .

well, actually because you need the gig . . . I really have seen it work
before . . . some cats I knew had a good thing going at this 3.2 club
for about four or five months until the group broke up. They were
pulling in about three hundred a night on Fridays and Saturdays,
and maybe a hundred on Thursdays, and a hundred on Sunday
afternoons. For four men that was all right bread . . . the trouble is
that it doesn't happen very often, and in the end you wind up getting screwed, as usual. That kind of thing never lasts. [*Piano player*]

The only way in which *playing for the door* is a good economic
arrangement for the group is when it has a sufficient following to at
least generate its usual one-night asking price, or to establish a minimum wage which the employer agrees to pay if the door is bad. Rock
musicians quickly learn that it is a managers' market.

So I go down to Chuck and ask him for a gig, and he says "two
hundred dollars for Friday and Saturday night"—take it or leave it.
It costs us at least twenty-five to get down there and back and buy
strings, and so what's left, about forty dollars a man for one week.
But I have to take it because we haven't played a gig in three weeks.
[*Guitar player*]

In this case the offer is way below the expectable door, and so a flat
price is, in actuality, *playing for a low percentage of the door.* The manager knows that he can buy local entertainment cheaply because he
knows that the existence of his bar is a significant slice of the total
market to which a local group can expect to sell its services.

The local group's bar gigs are shaped by the existence of another
form of rock economics: the travelling group. Groups from out of
town are *booked into town* through contacts and contracts with booking agents who, in turn, have booking agreements with local bars.
The ability of a bar manager to buy the services of a seemingly infinite number of rock bands through an agent enables him to establish an entertainment policy which consists of a "new group every
week." The bar gigs then split into two relevant categories for the

local group: agency-booked gigs and individually booked gigs. There is the ability to gain entrance to agency-booked gigs through a contract with an agent, but from the agent's viewpoint there is only limited use to a local group, for once they have been exposed to the local market their novelty is missing, and it is the entertainment policy of novelty which is the monetary return of the agency that books rock bar gigs at prices that most managers can afford. For the group that does not travel outside of a limited region, the bar-booking agent's services are similarly of limited use.

The number of bar gigs that are left for the local group after imported groups have taken their toll, plus the occasional agency-booked job, constitutes the local bar market. In economic terms, the travelling group's bookings constitute a salary, whereas the local group's piecemeal bookings constitute wages.

> We never know where the next gig is coming from. Last week was the first time we'd played in three weeks and that was because some out-of-town group cancelled at ——— [*a local bar*]. Spring is coming, though, and things always pick up . . . more dances and parties, and proms—we clean up on those—and the occasional concert pops up . . . probably on a night when you've got another gig—that's typical for us. . . . We could sign with an agency, and play steady gigs, and get steady money . . . we've talked about it enough. But that means travelling and hassles and somebody always telling you what to play . . . and we've talked about that too! Maybe that will happen, but we've been living from week to week for three years now, and we're sane—poor, but still sane. [*Guitar player/leader*]

The ability to make steady money means playing steady gigs, which, in turn, means going on the road and no longer existing as a *local* group. With the resources of a local market, there is no choice but to participate in the piecemeal economics of a wage income.

The concert gig is only an occasional event. Local groups typically get a concert gig when a *name group* (i.e., one that has a recording contract) is booked for a concert and a second or perhaps a third act is needed. Although the group is usually well paid for its services, the chance to play to a concert audience is usually considered a valuable chance for "big-time" exposure. Playing the first set at a concert gig is usually as close as a local group gets to actualizing its dreams of being rock stars, and the event provides a set of recognizable names to drop in future accounts of one's performance activities. The concert gig's rarity makes its existence as an economic resource no more than a fortuitous event to be pieced together with social, ceremonial, and bar performance realities into some semblance of economic stability.

MIDDLEMEN

It is significant that those who assemble audiences for local rock music are not the performers themselves, so that whenever there is a gig there is virtually always a middleman between group and audience. The essential trait of the middleman is his attachment to the physical and social environment in which the performance is to take place—something which the group can only have access to by invitation. As I have pointed out, the gigs which are available to the local group come from a diversity of social realities in which the demand for a rock music event is uniquely constructed. The economic problem is to disseminate information of the group's existence and readiness to play to each of these independently constructed markets. Agencies, of course, provide this service, but self-producing musicians are, by definition, their own managers and agents, and getting gigs depends on making and maintaining direct contact with local rock middlemen.

In this sense, the *bundle of tasks* (as Everett Hughes called it)[9] which local musicians consider to be part of their enterprise includes activities that are conventionally purchased as specialized services in the bureaucratically administered commercial music business. For example, managers, agents, and independent producers are distinguishable occupational roles in big-time music, and their contracts command healthy percentages of their client's fees. Managers tend to work closely with musicians; they publicize them, shape their image, and represent them in business transactions. Agents tend to provide the service of finding employment, and are rarely involved with a particular musician's personal problems, image, promotion, or representation in business deals. Independent producers tend to organize and finance recording sessions, choose material and arrangements, and attempt to sell the finished product to a record company. Small-time agents are typically available to book local groups and often specialize in bar gigs, but where musicians and bar owners are independent businessmen they trust their own abilities to arrange for musical work. Most local groups simply cannot afford the services of a manager or an agent, and do such work themselves. On the other hand, most local groups would jump at the offer of an independent record producer's services, but such offers are rare and often involve huge profits for the producer should the even more rare event of a large recording company contract come to pass. The most typical situation is that a local group manages its own publicity, image, job contacts, and physical presentation, as well as producing whatever demo (demonstration) recordings that might be necessary for potential employers to listen to. Ironically, if the group is successful at handling this task bundle for themselves they can afford to farm out that work to specialists and not do it themselves.

Before the time of financial success, business cards, personal calls, and friendship networks account for the bulk of a local group's gig contacts. Business cards with the name of the group, some indication of the group's musical identity, a name, and a telephone number appear on college bulletin boards, public bulletin boards, and in music stores. Business cards and letters of solicitation are also mailed to social chairmen of organizations that are known to hire bands: high school classes, college student organizations, fraternities, sororities, bars, and the like. A personal visit is the standard form of contact with bars and agencies. However, for most local groups, friendship networks account for the majority of gig-producing contacts. The simplest kind of network is the dyadic relationship of an audience member who approaches a group member at a performance event. Friendships between satisfied previous employers and new employers produce gigs, since the social conditions which produced the demand for rock services in the first place are likely to arise in a friend's similar situation.

Party gigs are examples of this kind of contact: The social committee of a fraternity exchanges the name and number of a good group with a contemporary in another fraternity, or the Jewish housewife seeks the name and number of the band that played at her friend's son's bar mitzvah. Friendship networks between musicians result in gig contacts, as well, although the competitiveness of the local market makes a group's contacts a valued part of its economic attachment to the locality. When a group encounters a gig it cannot play, or when personnel move from group to group, gig contacts are passed along from musician to musician. Both the employer/employer friendship and the musician/musician friendship channel contacts in such a way as to form local *circuits*.

> We just sorta stumbled across the fraternity party scene, man . . .
> a friend got us this one gig, and pretty soon we had a lot of gigs
> booked with different fraternities. I guess they must come and
> check out each other's bands or something because we sure didn't
> hustle ourselves. Between Fort Collins and Boulder that keeps us
> fairly busy. [*Bass player*]

What keeps a local group's contacts intact is its ability to establish a history of satisfied employers and audiences from which the new client is virtually always referred.

Bars and agents will normally ask the group for an audition prior to any actual job negotiations. There is no monetary return for an audition, and therefore it always represents an economic loss to the group. The chance of getting a good gig or set of bookings is the only incentive of the audition event. The complicated management of impressions by members of the group and by the entrepreneur are complex and difficult to describe in detail. In essence, the group tries to perform the parts of its repertoire which it thinks will most impress the employer (that is, what the group thinks the manager or agent conceptualizes as entertainment) while the employer takes a very critical attitude, requesting certain songs, or perhaps paying no attention at all. Many auditions are simply opportunities for bars to get free entertainment for an afternoon or early evening, or for an agent to reinforce his or her own role as rock music expert-entrepreneur with no real thought of hiring the group.

> Well, here we are at the same old sleazy bar, with the same old sleazy managers, doing another audition for nobody. The cat that wanted to hear us didn't even show up, the agents he was gonna bring—they didn't show either. Even the manager of the bar split before we started playing. . . . We've got just about the best zero band around, man . . . why if we can keep on doing auditions in Denver and Boulder maybe in five or ten years we can work ourselves up to auditioning in the big clubs—Chicago, Las Vegas, New York. . . . [*Guitar player/leader after an audition*]

When the group initiates interaction with a bar or agent, it can expect the ritual of the audition to be invoked. What the group sees as a big chance, however, turns out to be business-as-usual to the rock entrepreneur, and even if a gig ensues, the audition event has established the superordinate/subordinate interactional form between the assessments of the middleman and the music of the group. The ability of months and perhaps years of practice to produce monetary return for the group stands or falls on the assessment of an entrepreneur—someone who auditions groups in search of a marketable musical product.

STEADY GIGS

The local group's problematic access to audiences creates an ideal type: steady gigs. Establishing contacts with the disparate realities which social, ceremonial, bar, and concert gigs represent, and even participating in an audition or free performance, creates an audience of followers (a *following*) which is the socioeconomic indicator of steady gigs.

> When the group is going right, you'll have steady gigs—they just appear, because somebody has heard you and liked you and they're in the position to hire a group. When you don't have steady gigs, everybody knows there's something wrong. When things dry up too much, the group just dies . . . after all, you gotta eat. [*Former drummer*]

The lifetime of a local group is directly related to the number of gigs which are available in its locality. Large urban areas may be able to sustain a local group, but ten or twelve bar gigs, the fraternity-sorority or student activities gigs of a large university, and the unknown number of high school and party gigs in what might be considered a more typical setting are not likely to provide musicians a sufficient economic base for steady gigs. New groups may be able to manage the steady gig existence for a few months, but when the market has been exhausted, when the illusion of local economic stability passes, the group ceases being a local group and hits the road by seeking work outside the immediate locality, or it breaks up. Whether or not it is so conceptualized by the musicians, a local group is a transitory phenomenon which exists by virtue of a local demand for rock events which require only a small investment on the part of a casual employer. In this way the local market provides an experimental training experience—"a place to be bad"—for the career of becoming a popular musician; but it does not provide a place for full-time employment as a professional popular musician.

Part III

Mastering the Technological Component

6

Technology and The Music

So far I have described a set of cultural arrangements which surround rock musicians without offering a description of rock music itself. There are a number of ways of going about this task, and since none tells the whole story I feel that the insight gained from several descriptive methods promotes a more complete understanding than any one method standing alone. Perhaps the richest and most obvious of approaches is to trace the cultural origins of American popular music. However this is much easier said than done—especially since the research and literature which are available on the topic remain contradictory, and a coherent historical account does not neatly appear after the data have been consulted and sifted. Nevertheless I will sketch several of the influences that seem worthy of consideration when responding to the question: Where did American popular music (and especially rock music) come from?

AFRICANISMS

First, the influence of African music is both historically recognized and musically noticeable. The problem with many accounts of "Africanisms" in American music, though, is that they consider the vast continent of Africa, with its tremendous geographical and cultural diversity, as if it had only one kind of music. Obviously this is untrue, and a more sensible approach (as suggested by Oliver) would be to trace the specifics of the slave trade and discern the features of the African music cultures that were most able to affect America.[1] This is complicated not only by immense historiographical difficulties (for example: Which people from which parts of Africa went to which North and/or South American regions?), but by the twin processes of acculturation and enculturation in a repressed social atmosphere. Did, for example, the public dancing and music-making that existed in New Orleans until the first part of the nineteenth century (when it was outlawed) represent intact African traditions or American modifications and amalgamations of African memories? Or, to take another example, was the plantation entertainment produced by slaves in a forced situation (which, therefore, included double meanings, inside jokes, and coded language) a wholly new response to new conditions, or did it retain identifiable "Africanisms"? The mixing of African-based musical ideas once they got to the Western Hemisphere (in the Caribbean region, for example) adds to the confusion. In this way what is commonly known as Latin American music exhibits fundamentally African qualities to some people and fundamentally European (Spanish) qualities to others.

Despite these caveats in favor of specificity it is often possible to isolate (general) Africanisms in music by listening for certain qualities that have been conventionally labelled as such: an unchanging pulse or a *metronome time sense*, a dominance of percussion instruments, multiple overlaid rhythms or polymeter, off-beat melodic phrases, and overlapping call-and-response patterns.[2] Notice how rhythmic concerns dominate this list. To the ears of people who are used to European-based music an emphasis on rhythmic features and the failure to treat harmony and melody as the first items on one's musical agenda seem strange and simplistic. Similarly, to the ears of many African people an accelerating or decelerating pulse or the existence of a single meter (a time signature) signals a lack of musical interest and complexity no matter how elaborate the harmonic features of a piece might be. The "monotony" which is so distasteful to the critics of contemporary rhythm music may simply indicate a lack of aesthetic concern with melodic and harmonic elements in that music. Since aesthetic criteria other than the traditional Western European concern with harmony may be operating in music, and even if it is spurious to make such cultural generalizations, most American popular musicians tend to use the label *African* as a conventional way of indicating that rhythm—especially multiple interlocked rhythmic parts—is a primary (and not merely supportive) quality of a piece of music. It should also be noted that the kinds of (native) African music which actually do exhibit a focus on percussionists who spontaneously compose complex *locking* rhythms tend toward an indeterminately long performance time (twenty minutes, let's say, or an hour or more) in a setting (often outdoors) where dancing takes place, and where a large group of people actively participates in making music. This intentionally social music blurs the distinctions between musicians and non-musicians (or, performers and audience members) that seem so important to the non-participatory audience role that characterizes European music.

EUROPEAN MUSIC

A second major influence on American music can be identified as European-based popular music, and for the particular case of the United States it is useful to recognize that English (and Irish and Scottish) folk songs were more accessible than continental musical materials.[3] The long-standing European tradition of delivering history and news through itinerant human musical media (consider the *troubadours* and *trouveres*) lays a groundwork for the social and political comment that is an obvious feature of contemporary American popular music. Telling stories through music places an emphasis on the narrator—the singer—and on dramatic speech patterns even in purely instrumental music. European-based popular songs, then, are likely to exhibit qualities of insightful communication that go beyond the general understanding that songs are short, simple, musically vocalized presentations of poetic text. A modernized example of this is to be found in English broadside ballads which made use of the popular medium of the printing press to print many stanzas of social and historical revelations or political criticisms on large sheets of paper which were then sold by enterprising cultural workers. Most likely these humorous or mordant or ironic words were meant to be sung to the tune of a traditional melody and their success as mass-distributed culture had more to do with innovations in viewpoint than innovations in music. However this is exactly the state of affairs that characterizes early American music. Although songs which are strongly identified with America (like "Yankee Doodle") exhibit patriotism and an independent fighting (revolutionary?) spirit *in their words*, the musical compositions are imitations—sometimes direct copies—of British and continental tunes. In much the same way contemporary popular music places timely lyrics "on top of" derivative or recycled compositions with which the audience is presumed to be familiar.

It is interesting to note the historical and cultural connections of North African music and Scottish or Irish folk songs and dances. In general, however, the so-called modal tunes and distinctively designed instruments which exemplify these relationships constitute a minority report for present-day popular music. Certainly the folk music of the Appalachian region and its (partial) effect on commercialized country music is tangible evidence of a way of making music that emphasizes the use of *tunings* and *drone* tones—(often referred to as *modal* technique)—over harmonic modulations. Today this kind of thing can be seen in the five-string banjo (which includes a drone string) and other instruments (such as the guitar) when they are uniquely tuned to accompany particular songs. However popular these "middle eastern" derivations may have been at one time, the advent of radio and recordings marks the time of their decline as a resource for American popular musicians. Even though these ways of approaching music are now heard only as a minor influence (pun intended) in the world of popular music, some jazz players keep modality alive and even use instrumental sounds, like that of the soprano saxophone, which are reminiscent of North African instruments.[4] Of course old time country music and fiddle tunes, which are often used to accompany square dancing, also hint at a music which has no need for the equal temperament system upon which both Western European art music and contemporary American popular music are based.

Obviously European art music is heavily implicated as an influence in all phases of American musical life. In the same sense that the colonies and original United States had no indigenous folk music, they had no indigenous art music either.[5] The Western European art tradition was appropriated to fill this gap, and to this day what is considered to be "legitimate" music in America is dominated by European compositions and approaches to music. The unique aspects of European art music can best be understood in an appreciation of the development of the mensural notation system—the printed five-line system with which we are all familiar. The monks who invented this symbolic breakthrough in music communication rather effectively standardized the relationship of music and liturgy in the Roman church and distributed it to all parts of the world. The unintended consequence of their innovations was the secularization of the use of the notation system and the rise of the composer as an especially statused and empowered individual in the musical world. By composing on paper and committing compositions to the scribe or the printing press (instead of to memory), composers could simultaneously align many complicated voices into a single *polyphonic* presentation. By being trained to precisely render what was written on paper into sound, musicians became the interpreters of a composer's literary orders, and the complex polyphonic possibilities of the large orchestra became possible to organize. By rationalizing the time value of notes and instituting the concept of uniform meter with bar lines (*measures* of music), the authors of the mensural notation system facilitated complexity in the melodic possibilities of music by simplifying its rhythmic possibilities. The simultaneous and sequential interaction of many melodies has come to be the focus of Western European art music, and is the feature which most of its devotees point to when claiming its superiority over other kinds of music. Certainly this is the ideology which has been promulgated by the academies of European music which have been established at American colleges and universities. These schools, in turn, supply the music curricula to secondary and primary schools and also train players for American orchestras and smaller ensembles.

Although much more could be said about the European art music tradition in general its specific influences on American popular music can be exemplified by church music and Italian opera. The concrete presence of churches, where choral singing and polyphonic accompaniment were placed in the routine of everyday life, cannot be underestimated. Many people have their first exposure to the situation of performing music in church. Songs of praise and celebration sung in close harmonic intervals (thirds and fifths) have obvious counterparts in gospel and soul music as well as in the *tour de force* arranging style found in many big bands (or, for that matter, in the horn sections which accompany many popular music groups, large or small). Many hymns incorporate sections of eight bars in duple or quadruple measure, often including a release which returns to the initial strain—aspects which are similar to secular popular music. Operatic music, by combining music and theater, is an obvious model for the dramatic singing style which is affected by many American popular vocalists. The soaring virtuoso solo form of the operatic *aria* has certainly been available to American audiences ever since the early nineteenth century when tours of "the states" were first organized by European impresarios who made a business of pushing generation after generation of cultured "stars" to the very edge of the rough-and-ready American frontier. It should be remembered that the combining of theatrical, musical, and dance forms (an expensive operation) has brought opera both popular appeal and expert criticism for being "unartistic." The onstage dancing and theatricalism of contemporary popular musicians—a tendency toward using multiple media—is comparable to opera both in its widespread accessibility to audiences and its unattractiveness to purists.

SOME MUSICOLOGICAL PROBLEMS

Although it is useful in providing precedents for some rather diffuse qualities of American popular music, a consideration of African and European art and folk music does not result in a precise definition of the workings of such influences where actual pieces of music are concerned. An alternate way of approaching that description would be to make an abstract musicological study of the similarities and differences found in a sample of contemporary popular compositions. Standard academic musicology has accomplished such a task for Western European art music, and academic ethnomusicology has made an interesting start toward a taxonomy of compositions from the rest of the world's music cultures, and so it would seem that academic methods could make short work of something like rock music. From this viewpoint, for example, it could be known that virtually all rock music is in quadruple or duple meter; that its sections measure sixteen or thirty-two bars each; that there are one or two verse sections before a section known as the *bridge* or *release*; that the melody and accompanying lyrics often repeat a strain; that harmonic sequences are based on triads and dominant seventh chords of the first, fourth, and fifth tones of the diatonic scale, and (to a lesser extent) minor chords of the second, third, and sixth tones of the diatonic scale; and so forth.

There are several kinds of limitations inherent in this kind of musicological analysis of compositions. For one thing the process assumes that some way of documenting all the defining aspects of any particular composition is available. This works well enough with printed scores but becomes problematic when music is neither written nor read, but passed along to others only as a performance (or a recording of a performance). Transcribing performances with the aid of some symbol system is typically the literate person's solution to the "problem" of non-literate musicians. In fact, much of the sheet music which is commercially available for rock compositions is created *after* the final recorded version is approved for distribution and is marketed by the publisher as a companion product to the album upon which the composition appears. Usually a specialist at transcription and music copying is contracted to handle this task (and to copy the parts used by whatever extra studio musicians are hired for a recording session), and the process is undertaken in much the same spirit that an academic musicologist might employ in analyzing a field recording. Because the five-line (mensural) notation system is not equipped to precisely indicate many of the pitch and rhythmic aspects of rock performance conventions, a reading of the sheet music often produces something less than satisfactory in comparison to the original recording. This is in distinction to an earlier era in American popular music where composers—usually supplying music for Broadway stage productions—worked with the written system in much the same manner as academic art musicians, and produced faithful renderings of their often sophisticated songs (so faithful, in fact, that publishers often hired specialists to write simplified versions for the "home" market). The point is that comparing the details of commercially available printed versions of rock songs for analytic purposes might lead to spurious generalizations since the compositions may not have been conceived in terms of the rules of the written notation system in the first place.

Another way of going about the musicological task of describing rock music is to deal with recordings as the unit of analysis. This is, in fact, what both performing musicians and analysts of the style tend to do. There are a few attempts by academically trained musicologists to present "purely musical" conclusions about rock music. Mantle Hood's findings about the Beatles' recorded music and Ronald Byrnside's analysis of 1950s rock recordings are examples in this regard, especially since they both seize upon the idea of a deceleration in time sense as a latent aspect which unifies the selections in their samples.[6] The idea that *embedded* compositional devices distinguish rock music from other kinds of music is attractive to those who wish to "scientifically" isolate types of musical technique, but it tends to overestimate the intentions and abilities of rock composers and performers. In this sense the motivations of researchers become a limitation in and of themselves. Even the best and least prejudiced compositional analyst is making the assumption that compositions are the primary item of interest in understanding a music culture. Undoubtedly this happens because musicologists have learned their craft in the context of the European influence where the written score is the focus of attention within the music culture. It is possible, though, that popular music cultures have not elevated compositions to primary importance either for players or listeners, and that attention to performance techniques (improvisational solos, for example) outweighs attention to premeditated compositional creativity. This points to the existence of aesthetic differences in various kinds of music and the poverty of assuming that an analytic technique that is appropriate for one is appropriate for all. It turns out that rock compositions are considered to be so simplistic as to be boring from the viewpoint of most academically trained musicians, yet from the viewpoint of most rock performers, there is nothing quite so boring as to endure the performance of a popular song as it is interpreted by a player who uses the conventions of the academic tradition.

Beyond the drawbacks of an overwrought attention to compositional techniques in either written or recorded form, standard academic materials that typify music are burdened with a cumbersome sampling problem. If, for example, there were but one composer of the materials of a particular music culture, a comparative analysis of all those compositions could plausibly lead to the isolation of certain identifying characteristics. Although this is never the actual case, the works of particular composers which have been analyzed in this way are often taken to exemplify a style which is called characteristic of a certain culture or a certain historical period. The question then becomes: How are we to decide the *representativeness* of this sample of compositions? What about the other composers? How many of them were there? How many works did they create, and with what compositional techniques? Questions of this sort are suppressed by assuming a knowledge of which compositions are *in* and which are *out* of analytic consideration. For example, the "stars" whose compositions compose the expected repertoire for most

European art music concerts were included in a discernible grouping by promotional entrepreneurs,[7] and without questioning any "classical" composer's musical genius we can easily question whether these works are representative of the works of their unheard-of cultural contemporaries. To be scientifically accurate one has to be able to make an exhaustive list of every member of a population before that population can be sampled. Therefore to say that rock music compositions are distinguishable according to certain analytically known characteristics presumes that an exhaustive list of all rock compositions has been compiled and sampled. Are Delta blues or Chicago blues songs to be included? Are "hit" versions of Broadway show tunes to be included? Are the compositions of Frank Zappa to be included? Are Muzak versions of top-40 hits to be included? Or, looking at it another way: How many popular composers and compositions are unknown because of lack of publication, or because of erroneous credit lines? These questions barely begin to lift the lid on a Pandora's box of definitional problems which make sampling the compositions of rock music—or any music—an uncertain procedure. Ultimately we recognize that the rules for categorizing compositions into types have been created for promotional or historical purposes, and that taken-for-granted classifications represent qualitative valuations based on special—often economic—interests to a much greater extent than they represent "natural" groupings of style or creativity. To define *rock music* by comparing a sample of recordings found on *Billboard's* "Hot 100" list from the early 1950s to the present would suppress compositions that were never recorded or were never promoted by record companies. Such a procedure would also turn up an amazing diversity of compositional techniques and a corresponding equivocality of results if the perceivable differences between selections were detailed. On the other hand the scientific musicological method could handily distinguish rock music from other kinds of music if a few similarities between the selections (say, the use of *one-four-five* or *blues* chord progressions) were used as the criteria for categorizing the sample. In short, no matter how rational and rigorous the comparative compositional analysis, the compositions selected for analysis are ultimately *assumed* to belong together because a category name has been rather arbitrarily assigned to them by cultural tradition or by a promoter or by a historian. Furthermore, striking technical similarities can be demonstrated for a multitude of compositions from a variety of the world's music cultures (an enlightening ethnomusicological pastime), but in no way does such a demonstration prove that those far-flung selections belong together in a natural way.

Finally, it should be noted that these same problems also arise when only the *lyrics* of songs are sampled and compared. A number of published works that have passed as "sociology of popular music" in recent years have dealt with an analysis of songpoems,[8] and categories of popular music (like "protest songs" or "courtship songs") have been established on this basis. Of course any approach that treats meaning as a legitimate part of the sociological enterprise is a refreshing relief from the war on meaningfulness that is often waged by rigidly numerological sociologists, but to leap from the literary analysis of popular song texts (no matter how they are sampled) to conclusions about popular *music* pretends that sounds and performances are irrelevant to music. Not only does this erode the credibility of those who would mistake poetry for the whole of music, but it displaces textual analysis from its appropriate use—as one of many things that would have to be considered in an attempt to unravel the socially meaningful aspects of music.

RECORDINGS AND THE MUSIC

I have introduced some of the drawbacks to using the prevailing academic methods of tracing cultural origins and "scientifically" comparing compositions in order to explain my omission of them in offering a sociologically satisfying definition of what is commonly called rock music. It is not that I reject these approaches; quite to the contrary, I have made good use of them in coming to whatever understandings I have about popular music in America. Rather, I see the need for a supplemental approach which emphasizes the social production of musical reality. From this standpoint the drawbacks associated with conventional definitions of music illustrate the focus of my approach: the *taken-for-granted* as it applies to music. While most musicological investigators assume that patterns of composition can completely describe types of music, I assume that types are culturally produced categories which could be applied to diverse compositional patterns. The problem of uncertainty as to whether certain performances or compositions should be grouped together is, *itself*, the phenomenon of interest. Since, in actual life, category names tend to be taken-for-granted, what actually defines rock music is that certain compositions and performances are distributed with that label attached. Cultural leaders (such as record producers, disc jockeys, or record reviewers in this case) make it their business to define what is *in* or *out* of the rock world, and the followers rarely question those definitions. Of course the leaders take care not to shock the followers with sonic experiences which are radical departures from what was last presented as rock. Those who consider popular music to be business have a vested interest in creating and maintaining the taken-for-granted definition of their product, and are therefore the perpetrators of a variety of accepted category names for music—names such as *easy listening, country*, and *disco*, as well as *rock*. That some 1970s country music sounds a lot like 1950s rock music, or that some 1950s rock music sounds very different from what is often called rock music in the 1980s, does not cause the culturally accepted label to change.

The point here is that what is taken-for-granted by some is induced by others. There is no reason to believe that this has not been so throughout the history of music (or any other cultural enterprise, for that matter). On the other hand the existence of electronic devices has brought about a unique state in the art of making music acceptable to audiences. Until less than a century ago those who would attempt to institute the acceptance of music relied solely upon the ability of live performances to present that music to assembled audiences; now performances can be distributed to dispersed audiences without the services of live musicians. In either case it is only a repeated exposure of music to people's ears that can change novelty into long-term identification with that music. By recognizing the existence of this simple but basic principle, the means of managing the "taken-for-grantedness" of music has become the focus of my sociological understanding of music types. It is *how* the labelling of music is organized, and not simply *that* it is labelled, that promotes an audience's desire to hear music again and again.

Interestingly, the promotion of music is most successful when an audience is so saturated with the sound of the music that it no longer bothers to describe it with linguistic labels. When this process has been accomplished I speak of the existence of *the music* to represent a perceiver's taken-for-granted attitude toward what has been successfully distributed and culturally accepted. In this sense people throughout the world have access to musical sounds through a variety of sources; and, for any particular person, some of these sources may be labelled objectionable, and others may be allowed to carry the identifying label of their presentors, while only a few sources will be able to be perceived without the need for a label. This is *the music*. It is a member's attitude toward a group's *own* music. Of course where people have no particular cultural identity *the music* is not a relevant concept. On the other hand, in settings where there are strong identifications between individuals and groups there are inevitably cultural events which include *the music*.

In order to identify American popular music which is distributed through electronic means without the presence of musicians I have coined, somewhat ironically, the phrase *The Music* (with the capital letters). By this I am representing both the taken-for-granted aspect of electronic distribution as well as the larger-than-life, never before possible (and, even now, not quite possible) sharing of a musical and cultural identity across thousands of miles and thousands of alternate cultural possibilities. While local musicians use the resources of The Music in the development of their own musical skills, as a source of compositions, and as a definition of their economic relationship with employers and audiences, they are also in direct competition with it as a limitation on the perceived quality of and need for their live services. These contradictions point to the existence of *secondary* popular culture: the response of those on the receiving end to the primary, centralized, and industrialized, producers and distributers of cultural objects.[9] The contradictory existential state of local popular musicians is mainly due to the fact that they get their materials from the same source that others consider to be the source of finished products.

As a product The Music takes the form of vinyl discs (records), plastic strips impregnated with magnetizable substances (tapes), and the broadcast signals which are derived from them (radio). Even a "live" radio or television broadcast must also be included in a definition of The Music since its sound is manipulated as if it were a recording. (Actually the occurrence of live broadcasts is rare in comparison to broadcasts which are mechanically reproduced). The Music enters human lives from car radios and tape players, home stereos, portable radios, portable record and tape players, and specially broadcast "background" music in places of work, business, and leisure. Any site where a speaker may be placed can be defined by The Music: parking lots, patios, beaches, sidewalks, elevators, airplanes, ski slopes, and swimming pools. Even if people do not desire The Music they are subjected to it in public space, and often irritated by its entrance into private aural envelopes through thin apartment walls or open doors or windows. Electronic playback systems are integral with contemporary environmental design, and The Music is the sonic environment they create. Their patterning of compressions and rarefactions in air exists everywhere in the same form. The playback system on the west coast puts out a sound which is virtually identical to the playback system of the east coast. It is not simply the same *song* that millions of individuals share, but the same experience of sound— from the same recording take, with the same amendments, deletions, augmentations, and effects. The Music is a phenomenon of a society which is literally wired for sound.

All of this has an overwhelming effect on the ways in which living musicians are able to present their music to audiences. As with any musicians in any music culture, musicians in modern settings find it necessary to develop an awareness of the soundscape which surrounds them. For example: What instruments are audiences used to? What sources of sound generation are experienced in the course of everyday life? What times of day go with what sounds? Only by developing a sense of the aural contexts which surround them can musicians know when and how to play. Of course musicians can simply be trained to perform on command, but in that case someone associated with the employer is presumed to have this vital information about what kind of music is appropriate. After some experiences with performing it would seem that only the most unobservant players would fail to perceive the customary patterns which hold social and musical events together. This kind of knowledge is essential to professionalism, and deteriorates rapidly when it crosses the boundaries between music cultures. Indians, for example, have the choice of remaining in motionless meditation while listening to hard-driving American rock music, while I have the choice of hearing a twilight *rag* at high noon. Such things would not be possible without recordings. In person and in their own cultural contexts musicians would not promote a disrespect toward the social expectations which conventionally surround their performances.

For beginning rock musicians it is interesting to note how much of this learning-of-context occurs during events which are defined as parties. Often the mere presence of The Music serves to invoke the party reality. When a living musician is also present at a party he or she may be invited to perform.

HSB: Do people ever ask you to play when you're a guest at a party?

S: Yeah. Sure. I really hate it though when everybody's been listening to some group on the stereo and then you start playing alone with your acoustic guitar or something. . . . It's like everybody's gonna go to sleep or something; or they get fidgety and nervous. You can feel that energy level go right down. And if you don't know enough to stop somebody's gonna just go right over to the machine and put a record on. Right while you're playing. . . . Actually you should have enough sense not to get into a situation like that. [*Guitar player*]

Sometimes parties are arranged to be music parties even when it is known that not all the guests are musicians. These tend to result in music when the participants have played together before and when one or two experienced musicians are present to sustain things. This is social music in the traditional sense of the term, and it is my suspicion that it is not a common event in America. More likely is the situation where only those who think of themselves as musicians *want* to play.

> Jack came with his banjo and his harmonicas and of course Vern came with his harmonicas and there was the usual noodling of the guitar by Jan. People were up for it at first, but after about an hour of noodling and talking things over and Jack getting drunker and drunker on wine, somebody went over and put on a record . . . they tried to play along with records for another hour before they finally gave up. [*Non-musician*]

Even when an organized group is playing at a party there can be guests who have "just happened" to bring an instrument with them. And even though "sitting-in" is a custom among musicians who know each other and have some reason to believe that they can play with one another, it becomes a problem when a "stranger" wants to play.

> That guy . . . yeah *that* guy. He hit us with it right at the first break and I could tell right then he was gonna be trouble because we couldn't get away from him. All the usual lines only stalled him off. . . . Then next break he really started bugging us to play and so Ed said "Why not?" So we put him on and he wanted to play "Johnny B. Goode" and he was horrible. . . . A fucking disaster! . . . Ed had lent him his guitar but he couldn't get it back from him. Finally the rest of us just left the stage to get him to stop. . . . Of course he could have been great. Then he makes you look bad. . . . It could actually be a disaster either way. [*Drummer*]

Even for established professionals, though, the main source of musical competition is *the box.*

> It was really packed . . . during the break between third and fourth
> sets some guys loaded up the box with quarters and played Eagles
> songs over and over. There were some people dancing and . . . the
> typical rowdy situation. . . . It was time to play the last set and
> this scene was still going on. After about ten minutes John went
> over and pulled the plug on the box. You shoulda seen the reac-
> tion from those guys—something like "What the fuck do you
> think you're doin'?" They were pretty drunk. It was like somebody
> pulled *their* plug or something. I really think John would've got-
> ten punched out if he hadn't run back to the stage and we hadn't
> started playing right away. . . . Hell I can't really blame people
> (for wanting to listen to records). I can't really come up with the
> sound of ten dynamite studio musicians and thirty-two tracks
> with dbxs. I like what that sounds like, too. . . . And to be honest
> that's where I cop licks myself. If people want to listen to records
> then I usually quit trying to play because I figure you can't force
> people to listen. . . . There's just some times when live music isn't
> best. [*Guitar player*]

To the extent that contemporary popular music is dominated by commercial recordings, audiences form not only their sonic expectations but their expectations about appropriate musical presentation from experiences with recordings. The Music is, after all, under the direct control of those who listen to it; they start it and stop it by flipping switches and turn it up or down by twisting knobs. When faced with live musicians, audiences tend to assume that the same kind of control relationship will define their role. Obviously this presents a variety of problems for live performers. Beginners often pass through episodes of resentment and anger at the insensitivity of their treatment in this regard before recognizing the origin of the phenomenon and the possibilities of working within its context.

Both The Music and the awareness of sound that it creates raise questions about the description of contemporary popular music that cannot be answered by resorting to historical, compositional, or textual analysis. Rock music, the specific case in point, takes its shape as a finished product because of controls over sound that take effect *after* performers have relinquished their control over what and how they play. When sound has been converted to the form of an electric signal, the way in which it was created becomes less important than what can be done to it after it has been played. Technical innovations at this intermediary stage—after creation and before reception by an audience—have had an enormous effect on the kinds of sounds which can be assimilated by rock musicians, and, therefore, on the music they make. The actual manifestations of this innovative activity are recording studios.

Understanding the technical details of how a recording studio works is not so important as understanding the possibilities for controlling hearable experiences which the studio provides. In order to give this kind of account I have chosen some fundamental categories of studio sound control which leave their distinctive mark on The Music. Later these categories will be related to the types of sound control which are available in live performance. The categories are: (1) polyvocality, (2) dynamics, (3) equalization, (4) resonance and delay, (5) signal-to-noise ratio, and (6) editing.

Polyvocality is the master trait of studio sound control. Polyvocal music, in a literal sense, refers to many consciously separable sounds that occur in simultaneity. In performance polyvocality is only achieved through an actual separation of players, instruments, and musical ideas into what are generally referred to as *voices*. When voices are tonal in quality, polyvocality can be called polyphony; when they are primarily percussive, polyvocality might be referred to as polyrhythm. In any case the studio makes it possible to produce a sound experience with as many different voices as one desires without the need for their simultaneous performance. Two main methods contribute to this: the use of many microphones and a mixing board, and multiple tracks on recording tape. Placing a microphone at a particular point in space creates an *earpoint* (like a viewpoint) which biases its signal in favor of the particular sounds which occur in its immediate vicinity. Using many microphones at many sites creates a variety of earpoints for the performance situation—something that is physically impossible for humans who are encumbered by the considerable bulk of their bodily form and the fact that they are supplied with only two ears which (hopefully) retain a constant spatial relationship. The studio environment affords an electronic separation of musical phenomena by a physical space-partitioning system which can acoustically isolate microphones and virtually eliminate overlap between their signals. The definition of space in a recording studio is a major parameter of the sound of the recordings that are made there, for it is the spatial isolation of microphones which allows the complete electronic isolation of their signals. The sounds of one instrument (such as drums) may even be separated by the use of multiple microphones, creating more than one voice from only one player/instrument system.

There are enough microphones in the studio situation to sense the specific vibrational qualities of each part of each instrument without being overwhelmed by the total volume level of the players, since signals may be electronically attenuated and mixed with other signals. The close proximity of a microphone allows it to respond to fundamental vibrations that have yet to take on an interference pattern from nearby sounds. The ability to place a variety of microphones, each type having its own response characteristic, in physically—acoustically—separated spaces in the studio, and then to mix their simultaneous signals produces a unique way of hearing that humans cannot possibly achieve by putting their ears in the air. This way of hearing is an acoustic expectation for anyone who listens to contemporary recordings. It cannot be achieved without the aid of electronic devices. It has never before existed on earth.

If the polyphonies of many microphones and a way to mix their signals creates a whole new way of hearing, the ability of each of these earpoints to be *recorded* as a separate entity allows an amount of control over musical experiences which must seem, to some, an electronic polyvocal paradise. As long as some kind of continuity is established for a performance on tape (a *rhythm track* for example), separately recorded tracks may be added, subtracted, independently varied, and integrated with voices which are recorded independently of the original track. This last technique—commonly called *overdubbing*—means that the final recorded product can be composed of discontinuous episodes of performance, and yet result in one built-up sequence which simultaneously represents the originally unsynchronized voices. An ability to reverse the direction of the tape and start over again allows the recording to become the vehicle for a process of re-recording which is somewhat like the editing of a book, and more like the editing of a film. During the re-recording process each track is available for independent manipulation, and the entire passage is dissected, corrected, and augmented while retaining the time sense of the original performance. To understand the recording and re-recording process is to recognize that the layering possibilities for polyvocality are ultimately more complex than the polyvocal potential of compositions which were conceptualized (with the aid of written notation) before the invention of sound recording. The *idea* of sound control inherent in both written and recorded music, however, is identical.

Not only does the studio allow for the complete control of absolute dynamics (the ability to change the volume level of the entire performance), it enables the relative dynamic of each of the microphones and tracks to be independently adjusted. Dynamics have traditionally been the most subtle parts of a musician's knowledge, and a large part of a symphony conductor's responsibility is concerned with rehearsing and nursing the imprecisely noted dynamics of various passages into a continuity which makes sense in performance. Dynamic peaks in recorded material are available in infinite variety simply by boosting or backing-off on an appropriate level control in synchronization with the performance. Although it is possible to have this control in simultaneity with the recording process, it is customarily reserved for the re-recording process (or *mix-down*) where sixteen, twenty-four, or thirty-two distinct tracks become a two-track stereo tape. It is a common practice, for example, to crank up rock guitar solos so that they reach an ear-shattering climax that was not necessarily performed that way. Absolute dynamic control has been used in the popular recording business to provide a musical cliché in the form of the "fade" ending. The dynamic control possibilities available in the studio easily surpass the dynamic range which is available to an orchestra—and all without rehearsal or the conductor's set of prearranged signals. It is, rather, the emotive pull on a potentiometer which extracts dynamics of apparent virtuosity from a studio performance that often originates within a fairly narrow range of levels.

In the recording business it is conventional to make use of standardized *loudness contours* (see Appendix). As a technical term *loudness* means that the overall volume level of an entire recorded performance is controlled as a function of frequency. It has been experimentally established that the human ear is differentially sensitive to vibrational intensity as a function of frequency (pitch), and that at relatively low levels the low end of the sound spectrum must be several orders of magnitude greater than the middle and high ends in order for the ear to hear both registers with equal loudness (the *psychological* measure of intensity). In accordance with experimentally derived data standard loudness contours are used to provide a guideline for the final boost or attenuation of signals which appear at various frequencies—the low end usually getting a healthy boost. The kind of speaker which a listener is likely to use in receiving the performance is often anticipated in a similar way by boosting the octave components of the bass line so that they will not *drop out* on small radio speakers. Consider, then, the variety of ways in which volume levels may be shaped, since studio sound control not only provides for the setting of a level for each voice (and for the master level as well) and for the *change* in level for each voice (and the change in the master level as well), but the final product is controlled to an assumed loudness level contour to match the characteristics (some would say deficiencies) of the listener's ears.

As soon as a musician's sound has been converted into an electric signal its various component frequencies may be drastically modified. The *timbre* of a musical sound has traditionally been controlled by the design, materials, and condition of the instrument that produces it, and the ability of the human mind and musculature that plays it. When a performance is recorded in the electronic-magnetic medium the *character* of each voice can depend almost completely on the manipulation of various *filtering* devices that select distinct frequencies from a particular signal for alteration. The transformation of a bland vocal performance with few recognizable qualities into a distinctive sound is a possibility of studio sound control, and many popular singers have disappointed their live audiences with a singularly unmusical voice that did not match the vocal sound of their popular recordings. This process of controlling frequency characteristics is referred to as equalization. An *equalizer* can be one of a number of electronic filters that split signals into parts (or *bands)* on the basis of frequency. A *graphic equalizer* provides a level control for each frequency band, and there may be ten or more bands to cover the entire audible frequency range. A *parametric equalizer* produces a similar kind of frequency shaping without the huge array of controls or notches in between bands that are encountered with a graphic equalizer. Of late, circuit designs derived from computer electronics have provided *digital equalization.* No matter which type of device is used the resulting sound control possibilities are similar. Each channel of the mixing board (or track of the tape) is provided with an equalizer (typically a three- or four-band filter). In addition, the entire output of the board may be shaped with separate equalization devices that typically allow the control of many more bands than the individual inputs. Finally, effects may be achieved for either individual voices or mixed voices by using special signal processing (with the aid of accessories like phase control devices or envelopers) which produces frequency-related results. By combining all this with the basic volume level controls for every channel of the mixing board, each voice may be shaped in such a way that it blends with the others (clashing frequency characteristics are tuned out) and, at the same time, is audibly distinguishable from the others (it has its own characteristic frequency emphasis).

The design of a studio is meant to cut noise (or unwanted sound) to a minimum, and therefore produces a high signal-to-noise ratio. The interior space is usually carpeted and walled with sound-absorbing materials. A vibration-damping spot is often provided for drumming, a double-thickness window is provided between the control room and the studio to isolate the mechanical noise of the recorders and the human noise of their operators, a soundproof door exists, and a visual signal (maybe a red light) warns people in the area to be quiet when the tape is rolling. There are enough *earpoints* in the studio to get close enough to each instrument to produce an amazingly high signal-to-noise ratio for each microphone channel and tape track. In this case *noise* would be any sound coming through a channel other than the single voice that is intended to be there, and it is a subtlety of the studio concept that what is *noise* at one point may well be *signal* at another. Each of these *clean* point-signals can then be combined into the whole of the recorded performance. Environmental reverence toward silence makes the main source of noise in the studio electronic in origin. The recording amplifiers, mixing and equalization controls, and the physical movement of the tape over the tape heads produce an ambient studio noise level. It is the propensity of a grouping of electronic equipment to produce, by virtue of interconnections and simple physical proximity, the phenomena of ground loops and antennae. Ground loops tend to provide the familiar sixty-Hertz "hum" which is derived from an interaction between standard alternating line current (AC) and audio circuit power supplies, while antennae provide spurious signals radiated from broadcasting stations. Both of these conditions may be practically eliminated by the experimental arranging and rearranging of equipment, isolation transformers, and other gadgetry; but every new studio goes through a period of de-bugging while extraneous noises are eliminated from the electronics.

All of this means that the signal-to-noise ratio in a studio may be kept extremely high (that is, the noise component is kept very low)

through a general worship of silence throughout the entire operation. Innovative electronic circuitry such as the Dolby and DBX configurations have been specially designed to reduce noise in recording,
re-recording, and playback situations. Often the use of the thirty-
inch-per-second tape speed provides an outstanding signal-to-noise
ratio without additional noise-reduction circuitry. It is interesting
to note that noise-reducing circuits are also included in relatively
low-priced playback equipment intended for a mass market. Their
appearance is indicative of the widespread respect for a high signal-
to-noise ratio which studio sound has emphasized. However successful one is at increasing the signal-to-noise ratio of a recording,
though, there is always noise left in the system which, in the playback
experience, must be taken to be silence. It is the general nature of
any musical experience that it must compete with other sounds, but
even so the noise level which is provided as silence in a good studio
is at a level far below anything which has ever been heard on earth by
human ears in a natural setting.

Because of a studio's silence-providing environment, the acoustic
presence which a performance site usually adds to musical sounds is
absent. The effort in a studio is to achieve an amount of acoustical
deadness (or lack of sound-reflecting surfaces) so that the separation
upon which polyvocal sound control is based may be easily achieved.
The musically desirable effects of resonance and delay, which are
usually associated with natural performance environments, must
be somehow added to the studio signal. Some studios are equipped
with a separate room in which the sounds that are being recorded
may be reproduced by a speaker system and then reclaimed by a
microphone. The natural, architecturally produced delay between
this special speaker's output and its microphone's input results in a
resonant signal which can be separately channelled and mixed in the
same way that a single voice is controlled. In addition to this there
are a variety of electronic resonance and delay devices. Echo effects
can be achieved by means of a tape delay which records and momen-
tarily plays back a signal (a so-called echo chamber). The delay of the
echo is determined by the physical distance between the recording

and playback tape heads, while the quality of the effect is determined by electronic control over the number of repeats which the signal is allowed. Tape-produced delay is notoriously noisy. Purely electronic digital delay devices provide the same kinds of control, but with an excellent signal-to-noise ratio. Other devices (such as reverberation units that use steel springs) are also available. In this way the apparent acoustic space in which recorded performances take place is most likely a purely synthetic entity.

By re-recording, cutting, and splicing magnetic tape an edited musical passage composed of discrete segments encompassing many *takes* may be produced. For example, a recording of an introduction or a solo from one take may be attached to a passage from another take by physically joining two pieces of tape. The tempo of a passage may be speeded or slowed by driving the motor of the recorder at differential voltages. The existence of high-speed recording equipment (fifteen- and thirty-inches-per-second), precise methods of tape speed and synchronization control, and finely developed editing techniques makes the layering of sound a familiar studio practice. For example, it is possible for performers who are located in different parts of the world and who have never even met one another to "play together" on a final edition of a recording; or, it is possible to "beef up" recorded vocal performances by mixing several separate but virtually identical vocal takes into a humanly impossible but strong-sounding final version; or, it is possible to have many more voices appear on the final edition than could ever physically fit into the studio at one time.

It should be emphasized that there is nothing inherently musical about the ability to control sound. That is why I have been careful to describe the studio environment in terms of possibilities—options for action which may or may not be used to create musical experiences. Whenever these possibilities are used there is always a set of musicians in evidence to provide input to the studio system, and it is their ability to make music together which allows the finished recording to be heard as music. What happens in the studio, however, is accomplished not only by pedagogy and persuasion, but by an intrusion into the distribution route of the performer's sounds. The ability of people other than the performers to manipulate a performance before it is distributed to listeners is an essential feature of The Music.

The business of sound recording is carried on in an economic universe of discourse in which *product* is the key term, and to negotiate economic exchanges as a studio performer one must be willing to conceptualize performances as products, enter into contracts in which services are understood to be converted into products, and therefore assign the final measure of control over the sound of the product to an electronic entrepreneur. As a live performer, on the other hand, a *production* (and not a product) is the exchangeable economic entity which is recognized by members of the audience. The ability of products to get to mass markets is the mainstay of American economics, whereas the ability of productions to get to mass markets is practically nonexistent. Local rock groups deal exclusively in live performances, and therefore in an exclusively small market for their services. They are overwhelmed by their audience's attention to the product of The Music.

Traditionally all the performing arts were limited by the constraints of presenting works in real time ("the show must go on"), while the plastic and literary arts could use time in a different way—stopping for rest or inspiration, or going back and modifying or eliminating things that, in retrospect, were seen as mistakes. Recording technology has brought the editing possibilities of *time out* to the previously *all real time* of music-making. This has spurred a recognition of recording techniques as literary techniques by studio musicians and other studio workers. Just as editing a book might involve bringing distinct sections into some kind of uniformity and sequence, or choosing type faces and binding materials, or searching for errors and correcting them, or perhaps even censoring material for some reason, editing a recording involves similar mental and physical processes. And just as some editors of written material are notorious for mangling the literary constructions of authors, so are engineers, producers, and executives notorious for making musicians' performances unrecognizable to their originators. This right to intervene electronically has, until recently, been assumed to be an integral part of the recording business. Now those artists who have some bargaining power request a contractual specification of the boundaries of *artistic control* afforded to the musicians and to those who manipulate performances *ex post facto*. It is important to see that the studio's inherent sound control possibilities lay the groundwork for the intricacies of the musician's relationship with it, its owners, and its operators. There can be little doubt but that the experience of a mechanically reproduced performance involves not only the musicianship of the original performers, but the musicianship of the manipulators of the studio. The musical expertise of one of these groups is often called into question by the other. Both groups, however, recognize the studio's identity as an instrument, and the manipulator of its controls as a musician—however incapable or inspired he or she may be.

THE RECORDING CONSCIOUSNESS

When studio sound vibrates a beginning musician's eardrums, expectations about how sounds can be made and controlled come into being. Once this distinctly contemporary awareness of sound is made possible, the hearing, noting, forgetting, and remembering of sound events *in general* may be perceived through the parameters of studio sound. Even stubborn traditionalists who take on the role of "enemy" toward studio sound are changed by exposure to it. They can then imagine sounds which were previously unimaginable, and their distaste is all the more adamant for the undeniable alteration which that exposure produces in their sonic surroundings. Beginners, on the other hand, have no deeply instilled expectations about how things *should* sound, and, for them, the main feature of experiencing studio sound is an opening-up (rather than a closing-off) of musical possibilities. The flagrant sound of synthetic delay or overdubbing or flanging, which might pull profanity from the lips of a stubbornly traditional musician, is a peak experience at some point in the career of a rock musician.

> How could you forget the sound of "Heartbreak Hotel"? . . . The way the vocal just jumps out at you. . . . When I first heard that it just drove me crazy—I couldn't figure out how you could get somebody's voice to sound like that; sorta eerie and hollow. I'd heard people talking about echo chambers, but at the time I couldn't imagine what that would be. All I knew was that sound just grabbed my ears every time . . . and the thing was, I never really dug Elvis Presley. [*Guitar player*]

> "Whole Lotta Love" just blew my mind away when I first heard it . . . it still does. The way that fucker just screams into the echo . . . wow. You get stoned and listen to that over the earphones and you get lost fast. . . . I can never decide whether they purposely double-tracked the vocal that way or whether the vocal just leaked from the instrumental track and they just left it. The more you listen to that, the more of a mindfucker it is. [*Bass player*]

The lingo of sound control, the awareness that recordings have overall *sounds*, and a fascination with unravelling the mysteries of how certain studio sounds were made marks the attitude of these responses. Even disbelievers can be converted:

> I'd always been into jazz pretty exclusively—Brubeck, Parker, Mulligan maybe, and of course Coltrane—and I put down studio tricks pretty bad . . . but then I got turned on to Don Ellis playing harmonies with himself into echo. I really wanted to say "it's just a trick," but it sounded *good*, man, you know? . . . There was something there. Then I started thinking of stuff like that—not Ellis, or Weather Report, or anything else I'd heard, but stuff out of my own head . . . only it was in that same harmony-echo trip. I guess it'll get to you if you give it a chance. [*Sax player*]

To the untrained ear studio sound is a mystery, a curiosity, and an example of virtuosity. To a traditionally trained ear it is either lunacy, heresy, or a mind-changing possibility. In any case it enters the musical consciousness as a *way of imagining* (of hearing music *in the head*) that was impossible before electronic sound control devices could be heard from.

My point is that the interaction between the aura of the studio environment and the ear/mind/musculature system of the human organism can produce a specialized way of imagining sounds.[10] Vladimir Ussachevsky describes this manner of musical awareness as his "habitual imagination of a sound as if it were changed by (various) mutation techniques." Examples of these mutations include: "pitch transportation through variation of the tape speed; snipping of the attack and listening to the body of the sound; playing the sound backwards; depriving it of some of its harmonics through filtering; and reverberating it."[11] I am not proposing that Ussachevsky, or any of the other so-called serious contemporary composers who have recognized electronics, be classified as a rock musician. What I do propose is that many of their musical ideas have been created by an imagination of the sound control possibilities inherent in the recording medium, and therefore that they share a type of sonic awareness with the local rock musicians I studied. The quality and originality of the music which that shared awareness produces might vary greatly, but that is not the question at hand. It is, rather, the ability of new technical possibilities to influence the perceptions and imaginations of musicians that I wish to emphasize. In this sense, neither the existence of the studio environment nor the existence of its audible product are as important as the existence of the mutations of musical imagination it makes possible.

I will refer to that imagining process as the *recording consciousness*.[12] By this term I mean not only to convey a connotative connection with the recording studio's sound control environment, but a denotative description of the workings of such a consciousness. The recording consciousness, by virtue of exposure to recordings, allows people, as a *purely mental activity*, to multi-track, alter dynamics, achieve reverberation and delay effects, equalize according to frequency, and manipulate signal-to-noise ratios, and to sequence, splice, and edit their musical ideas. Perhaps these abilities have been the essentials of any musician's consciousness at any point in time. However, the ways in which that consciousness is now developed—the ways of talking and playing and generally attending to music which typify the interactions of the local rock musicians I studied—are directly and explicitly related to recently invented magnetic and electronic devices. As such the recording consciousness specifies the sociological unity of a local popular musician's career as distinguished from the non-electrified careers of other musicians. It assumes an intimate relationship between the technical construction of the studio environment and the mental creation of popular musicianship. This is, of course, an ideal-typical formulation of musical consciousness that may exist alongside other types of musical consciousness in actual life.

7

The Realities of Practice

COMMITMENT TO A SCHEDULE

The first consideration of the practice session is that it is a prearranged meeting, and there can be as many or as few sessions as the group cares to arrange. Observation of many groups shows that there is a great variation in frequency of practice schedules (from "never" to "every day"), and further that the categorization of groups by their practice scheduling yields an indicator of group career stages. It is, of course, not the number of practices, but the ideological framework which creates a particular practice density that is indicative of the group's stage of development. When there is not enough material to play a three- or four-hour gig, the group is at an early stage, and the need for practice is great. If the "every day" schedule is actualized at this point, the shortest possible lag time ensues between the group's formation and the playing of its first gig. As the number of practices decreases from the practical limit (i.e., "every day," which means "almost every day") the time it takes to construct a repertoire increases. Since the ability to accept an engagement depends on the existence of a repertoire, the practice schedule of a newly formed group determines its possibilities for succession to the steady-gig stage. It is, however, the fate of many groups to break up after initial formation because a workable practice schedule cannot be maintained.

Here are some typical examples of non-musical factors affecting the existence of group music.

J: There's one thing we're gonna have to do, and that's practice every day. If we don't do that there's no use in saying we've got a group together.

S: That was the reason my last group broke up. We coulda had a good band, too—Mike was a really steady bass player, and Jones was really into drums—but when nobody showed up for practice except every other Tuesday, all the energy just went down the drain.

J: Bob is working until five on weekdays, so we'll have to practice at night. . . .

B: If things work out with the group I'll quit that job. I just need enough money to pay off my amp and have something to live on.

S: Well, I know we can't play in here past about ten or something like that or else the neighbors will get pissed off and call the cops or something.

J: Let's do it between seven and nine then—no, six-thirty and nine, O.K.?

S: If we do that every day for two or three weeks we oughta be ready. [*Group conversation after first session*]

S: [*Phone rings.*] Hello.

M: Hello, this is Mike. I just wanted to call and tell you that I can't make it to practice tomorrow 'cause I'm sick.

S: You were sick yesterday and Monday.

M: Yeah, I know, but I just can't make it. Really, I'm sick.

S: Well, when are we going to get this thing together?

M: Look, I'll call you when I can practice again, O.K.? [*Silence.*] Hello?

S: Yeah?

M: Well, is that all right?

S: Whatever you say. It's up to you.

M: O.K., well, I'll see you maybe the beginning of next week sometime, when I'm feeling better. I'll call you then, O.K.?

S: Goodbye, Mike.

M: Goodbye. [*Telephone conversation between members of a dissolving group*]

It is obvious that the practice schedule must coexist with a variety of non-musical contingencies and yet produce enough sessions to generate a performable repertoire. One of the perennial signs of a group in trouble is the absence of members from called practices, for when there is "something better to do" the special nature of the commitment to rock music is bastardized. Groups are founded on the commitment that *nothing comes before music*. When group members fail to show up for practice they are doing more than breaking commitments to the other individuals in the group. Their absence demonstrates that something means more than music—that, in short, they are not *musicians*. The ability of an individual to schedule everyday activities around the schedule of band practice, is the ability of a group to exist.

> You know, if I had the most beautiful girl in the world, and she said, "You're spending too much time with the band and not enough time with me; if you don't quit the band, I'll have to leave, because you love music more than you love me," I'd say goodbye to her, even though I loved her and all, because nothing can get in the way of your music. Nothing. [*Drummer*]

Once this degree of commitment is obtained for the practice schedule the group moves along to the business of "getting down some songs."

SONG GETTING

What separates the rock musician's musical consciousness from that of rock audiences is the knowledge of how to *get* a song from a recording. This requires the resources of an instrument and a playback system. At first the process seems so simplistic that it might be unworthy of attention, yet its naive simplicity is its essential trait and is not to be overlooked.

HSB: How do you get your material?

G: Mostly from records.

HSB: Say some more....

G: There really isn't much more to say, you just set [*sic*] down in front of the stereo with your guitar and play the record over and over until you learn it.

HSB: Do you think everybody does it that way?

G: I guess they'd have to . . . I can't think of how else you'd do it. Everybody I know does it that way.

HSB: What about buying sheet music?

G: I wouldn't know what to do with it—I can't read. Besides, I want to hear what the thing *sounds* like, and there ain't no way a sheet of paper sounds like Jimi Hendrix. [*Guitar player*]

What this account leaves out is a minute description of song-getting episodes, and therefore suppresses some of the most significant and problematic detail. Most musicians assume that this is "the way things are done" and lend it little importance, yet it is the event which is the key link in the transmission of musical ideas from the mass product to the individual mind, and bears further analysis.

In order to gain more detailed information I asked musicians to reminisce about their first song-getting attempts. Here is one of the richest responses.

HSB: Do you remember the first song you ever got off a record?

B: Yeah, it was "Sunshine of Your Love," you know, the Cream song.

HSB: How did that happen?

B: Well, it was mainly because I'd just gotten my guitar . . . just had it for a few weeks, and I would get somebody to show me a few chords and I'd practice them for a while and then I'd get frustrated. I mean I wanted to play something *specific* . . . a song.

HSB: And so. . . .

B: And so that riff kept going through my head: da-da-da-da-dum-dum-dum-da-da-dum, and I tried to play it but I kept losing it . . . forgetting how it went. So I'd get frustrated and put down the guitar, and then the damn riff would run through my head again, or I'd hear it on the radio or something, and so I'd try to play it again, *but for the life of me I couldn't remember it while I was trying to play it.* [my italics]

HSB: So what happened?

B: You got to remember that this was four years ago and I'd never played any music in my life. I got so frustrated I just gave up . . . put the guitar in the corner and forgot about it. But it seemed like everywhere I went that song was on the radio or the stereo or something.

HSB: Well, you obviously went back to it.

B: Yeah, what happened was we got the album and so one day I got up all my nerve and tried to play along. Of course the guitar wasn't in tune with the record and I didn't understand about that, but somehow I managed to hit a note that sounded reasonably close and I kept putting the needle back in the grooves and trying to play along, and eventually I came up with something that resembled that riff. Some of the notes were wrong, but I had the rhythm down cold. I knew it wasn't much, really, but it was like I had won. [*Guitar player*]

Interaction with The Music is inescapable, and for the new instrument owner it provides the first "something specific" to play. It may not be obvious at first that a piece of The Music which has saturated a beginner's mind to the extent that it is completely memorized could be forgotten in the attempt to play it, yet this is the empirical evidence for which I have not found a negative case. This could be the point of departure for a deep discussion of the phenomenology of musical memory processes, a discussion that could be extended to include another piece of empirical evidence, which is that musicians report that they have the experience of hearing "music in the head," while some non-musicians claim they have never had such an experience. I will save the phenomonology of music consciousness for another time, however, and simply point out that recorded songs are not *gotten* through the usual mode of audience exposure to playback events, but by the specifically defined event of copying a recording by playing along with it and using the technical ability to play parts of it over and over again.

The most important thing to notice about the initial interaction of recordings and musicians is its privacy. Although the self-taught student does not have the benefit of a more experienced musician as a guide, there is also freedom from the human expectation system of pedagogy. A beginner can therefore proceed at his or her own speed and, by manipulating the controllable electronic playback system, select certain temporal segments for focussed attention. It is the conjunction of naive determination and the controllable repetition of recordings which makes an individual's song-getting skill possible. Similar learning techniques have long been employed in hard-sell radio and television advertising, and, of late, educational theorists have caught up with advertising practices by conceptualizing learning as repetition delivered by an electronic device (one notable example being *Sesame Street*).

One musically significant difference in song-getting appeared in the case of a drummer.

HSB: Did you ever have any drum lessons?

J: Yeah, but I was playing in groups before that.

HSB: How could that be?

J: Well, I had my drum set—which was a Christmas present—in the basement along with my record player . . . I guess that was before stereo. And I would get a record and try to play along with it.

HSB: Did you ever play just certain parts of the record?

J: No, never. These were singles, see, and you'd put one on and then run over and sit down and try to play from the beginning. Sometimes when I was having a hard time I would just listen to a certain part, but I wouldn't try to play along—just listen.

HSB: And you did this alone?

J: Sure. I would have been too embarrassed at first to have anybody watch me, 'cause I was making a lot of mistakes. I didn't know what I was doing.

HSB: But you were just learning.

J: I'm still that way though. I don't like other people around when we practice—it makes me nervous . . . you know, I was just thinking . . . it's really pretty hard to play drums along with a record—even now.

HSB: Then you started the hard way?

J: Maybe . . . but it sure makes you listen. [*Drummer*]

The career of a local rock musician starts when the resource of the instrument is combined with the resource of The Music in a private copying episode. That it is possible to learn to play this way attests to the simplicity of The Music, but it also is indicative of the results of a private human/machine interaction where the human is in precise control of the stimulation which the machine gives.

The next career step is to expand the song-getting experience to the group situation. Here the individual's unique learning experiences are negotiated into a set of song-getting rules, and a group recording consciousness is invoked.

The first big fight we ever had was about who had the song right. It was a four-chord change—regular old schlock rock . . . I don't even remember the name . . . well, anyway Pete had decided that the third chord was—let's say this is in G—a C, and I said it was an A minor. We'd play the song over and over and Pete, being the bass player, would play the C that the bass player on the record played, and I being the guitar player, would play the A minor which the guitar player of the record played. He was hearing the bass part and I was hearing the guitar part, and we both were right. It finally got to "you stupid asshole, you can't play for shit anyway" . . . something like that . . . and I was so pissed off I just packed up my guitar and got about ten feet of rubber pulling out of the driveway. [*Guitar player*]

If an academic musical universe of discourse could hold in this situation, the concept of *relative minor* might be injected into the argument with some chance for resolution, since Am and C are closely related chords which can harmonize with or substitute for each other under certain circumstances. What is determining these musicians' music, however, is not a body of knowledge—a *theory* of music—but the aural experience of the recording. The conflict about who was *right*, i.e., whose interpretation of the recorded sound was to be considered legitimate, did not admit a consideration that varying interpretations can be derived from various ways of listening (aesthetics). Throughout it all the recording remained an unquestionable standard to be referred to "over and over" with expectations of revelation and resolution of doubt. Musicians may fail to reproduce recorded sounds, but the electronic god never fails.

It is such an important point to recognize this group song-getting sequence that I will give another detailed example. The song in this case is "C'mon," recorded by a group called Poco. It goes through a few more changes than the average rock song.

R: [*At the turntable.*] O.K., now I'll play the introduction . . . you got that?

S: I'm not sure. How's this sound?

R: No, no, it's "dah dah dit, dah, dah, dah."

S: Play it again . . . [*He does*] damn that goes by quick.

R: Well, that's close enough, how about running through the first verse.

S: O.K.

R: Shit, what are those words there: "Dah, dah, dah . . . and it won't take long."

S: I'm gonna sing this song?

R: Yeah, of course, and it's just F and C.

S: And then there's that little lick, which actually should be in harmony.

R: Well, just play one note for now. But remember the C after the second one: "bow, dah, dah, dah" [*etc.*] [*Getting "C'mon" from the record*]

To get this song took at least two hours, and to be able to play it "all the way through without a mistake" took many rehearsals—perhaps fifty run-throughs over a three-day span. During that span the record was considered a few more times to clear up minor confusions about specific parts. After that the group agreed that they could play it "just like the record."

It seemed unlikely to me that *everybody* learned to play rock music simply by listening to recordings. I searched for negative evidence, which produced itself in the following way:

HSB: Would you say that you got turned on to playing music through recordings?

B: No. I mean records turn me on, for sure, but I started playing because I knew this guy that played, and I used to go over to his house and play, and then he had a band and I went to hear them practice and then I would even go with them to jobs. It was more like that.

HSB: What kinds of things did you learn that way?

B: I guess I learned all the songs he knew, which was all the songs the band knew. I used to know all his licks . . . the two of us would just sit around and play and when he would do something I wanted to learn I'd make him show me. [*Rhythm guitar player*]

Obviously one alternate account for learning to play rock music is the phenomenon of detailed face-to-face transmission, i.e., pedagogy. The empirical question then becomes: Where did the teacher learn what he knows? There is convincing historical evidence that the chain of connections between students and teachers of rock musicianship is not an infinite regression and that it ends in the process of white musicians copying recordings of black musicians' music. In the 1950s self-styled anthropologists of American black culture turned the uniqueness of black music into a product which was salable to white audiences, i.e., *rock and roll* music. The generalities of the process of American whites stealing American black cultural products (especially music) for their own economic gain are too well known to elaborate here. What is more important for the present is that the apparent negative evidence for my findings of transmission of rock musical knowledge through interaction with recordings, i.e., transmission by pedagogy, points to an entire historical process of impersonal interactional "pedagogy" through recordings. The point is that whether or not the initiate learns from a recording or from a teacher who has learned from a recording, the ability to get songs from records is the essential process for the transmission of rock music.

Here is another kind of alternate account:

HSB: How did you get into rock music?

K: I took classical piano lessons for twelve years . . . my dream was to be a concert pianist, and rock and roll was . . . well, you know, *commercial*, not really music. Then I got to college and these guys were starting a group and they heard me playing piano and they talked me into giving it a try. It was really hard for me at first because I had never tried to play without music in front of me, and so we went out and bought one of those books of sheet music from albums, and, of course, I could read that perfectly, and that broke the ice.

HSB: So you learned to play rock and roll from written music?

K: It's true in a way, but those transcriptions are so bad—they never match the record—so I stopped doing the sheet music trip really quick. It's so simple just to get things off the record, sheet music is just for people who can't hear. [*Piano player*]

The fact that rock sheet music exists as a salable item would seem to refute my song-getting argument. Much could be said about the market for those products. They are primarily aimed at the home market, but could conceivably be used by non-rock musicians who routinely perform from sheet music to "modernize" their repertoire. However, rock sheet music is itself derived from recordings in most cases, and although it is transcribed by experts into the conventions of traditional musical notation, the process differs little from the direct song-getting process which I have described. The generally poor repute in which rock sheet music is held among rock musicians is inherent in the limitations of the traditional notation system: Rock musicians tend to play in ways for which conventional notation does not exist. This phenomenon has promoted and will continue to promote experimentation with written notation systems which can more adequately convey unconventional sounds, just as the art music world is now filled with experimental notation systems. In either case the primacy of sound over literature is surfacing.

Wherever I have sought out the basic process of learning to play rock music, the human/recording interaction—"getting the song from the record"—appears. In its typical cases there is a direct interaction between the initiate, with the instrument in hand, and the playback system: in the case of face-to-face transmission there is only a series of pedagogical links which separate the initiate from the song-getting event; and finally, in the case of transmission by written notation, experience with recordings is both logically and temporally prior to the writing down of the music, and is therefore a special case of song-getting.

As a comparative case to the practice of getting songs from recordings, consider this account of the getting of a song in a Polynesian culture. The "musician"

will go to the ocean side of the atoll at a propitious time accompanied by an assistant. He will enter the sea before dawn and swim beyond the ocean reef, a feat in itself involving no little danger. There, just beyond the line of breakers he will lie and swing up and down on the rollers as they pile themselves to crash on the reef, and chant his *tabunea* (or invocation) as follows: "O-ho, for I seize the leaf of the tree, the leaf of the tree the ocean—one, the Ocean-One. Come down to me, come to me, my inspiration verse. Come forth and be-drawn-forth from below, for I begin above, under the blowing wind of the southeast. It is finished, the tune, it is finished its-begetting." The words and music then come to him and he sings them out line by line so that his companion will hear and repeat them until the song is done. The companion will never forget or vary the song thus obtained. Anyone rash enough to attempt the above process without full skill and preparation will certainly end in trouble.[13]

Whether the god is oceanic or electronic it is the unquestioned source of perfect music. Musical skill in both the Polynesian and rock examples is concerned with the process of *getting* music which already exists. The individual creative process of *making* music is not thought to exist in either case, and, instead, compositions somehow arrive intact and unquestioned.

RECORDINGS AND NOTATION

Our insight at this point is that learning to be a rock musician involves interacting with recordings in such a way as to copy their sounds—sounds which are created with the sound control possibilities of modern recording studios. The subtlety of this insight is that the control of sound available through recording technology cannot be duplicated in the acoustics of a performance, and therefore that recordings serve as a unique form of consciousness which the group must modify in some way before playing in the live situation. It is the aesthetic relationship between the "never-before-possible" possibilities of the recording consciousness and the uncanny possibilities of an eclectic and electric performance event that draws my sociological eye to local rock bands.

To better understand the socially constructed nature of a local group's performance aesthetic, it is useful to conceptualize the social nature of musical notation systems. The conventional notion of a notation system in Western cultures is paper with writing or printing on it. Notes for musical ideas have become so identified with music itself that musical phenomena are often referred to as *notes*. Although the "legitimate" music of our time is exclusively written and the process of composing music is commonly known as *writing*, no one argues that written notational systems preceded the creation of music. Notation in linear script is, rather, a later invention which certainly could not have been widely disseminated until after the invention of the printing press. The state of the written notational system today has been transformed in a way that disguises its sociological relationship to the playing of music. The idea of putting marks on paper cannot possibly be construed as a complete musical language—that is, the written system *always* leaves out information which is necessary to the performance of a passage.[14] If this were not so, there would be no need for the laborious guidance of the orchestra conductor, nor the obvious possibilities for the performance of the same piece in different ways by the same musician. The prevailing case in the European art music tradition of the past few centuries is that the notation system has been rationalized into a rigidly defined set of instructions from the high status composer to the less statused musician.[15] The "classical" musician is expected to reproduce the composer's "notes" *verbatim* and is accused of a bad performance if sonic experience does not precisely match the abstract score. Of course, attempts at rationalization have not achieved perfection. Indications of phrasing, for example, or the purely linguistic marking of dynamics are so vague as to be out of context in the precision of the system for notation of melodic, harmonic, and metric elements. It is interesting to note the movement toward scientific correction of these notational imperfections. For example, electronically measured power readings have been suggested to rationalize dynamics (*fff* could equal 95 decibels). The goal is that what is noted for the European art musician and what is played by the European art musician be virtually indistinguishable. The room that exists for spontaneous interpretation of the notation is confined only to some areas, and those, for the most part, are subcontracted to the conductor.

This does not seem astounding until it is recognized that the origins of the conventional European notation system are in a playing situation which is *meant to diverge* from what is literally written. At the beginnings of the present five-line, time-valued sign system, what was written was considered the basics or the *ground* of the musical ideal, and was all that the composer presented to the musician.

In this sense, the notation system was simply a shorthand guide to improvised instrumental moves (what American popular musicians might call *runs* or *riffs*), and to play only what was literally written was a gross misunderstanding of the system. The way in which a performance unfolded was by "breaking the ground," or improvising in conventional rhythmic and harmonic patterns upon the groundwork which the composer provided. What might look like a lethargic melodic passage in much early European music is only the *ground* which the musician *breaks* into a spontaneously engaging rhythmic and harmonic episode.

Contemporary "classical" musicians are so dominated by the authority of the composer that to place such notes in front of their eyes would bring forth only the sounds of the ground—unbroken, unimprovised, and uninspired. The idea that the marks on the staff are simply shorthand guides from which a spontaneous musical experience is to be created would never be included in the academically trained musician's field of action. Musicians are now narrowly defined as virtuoso reproducers of musical literature, and to ask them to "throw in a few notes of their own" would be heresy to the accepted relationship to the composer. Of course a typical sixteenth-note solo passage could be written out for them and dutifully played, but the thought of improvisation—a way of playing that is connotative instead of denotative in meaning—is wholly apart from their musical knowledge framework. The existence of this kind of musician is evidence of a specialized subordinate/superordinate relationship between musician and composer where musicianship consists of the precise expression of somebody else's musical ideas. The point is not that there cannot be beauty in this kind of musical experience, but that its human organization rests upon the ultimate assumption that print-on-paper—the score—*is* music. In this regard, A. N. Whitehead might remind us of "the fallacy of misplaced concreteness."[16] What began as a communicative guide to the playing of music has come to be treated as the concreteness of music itself. Sheets of paper upon which notes are written have even come to be called music. What has been created sociologically is a way of performing that cements the composer's ideas to the performance experience with only the faintest hints of improvisation.

Another example might illuminate the situation from a different perspective. Those who are known as jazz musicians certainly do not have the same relationship to a composer as academic art musicians have. Jazz notation systems make use of the European five-line rhythmic-mark system in that specific melodic and harmonic passages are written on pieces of paper and referred to in performance. There are holes in the system, however, places where no traditional notes appear, but simply a symbolic indication of harmonic relationships (i.e., chords). In the full-blown case such a sheet of paper is a representation of harmonic changes in the form of capital letters of the musical alphabet (A, A# or B♭, B, C, C# or D♭, etc.) with superscripts indicating additional harmonic information. Twelve bars of jazz blues in C might look like this:

1	2	3	4	5	6	7	8	9	10	11	12

$$C \mid F^9 \mid C \mid C\,C^7 \mid F^9 \mid F^{\#dim} \mid C \mid A^9 \mid D^9 \mid \underset{A^\flat}{G^7 G^7} \mid C\,A^9 \mid D^9 G^7$$

A performer doesn't replicate this notation in order to play the blues. What is written here is so fundamental as to be indelibly stamped on the minds of millions of people who have never even considered the problems of musical notation. Less expectable kinds of harmonic changes, however, might be the information which jazz musicians would want to convey to fellow performers, and in that case to have such markings on a piece of paper in front of you while performing would be helpful. However, no one would mistake those marks for *music*; one would use them as a negotiated device for performing the changes of the piece in simultaneity: *notes*—in the nonauthoritarian or egalitarian communicative sense. Jazz musicians have often ignored even this written notational rigidity in favor of notation by the human processes of memory. Being a jazz musician often means that hundreds of, possibly a thousand, sets of harmonic changes (the *standard repertoire*) have been committed to memory, and simply the mention of the name of a tune conjures up its particular harmonic sequence.

What I have hoped to convey at this point is that a notation system is a symbol system which helps organize the interactional episode of making music together, that when notation systems are written they may appear in a variety of forms, and, most importantly, that notes need not be written. It is a universal characteristic of human consciousness that one may make marks in the mind; that there is forgetting and remembering which does not stand or fall on a written symbol system, and, further, that acoustic phenomena (including recordings as the special case in point) are similarly markable and remarkable.

Contrary to most academic definitions of their situation, contemporary popular musicians do, in fact, organize performances with the aid of a formal notation system. However, it is not a *written* system. What is established in every rock musician's mind is the set of sound possibilities that are responsible for the recorded sounds that reach one's ears. Electronic techniques provide the possibility for acoustic phenomena which break with the limitations of sound-making which were in effect when the written notation system was developed. Therefore, an understanding of the acoustic control which is possible in the recording studio has promoted a unique consciousness of the make-up of sounds in general—what I call the *recording consciousness*. It is this consciousness that defines a group of people with expectations about the way things *sound* that are wholly different than the expectations of those who learned to listen without sound recordings in their environment, and demonstrably different than the expectations of those who learned to listen in an environment where reproduced sound was simply a poor imitation of an easily understandable acoustic event. A rock musician, through experience with recordings, conceptualizes acoustic phenomena in a historically unique way. Further, popular musicians know that audiences have also been exposed to the medium of recorded sound, and that their expectations about the way music sounds have similarly been given a context by the playback experience. The difference between the rock musician's acoustic consciousness and that of the audience is only derived from the manner in which interaction with recordings has occurred, i.e., that attempts have been made to play along with what has been heard on records. In this way the audience and the musician share an experience of sounds which have been produced through the various sound control possibilities that the recording medium has made possible, but only the musician can take on the task of delivering them in live performance. The special skills of rock musicians (or, for that matter, any contemporary popular musicians) involve the use of commercial recordings as formal notation systems.

THE WORK-UP

After a song is *gotten* it must be transformed into a performable entity. Although a song may be known in its individual parts it cannot be said that the *group* knows the song until the process of *working-up* (which is not so ironically also known as *getting-down*) has been concluded. This process is the *practice* of the business of rock performance, and includes the dual aspects of repetition and alternation.

R: The only way you're ever gonna get a good group together is to go over and over your material until it's perfect.

HSB: How do you know when it's perfect?

R: You just do, that's all. Everybody plays his part without making a mistake, and if you can do that two or three times, you've got it down to where it just *feels* perfect.

HSB: How many times would you say you'd have to play a song before it's perfect?

R: Yesterday at practice we worked on the same song for more than an hour—closer to two hours. The lead was hard to do without mistakes and about halfway through we realized that the rhythm didn't sound quite right, so the drummer had to unlearn one part and relearn another one. I'll bet we did it twenty times straight.

HSB: Doesn't that get kind of boring?

R: It depends . . . if everybody's concentrating on getting the thing down it's not boring. But it sure is work . . . no doubt about it. [*Bass player*]

At any one day's practice a song can be assessed as worked-up, yet at succeeding practices it might not be played with its original perfection. To be truly integrated into a group's immediately performable repertoire, the work-up must stand the test of time, and today's forgetting of what was familiar yesterday is a commonly understood part of the group's interactional form.

S: Let's do "Walk on the Water."

J: Which one is that?

S: Man, we only did it about fifteen times yesterday,

J: Yeah, I know but just play some of it and I'll remember.

S: [*Playing the song.*] Remember not to speed it up—O.K.?

J: O.K. How are we gonna start it?

S: Same way as yesterday . . . one-two-three-four—

J: Hold on man, I don't even know where to come in . . . let's just practice the introduction alone so I can get it straight in my head . . . [*etc.*] [*Drummer*]

Precise retention from day to day is neither expected nor expectable. Fairly quick recognition (re-cognition) is expected, however, so that every day that passes brings the group closer to the ability to perform its songs at will, without preparatory huddling or reminders. The technique of alternating songs is evidence of a particular knowledge of the learning process: that learning to play a song together is not a one-shot mechanism.

We always have two or three songs to work on at practice. We do one until we get tired of it and then start on another one. Of course, some songs go quicker than others. When you're practicing steady with a group you know you can always come back to it the next day, and that way there's no pressure and you really learn the song. [*Manager*]

For a group to learn to play a song each member must learn to assimilate a set of musical ideas (sounds) and then reproduce them at will. Yet at the beginning stages of a group and at the stage of introducing new material to an experienced group, the song materials are in such a state of disorganization that if there is to be willful reproduction of music, it will be of a quality which is unacceptable in the performance reality. The secret of group operation is, very simply, the shared knowledge that one has to be bad before being good. The cooperative understanding at practice sessions must operate with no negative sanctions for mistakes, and in fact must be conducive to the correction and amendment of another's playing.

L: Man, I don't know what it is today, I just can't play for shit.

G: You just have to take it easy man, we'll get it down. You remember how long it took to get "Sympathy for the Devil" down, and now it's one of our best songs.

L: I just feel so tight, I need to loosen up. . . .

G: Just play whatever comes out and don't worry about it, we'll get it together, if you'd just play simple and not try to throw in that extra shit, it would sound a lot better.

The existence of a mistake, amendment, or correction is a recognition that, at least for a particular moment or day, the member in question could not play well. When it works the practice reality is negotiated in such a way as to freely allow a member the ability to make mistakes and play poorly in front of his peers. The privacy of the practice session provides an offstage reality in which the privilege of actually editing the group's music is provided. To work up a song, then, is literally to repeat the various voices and segments of the song which were learned disparately from the recording until they flow together as a unitary performance experience. To the audience the practice reality, with its inevitable fumbles, is invisible. What is worked up in piecemeal over many days' time appears in the performance reality as an episodic whole, steadily unfolding and changing without apparent cues. To perform a song which is worked-up is to compress the temporalities of many repetitions of the song (with other life activities) into a form which is spontaneously available to the collective memory of the group by voluntary fiat.

> If we played that song once we played it a thousand times. We practiced it one day, forgot it completely the next and relearned it the day after that. We played it in bars and at dances and concerts, and over the course of six months it just gets into your automatic system. [*Flute player*]

The practice of rock music is the worship of a sequential precision which is to be projected into the performance reality. The song has been gotten in parts—in the dual sense of the polyphonically separated instrumental lines and the sequential division of the song into copyable sections, such as "introduction," "first verse," "first dah-dah-dah," and so forth, which recapitulate the sequential playback of the song-getting process. Putting it all together collapses the analytic divisions of the recording into a coherent experience. Having a song *down* is literally forgetting—removing from the group's awareness— the conceptual partitions which were constructed as an ordering or sequencing system so the song could be learned in the first place. The recording is a notation system precisely because its manipulation allows a representation of numerous segments and voices of the song outside of the temporality of the running-off of the recorded performance. Actually, the musician/recording interaction (song-getting) is a partitioning of the music for analytic purposes. Once that partitioning has allowed the copying of individual parts, the whole is reconstructed in performance from that note-taking interaction. Local rock musicians are no different from any other kind of musician in the sense that they create performance realities from notes;

it is just that those notes are remembrances of the partitions which the group placed in the playbacks of a recording while it was being *gotten*. As with any notation system, the notes provide an ordered boundary system which is elaborated in the play of the performance reality, but it should be remembered that transforming a song that is *gotten* into a song that is *worked-up* involves removing the original partitions of the notation process and assimilating the song as an unbroken unity.

THE SET

The processes of song-getting and working-up have delineated the procedure of note-taking and note-breaking by which the group's aesthetic is constructed. The first part of the process is a unique way of listening to the recording (with the recording consciousness) to ferret out the aesthetic which was operating in the studio reality—finding answers to the question: "How did they make those sounds?" The second part of the process is a unique way of reproducing the recording by using the recording consciousness as a notation system—finding answers to the question: "How can we make those sounds?" From a sociological viewpoint these can be seen as two interactional forms: the musician/recording interaction, and the musician/musician (i.e., group) interaction. A third interactional form must be seen in operation before an understanding of the practice of local rock is complete: the group/audience interaction.

I have shown that the economic category of gigs is the musician's avenue to audience access. Whether or not money exchanges hands at a gig, the musicians' services are exchanged with the audience, and it is in that sense that every event of audience access is an exchange event to the group. The stage at which the exchange idea and the idea of an aesthetic meet is in the process of *programming* the performance episode. The central concept of this practice is the *set*. A set is an anticipation of the exchange expectations of the audience; it is what the group knows about what the audience wants.

The physical evidence of the group's notion of a set is found in the phenomenon of the song list. A collection of song lists for different groups would provide the comparative cases necessary to see that although repertoires differ, the set form of local rock is the same. A typical song list provides an arrangement of titles and the key in which each song is played. I have seen some lists in which a small number of songs (say, five) comprises a set which is unified according to some programming standard (ballads or dance numbers, for example) so that after a set of five is played, any of the other sets may be chosen to fit the perceived "mood of the crowd." A more typical kind of song list is divided into sets that represent an entire playing episode from beginning to end. It is conventional to play forty-five minutes and break for fifteen minutes, so that each set is considered an *hour's worth of gig time.* This might represent ten or even fifteen songs per set, so that three such sets would mean that it is possible for the group to play a three-hour gig. The song content of such lists could provide a wealth of theoretical observations in and of themselves, but it is the *form* of the set which is of interest at the moment. It shows that the practice of local rock includes a projection of the group's future performance reality. The care and precision with which sets are constructed align the group's performance potential with particular markets for the group's services.

In this way the composition of a set is the product of group decisions which are made with particular types of gigs in mind. Consider this example of a local group with an established following that plays social gigs almost exclusively, with an occasional commercial or concert gig.

HSB: How do you get a set together?

B: By this time it's mostly a process of amendment of old sets that we're sick and tired of. Maybe there'll be one or two songs in a set that we keep and the rest we just throw out. Then somebody'll say, "Let's do this song," and if nobody violently objects, we'll do it.

HSB: Does that mean a lot of top-40 stuff?

B: No. We don't play much of that . . . I mean if it catches some-body's ear then we'll do it, but not because it's popular with the audience or anything like that . . . we only play songs we want to do.

HSB: How do you put those together?

B: We've always had a thing about continuous sets—we try to play for at least an hour without stopping. Putting them in order is usually the old ratio of three or four fast songs to one slow song—that just sorta falls in place—and then you think of those weird ways of ending one song and having some kind of transi-tional riff to get into the next one. That's really the most fun—especially when you can pull off some mind-fucking key change. [*Guitar player*]

Here is a comparative example of set formation in a group that plays bar gigs exclusively.

V: I don't know how it is out here, but to get gigs in North Dakota we were doing about half top-40 stuff, about four or five coun-try and western songs . . . and maybe we could slip in one or two good blues or rock songs a set. If you did too much of that the manager would come up and sorta let you know. . . . If you wanted to play steady gigs you had to pretty much be a top-40 or country group.

J: It's the same here, man. It's the same all over. [*Conversation between travelling and local musicians*]

When a group has established a local audience (i.e., a local market) in the economic setting of social gigs, set composition is primarily a function of perceived audience response—what *works* in the perfor-mance reality remains in the set, what doesn't work is replaced with something else, until an entire *good set* is derived by empirical test. Choice of material, however, is an option which the group retains.

When a group is playing in the economic setting of a bar gig, the set composition is almost completely determined by The Music of the day as perceived by the bar owner or manager. Choice of material may be so completely specified by the management that specific songs are advertised to the potential audience. This control was exemplified to me through the newspaper advertisements of a Denver bar which promised "exciting, *live* entertainment" and then proceeded to list the week's "top-10 songs" which would be performed.

To construct a three- or four-set repertoire is to transform an aggregation of musicians into a group that has audience access. To practice a set is not to practice the group's *music*, but to practice the programming of that music with a particular audience in mind. It is the subtlety of the set concept that it defines the rock event over long temporal slices, and therefore contextualizes "the next song" by what has gone before.

> What really makes them a fantastic group is the way their sets build. If you think about it, there are a lot better groups musically, but when ——— gets an audience going, the next song just keeps taking you higher and higher and higher. Then they break into a sort of laid-back boogie blues which would be just an average song if it wasn't at the end of this amazing set of changes; but the energy carries over, and your mind just gets cleaned out. [*Bass player referring to a local group*]

For a group to organize its songs into sets is to allow the musician/audience interaction to become an element of its aesthetic, and in that sense to share an aesthetic—a way of listening—with an audience. When a musician is getting a song the *studio aesthetic* is considered and assimilated. Then a *performance aesthetic* is invoked which allows the group an acceptable rendering of the original even though they do not have studio sound controls at hand. Musicians quickly learn that audiences expect the recorded version of a song, and are likely not to appreciate the innovative musicianship required to turn the professionally produced and recorded product into a locally performable item. An original recording with ten studio musicians and overdubbed vocals is impossible for the local four-person group to play just like the record. Given this divergence between commercial recordings and live performance potential, groups often seek other avenues of connection to the audience. This is why the third aesthetic of the set is so important, for it is an aesthetic of programming which both the musician and the audience can share.

> It's like last night . . . we slipped in a few blues tunes because we felt like blowing really hard, you know. Of course, the audience was there to hear top-40 and they just dug the shit out of that. When we took a break, a guy came up to me and said, "That was a really good set." Now, I know he wasn't listening to much of anything. He was drinking beer and hustling chicks, but that was the only way he could communicate with me, you know, the only way he could say "O.K." [*Drummer*]

If a group defines an hour as a *set of fifteen good songs*, the audience need only define that hour as a *good time*. In this way, the musician/audience interactional aesthetic of the set is program music; it is, for the audience, referential to experiences which the music accompanies. In fact, attention to popular music is programmed as a presentation of many selections in sequence. The radio station plays one *right after another*, or, if you are lucky, *four in a row* (without an advertisement); the album or the stereo at home plays *five or six in a row* and then the changer automatically programs another "set"; even the background music of shopping centers, offices, factories, elevators and air terminals is organized in this fashion. If local rock is delivered in set form, then the audience need not listen to the live performance in the way the musician listens, and the exchange of the performance reality remains both undemanding for the audience and economically viable for the group.

THE COPY GROUP

After the group has learned to get, work up, and set The Music, an ironic economic reality presents itself: The services of the group are now marketable. This means that the career of becoming a rock musician becomes engaged with the various (and to some, devious) careers of rock entrepreneurs. These entrepreneurs might vary from college fraternity social chairmen to managers of bars to producers of rock concerts, but the similarity of all entrepreneurs is that they pose as experts who require a specific product. What keeps the local rock band viable is that it can supply that product to the local rock middleman. Although the demand for the group's services is represented by what I have called social and ceremonial gigs (and more rarely, concert gigs), the economic possibility of the local group having steady gigs is in the bar market. Bars are stable environmental configurations dedicated to sociability, and because there are those whose ideas of sociability include the presence of The Music, certain bars can, from the musicians' viewpoint, supply steady gigs. The meeting of demand and supply is, in this case, ironic, precisely because the spontaneous institution of a local rock band is originally unattached to the traditional institutions of sociability which it eventually learns to service. Bars and bands, although economically dependent on one another, are two distinct institutions whose participants' needs and desires cross only superficially. The bar manager is the musical go-between for his bar's clientele, and if he does his job well he chooses whatever musical experiences his clients desire with their talk and alcohol. It is the fact that the rock entrepreneur acts on a knowledge of "what the audience wants to hear," and that creates the economically and professionally stable social phenomenon of the *copy group*.

Top-40 group, *bar group*, and *copy group* have the same denotative meaning: bands which can be counted on to play The Music. The more subtle implications of a group which has as its main enterprise the human reproduction of sounds that have already been mechanically reproduced are sociologically devastating. The copy group is an enigmatic ideal type; it is as far as the local career of playing rock music tends to go, and it finds a market in those who do not want that way of playing to come to an end. The ability to copy music (the sounds of The Music) is the exhibition of a group's technical accomplishment—the finger exercises of popular music. In the same way that T. S. Kuhn speaks of scientists who do *normal science*, there are copy groups that play *normal rock*.[17] Both the copy groups and the scientists are locked into a paradigmatic interactional form that suppresses the next stage of a learning career. The reality of this "locked door" is in evidence when the twin heresies of eclecticism and originality are brought to the market for sale.

> We went down to audition at this place and it was your average 3.2 joint with your average sleazy manager. We played a lot of stuff we'd written, some blues, and maybe an Allman Brothers tune or two. This guy kept asking for these particular tunes, you know, some stuff which I'd never heard of, which was probably that week's top-40. Needless to say, we didn't get the gig. [*Guitar player*]

The method of operating as a copy group is to keep up with The Music by adding new songs to the repertoire as they are selected for release by the recording companies, heard on the radio, and popularized by advertisements. Taking on the permanent stance of copyists means that a copy group's performances attempt to recapitulate the aesthetic which was used in the production of particular commercial recording sessions. That this is likely to be humanly impossible means that the goal of a copy group is to approximate impossibility. The economically determined aesthetic of precision reproduction (precise, that is, in comparison to recordings) meets the group at every turn. If it is the economic reality that The Music must be played, then it is the musical goal of managing the *impression* of precise reproduction which is left as a local musician's ultimate specialty.

Once one's repertoire has been so precisely specified, the copy group musician knows at least one thing: The ears of both employers and audiences have been exposed to, and most likely saturated with, the songs they request.

If you're playing steady gigs, you're playing the same songs over and over five or six nights a week. That will drive you crazy unless you can get into being as tight as hell. We've even gotten to the place where we can get off playing bubble-gum music. . . . The songs are for shit, but when you play one just like the record, you've got every part of the song straight in your mind. There's nothing sloppy about any of it, and it feels good just to be playing. . . . Besides, the audience eats it up. [*Drummer*]

Just like the record is impressionistic terminology. Left to their own devices a group of humans can rarely produce the sounds that a recording studio can produce, yet it can produce a sound which is *doctored* in such a way as to fool the ears of the typical bar audience. The intent of the members of a copy group is to see how close to identical-to-the-record they can sound. In the process of successive approximations to that impossible congruence, a universe of sound-making skills is created.

A lot of these over-produced top-40 songs are overdubbed a zillion times. For one thing, it gives the vocal a kind of presence . . . you know what that sounds like. The way we get that is to get the drummer and the bass player to just sing along with the lead singer and just do exactly what he does. Those guys can't sing for shit, but if you mix their mikes down a little bit it sounds really close to an overdub. Or, a lot of times there'll be a string section or horn section part, and the organ player and I will work out the exact part they play and try to get the tone and the harmony the same too. You'd be surprised how close we can get. [*Guitar player*]

Whatever has been pounding the ears of the country for the past few weeks, or even the classic poundings of years gone by, is the reproductional challenge of the copy group. There is some doubt as to what the audience actually hears during a performance of this type. They sing along, dance, and expect every change in The Music, even as it is performed by different groups who necessarily have variable skills.

It is as if the audience assembled at the American public house is not concerned with the performance of the here and now, but with some autonomically memorized set of sounds which is only sketched by the live musicians. As long as the copy group delivers its services, the collective memory of the audience seems to fill in the gaps between the sound of the group and the sound of the recording. When a copy group has fulfilled the expectations of its contractors, it has played what it cannot play, and the audience has heard what it cannot hear.

Part IV
Performance

Aesthetics and the
Technological Imperative

8

Playing

For copy groups the problem of performance is to find ways to use the instruments and equipment of the live medium to approximate aesthetics originally produced through the recording medium. As has been shown, the process of hearing recorded sounds and transforming them into performable sounds is the essential musical knowledge of local rock musicians, and it is in this sense that recordings serve as a notational system and that the copy group serves as its own pedagogical institution. Taking this approach a step further and applying it to a local group's performance, then, is tracing the ways in which the parameters of the recording consciousness are recapitulated in the live rock event. It is important to remember that the sound control possibilities of the media themselves—the studio environment or the band's portable audio environment—are not aesthetics, but resources. It is the unique combination of those controls that produces (and reproduces) the collectively negotiated *good* sounds—electronically emphasized ways of listening—that are aesthetics in this context. An aesthetic, then, is a way of playing with sound, and the means of electronic sound control can provide a practical infinity of aesthetics by the arrangement of their elements. For the copy group's purposes each commercial recording is exemplary of an aesthetic—a *sound*—which can be differentiated by parts and then re-integrated into a performance. Composers, musicians, producers, and engineers make recordings with identifiable sound control choices which are then approximated in performance by copy groups as "the same" sound.

HSB: What kind of stuff do you play?

D: A lot of Rolling Stones, some Johnny Winter, some Led Zeppelin, that kind of stuff.

HSB: How long does it take you to work up a song?

D: Not long. Like we set down one day and learned the whole *Sticky Fingers* album. . . . You get in the groove with their style, you know, and after you learn one song the rest get easier and easier.

HSB: Of course, they're all right there on the same album.

D: Yeah, I guess that helps, too. [*Guitar player*]

Although the calculus of approximating a sound can vary in ease, depending on the musician's familiarity with the aesthetic choices of the originators of that sound, each process of getting and working-up involves recognition of a unique patterning of the elements of electronic sound control. In this way the copy group's economic viability is maintained (it plays The Music), but in the process of that maintenance the boundaries of the recording consciousness are discovered, and after some months (or years) of practice the group can copy *any* of The Music. Through the use of aural phenomena themselves, local rock musicians master a conventional notation system which is unwritten and unread, and therefore establishes an innovative composer/music/musician relationship. It is this relationship which defines a new musical medium, and therefore a new form of musician/musician interaction in performance. In this case the wholly different musical and acoustical problems of sound on tape and sound in space, identically conceptualized through the experientially acquired recording consciousness, have *not* brought about an identity of mechanical and human reproduction. Instead, in the *attempt* at that reproduction, an innovation in musical performance has appeared. My description of rock events will assess the connections between the consciousness that electronic sound control media provide, and the unique application of that consciousness to the ears of live audiences.

PLAYING THE ROOM

In the sense that he or she deals with the practical problem of moving air to an audience's ears in a precisely controlled manner, there is nothing particularly unique about the constraints of a rock musician's live performance. All musicians must deal with the problems of physical and social definition which the performance site presents. The size of the room, its design, its interior space definition, the presence of the audience, the pressure of the entrepreneur, instrument failure, and human failure are sensible categories for boundary definition of any musical performance, although I will apply them specifically to local rock events.

A performance constraint is a limiting condition which is defined by the musician as affecting the sounds that get to the audience's ears.

> You've got to think about the audience, man. . . . What is it *they* hear when you play? That's why we always have some kind of sound check before we start. . . . Somebody goes out into the place where the audience is going to be and listens to the way things sound. If something is too loud or too soft or not in the right place it makes a big difference in what the audience hears. Sometimes you can take the whole first set just getting the mix to sound good in the back of the room. But you've got to do it. It's cool with me if somebody doesn't like what we play, but if they get turned off because the set-up wasn't right, then that pisses me off. [*Guitar player/leader*]

The assumption in this example is that the group has the ability to control the sounds that reach an audience member's ears. What is important in performance, then, is for the musician to have the ability to hear as *the listener hears*. In the sense that the musician's ears cannot be in two places at once this is a practical impossibility. What is possible is the ability to translate what is heard on stage into an approximation of what is heard in the audience by imagining an audience member's unique position in the aural environment.

> Some bands get really hung up in listening to themselves. It may sound fantastic to them if the bass is really loud because they can hear the rest of the instruments, too. In the back of the place, though, the singing or the guitar could be completely covered up by the bass. [*Organ player*]

Achieving audience reception of the intended sounds is not the same as simply listening from the stage. In order to fully understand the audience's listening point it is necessary to develop a way of translating onstage sound into back-of-the-room sound. Conspiracy in this illusory process is evident in the learning experiences of newly formed groups.

> It took us a while to learn to trust what John was telling us. He would go out and listen for a while and then come back and tell somebody to turn down and then play with the P.A. for a while. We would really get pissed off at him because that made it sound like shit to us. Finally he hauled us out in the audience one by one while everybody else played, and we heard how different it sounded, and the light began to dawn. [*Guitar player*]

The essential requirement for playing the room is the experience of being in the audience space at performances. This cannot be fully understood from attending performances of other groups and often requires the services of support personnel to "stand in" for the performers' ears. This, in turn, requires the negotiation of trust between the musicians and the sound mixer that there is in fact agreement about what sounds good. When there is a sound mixer or manager, he or she becomes a determining factor of the group's *sound* in the same way that the recording engineer becomes a part of The Music.

One simple technical innovation has refined the presentation of local rock performances, and is a good example of the developing consciousness of *fit* between recordings and live performances. I am referring to a system of monitor speakers which deliver a version of the large sound system's *sound* to the performers' ears as they play. Prior to the 1960s monitor speakers were rare items. Now a high-quality sound system is assumed to include a unique amplification and speaker system for the performers. When electric instrument amplifiers first filled rooms with sound they easily outshouted the microphone amplifiers, which were supposed to be providing a sound as loud as the instruments. In even moderate-sized rooms it was impossible to extend the dynamic range of the vocal music to match that of an electrified instrument. Even if the electric instruments turned *down* from an apparently comfortable volume setting and someone in the audience's position approved of the dynamic balance between voice and instruments, the vocal performer could not hear his or her own signal. While pioneering the filling of large rooms with electric sound, rock musicians tended to create new problems. As soon as the band's scale of sound became larger than human, the human-scale sound at the lips of a vocalist became effectively masked, and the natural channel of auditory feedback between vocal cords and ears was lost. This same problem was experienced (to a lesser degree) by instrumentalists who were so close to the very loud sound that was originating from their amplifiers that a neighboring player's sound or the sound returning from the walls of the room was masked. By removing a part of performing that was traditionally taken for granted, rock musicians discovered the desirability of instantaneous self-hearing in performance and the confusion that can result if musicians are not able to hear one another. During the last decade or so more powerful vocal amplifiers and speaker systems, elaborate equalization equipment, and monitor systems have effectively solved the problem—at least for those who can afford to purchase the solutions. It should be pointed out, though, that the separate *monitor mix* heard by the musicians is necessarily not the same as the *main mix* heard by the audience. The monitor mix is adjusted to let the musicians hear each other, while the main mix is adjusted to appropriately fill a particular room with music. All of this has elevated the importance of live sound mixing to equal that of the performance itself, raised the capital investment necessary to present live popular music, and edged performance conditions ever closer to studio conditions.

> The last group we were in was really an amazing idea. We had this guy who was backing us and he had put about twenty thousand into this amazing sound system. We would set up just like you would in a studio, with small amps and everything. . . . Then that sound would be miked into this big sound system and somebody could sit at the board and control everything, just like the studio. . . . Like, you could bring up a solo or the vocal mix could be different right when you wanted it. . . . [*Guitar player*]

The point is, of course, that "right when *you* want it" is not the same as "right when the *musician* wants it" when sounds are being controlled by support personnel. Only if the group's desired sound is understood by the sound mixer, that is, only if a sympathetic relationship exists between the performers and the non-performers, is a sound mixer's presence instrumental to the group, but this requires the precise rehearsal of that person's "moves" at the controls, and therefore a more complicated stone in the path of simultaneous improvisation on the part of the entire human organization. This is similar to the problematic situations that arise between actors, dancers, or musicians and lighting operators. Even though it is difficult, this type of operation is widely used by well-known groups in concert appearances where suitable equipment, a well-trained "dial-twister," and well-rehearsed sets are integral parts of the performance.

Local groups cannot always afford this kind of production cost, nor are they experienced enough in the intricacies of performance to be able to establish a relationship with the "outside ear" which is satisfactory to them. Local groups tend to originate in the form of performance where there is no actual division of sound control labor, but the illusion of that division exists in the group's specially constructed knowledge about "how it sounds out there."

HSB: Can you hear what you play the same way the audience hears it?

B: Well . . . yes and no. I know I can't *really* hear what they hear because I've been in the audience at other people's gigs and I know what the difference is.

HSB: Which is?

B: Which is mostly a matter of experience. You take a good look at the place, how big it is, how many people are there, and what you can hear yourself, and you get to the place where you can pretty much imagine how it's happening out there. . . . After you've played a while you realize how important that is . . . to listen to what you're doing the way you know it sounds *out there* instead of what's actually happening up on stage.

HSB: Doesn't that take your attention away from what you're doing?

B: No. . . . I'm usually so stoned, my attention is already away— a long ways away.

HSB: And you still know how it sounds to the audience?

B: Sure. After you do it for long enough. You can hear things any way you want. [*Guitar player*]

It is this phenomenon, then, which is of particular concern. Local rock musicians learn to "listen to things" in a particular way for the purpose of performance. This learning is the process which a newly formed group must undergo before what is heard as good in practice is good in performance.

The generalized notion of performance *sound quality*—the listener's *earpoint*—is the assessment of *good rooms* and *bad rooms*.

Man, there's some places you play in that you just can't hear anything . . . sounds like somebody's playing a transistor radio down in a hole. You get a gig at a place like that and you say, "Oh shit, another night of hassle." [*Drummer*]

I really dig it when we play the UMC (at the University of Colorado). It's got the best acoustics of any place we've played in the state. And the picture of Glenn Miller is nice, too. [*Bass player*]

That the room in which musicians play affects the sound of their music is clear in the parallel case of symphonic music. The thought of a symphony concert without a specially designed hall or shell for sound reflection is heresy, for, even if a listener were close enough to the orchestra to hear, *what* would be heard would involve the sounds of the individual instruments without the benefit of "the big instrument" which architecturally conventionalizes the kind of phase and delay effects that are an expected part of orchestral sound. On the other hand, no local rock musician is in the economic or cultural position to specify places of performance. Surroundings are typically out of the musician's control, and virtually never designed to even minimal acoustical specifications. Local musicians must, therefore, be prepared to play any room. That the categories of *good* and *bad* rooms are recognized must mean that there is an optimal aural environment which produces optimal conditions for the "listening as the audience" ability; however, environmental conditions never promote the refusal to play.

HSB: Would you turn down a gig in a place that you knew had bad acoustics?

J: If we did that we'd be broke. Half the places we play are so bad they stink. . . . Everything comes back muddy and distorted no matter how loud or soft you play.

HSB: How do you play a gig in a bad room, then?

J: Well, what usually happens is you start turning things up, and you play loud enough until you can get some sort of sound back in your ear. Turning the bass up helps, too.

HSB: Why is that?

J: I don't know, man, it just does. . . . It sounds fuller and more
         together, sort of solidifies the fragments. [*Singer*]

The point is that the local rock enterprise is based on the assumption
that it can produce its music in any environment that has electricity,
regardless of acoustical constraints.

Several recent technical innovations have made it possible to
have fairly precise control over the sonic characteristics of *any* room.
The most fundamental of these is high quality portable equalization
equipment (similar to that used in studios) which allows boosting
or attenuation of the sound system's signal at selected frequencies.
Graphic equalizers—the most common of these filtering devices—
divide the sound spectrum into distinct bands (usually from five to
ten of them) each of which has a separate level control, often in the
form of a sliding potentiometer. The physical array of these adjacent
controls graphically represents the shaping which has been accomplished on the total wave form of the signal which the sound system
is delivering. The result is that where a room would tend to absorb a
band of frequencies those frequencies can be enhanced, and where
a room has a natural resonance the affected frequencies can be suppressed. Even more sophisticated devices, such as parametric equalizers, achieve the same kinds of control. Figuring out how to use precise
frequency contour control to the best advantage in any particular
room requires an understanding of architectural acoustics and a lot
of experimentation. Also, delay devices can be adjusted to complement or overwhelm the natural reverberation of rooms. Although
they are often taken for granted, high quality cardioid microphones
(which pick up sound in a very limited area) allow sound sources
to be "pin-pointed" so that undesired sounds are not simultaneously amplified. Most of all, those who control sound systems seek
to develop a working knowledge of acoustical principles so that the
available technology can be put to use intelligently. However, at this
point in the development of knowledge about live performances, a
high degree of positive and magical self-image about the craft is typically coupled with actual incompetence.

The problem for the musicians then becomes that of selecting equipment and assembling techniques for matching the group's sound to many kinds of sites.

HSB: What's the smallest place you've ever played in?

F: I think it was that bar down in Lyons. The place could hold a hundred people—at the most. The bandstand was set up along the shortest part of the room, and everything was cramped up. The damned bar took up half the space, anyway. We were playing really low in there, as low as we can play, and everybody was screaming to turn down. [*Sarcastically.*] We never could figure out how we got fired. [*Bass player*]

HSB: What's the biggest place you've ever played in?

C: I guess that would be the field house at csu. It's really not all that big, but it's bigger than this p.a. that we've got. . . . Everybody kept telling us to turn up the vocals, and we had the thing up as loud as we could get it. If you were rich you could probably play a place like that, but right now we just can't cut it in a big room. That place just swallowed us up. [*Guitar player*]

The room-matching enterprise has its upper and lower limits in the instruments and equipment which the band possesses, and what may be a bad room for a low-powered group can be adequately handled by the high-powered group. The reverse example—that there is an impossibility of playing at minimal loudnesses—shows that room-matching is also dependent on the limits of a performer's perceptual expectations. It is possible, after all, to turn the volume control on any amplification device to an arbitrarily low setting, but it is impossible for most performers to give a good account of a performance which is below some habitual sound level. A *good room*, therefore, exists as a performance site which can be matched not only by the physical capabilities of the group's instruments and equipment, but in addition by the group's negotiated aesthetic, and is therefore a socially constructed category. In taking things a step further, the notion of a good room will be seen to mean not only the physical characteristics of a performance site, but the socially constructed aspects of the performance situation as well. It is in this sense that I have asked, "What makes a *good room* good and a *bad room* bad?" and received accounts of local rock musicians' performance aesthetics.

PARAMETERS OF THE PERFORMANCE AESTHETIC

A major constraint of the group's sound-matching possibilities is site size, as the foregoing examples indicate. This is the most general measure of the *fit* between instruments and the space in which they are played, but is also indicative of possible audience size, and therefore possible economic returns and future hiring because of previous auditioning. For all these reasons it is rare to hear an account of a good room which is also a small room. The size threshold is typified by the exclusion of most bars from the good room category.

HSB: Do you like the way the group sounds at bar gigs?

M: No, not usually. Most bars are too small to do anything with. I mean, you go in and start to play at your regular volume, and the manager starts to go nuts. So you've got to turn down.

HSB: Do you think the manager is ever right?

M: Oh sure, from his point of view. . . . He sits in there and listens to the jukebox all week and it's pretty damned loud to his ears. But he can still hear himself talking to the waitresses and shit. . . . We come in on the weekend and play one note and it's ten times that much sound because it bounces right back off the walls. It's like putting a firecracker in a tin can.

HSB: Have you ever played in a bar with good acoustics?

M: Yeah, sure, but they're pretty big places. Like —— in Boulder, and —— in Fort Collins, but that's the only two I can think of. [*Guitar player*]

The room size of the places indicated is at least a hundred feet along the long axis of the room, with proportionately higher ceilings, allowing them to contain many times the volume of air that the typical urban hole-in-the-wall bar design can contain. From a knowledge of the rooms which were reported to be "too small" in my data, the lower threshold of the good-sized room begins at an air volume of about twenty thousand cubic feet, which is the equivalent of a 50 × 40 × 10 foot room. This is, of course, a rough estimate of only one variable of the good room but is a good example of the order of magnitude of air which seems to be the absolute minimum size for an electric musician to report *good sound*.

An upper limit can be established with much less precision, since it is a common occurrence to place rock events outdoors where there is a practical infinity of air to move. Musicians' conceptualizations of an outdoor event's sound are most interesting on this point.

HSB: Do you like to play outdoor gigs?

J: In the summer we're always getting jobs outdoors. I guess it's really a good thing for the audience, you know, like a picnic or something, but I've never heard us play very well without something to bounce off of. . . . As a matter of fact that's just the point—you can't hear anything.

HSB: Say some more.

J: Like, we played this one job with a lot of other bands at a free concert which was outside in this farmer's pasture. We had about three really good sound systems which we put together into one gigantic thing for everybody to use. I'd say there was more than a thousand watts of amplifiers, four Voice-of-the-Theaters [*speakers*] and six other cabinets with good speakers in them . . . and you couldn't hear it, man, you just couldn't hear it. These other guys would go out front to listen and they'd come back saying you could hear the vocals for about a hundred yards and then that was it. Playing outside is like dumping all your marbles into the Grand Canyon. [*Drummer*]

The account of outdoor playing changes when the environmental design changes.

HSB: Have you ever played a good gig outdoors?

J: Yeah, there's one place I really like to play, and that's outside the student center at CSU. They have a lot of concerts there when the weather's good, and they've usually got the stage set up so that you've got the building behind you. Usually when you play outside you can't hear a damned thing you're doing . . . sounds sort of flat and dead . . . but you get a pretty good bounce off the building, and it's really O.K.

HSB: Would you rather play there than indoors?

J: For sound I'd have to say no. But it feels good to play outside, and I know the audience can hear better than we can, so that outweighs the other problems. Besides, we play a lot more indoors than out. [*Guitar player*]

The fact that outdoor concerts can be played at all attests to the air-moving capabilities of even minimally equipped rock groups. In a similar position the player of an acoustic instrument could only hope to play to a handful of attentive listeners. Whether or not one can estimate an order of magnitude for the upper limits of a local group's air-moving capabilities (and, therefore, a technical limit to the size of audience they can effectively reach), the need for some kind of sound reflexivity in large spaces is obvious.

Architectural design, as well as size, plays an important part in the designation of interiors as good and bad rooms. The most important aspect of spatial design seems to be building materials.

Every once in awhile you get to the new local high school gym, and it's all cement blocks and glass and hard-surfaced materials. Usually you know you're gonna sound like shit before you even set up. It's not that you can't hear yourself exactly . . . it just sounds all mixed up into one big roar, because there's nothing to soak up the sound. [*Bass player*]

Playing the room involves not only the constraints of not being able to hear, but also the constraint of hearing *too much*, in the form of reverberation effects which are uncontrollable by the musicians, and yet easily confused with sounds which are supposedly under control. The musical effect of this situation is an uncertainty in the collective time sense of the group, which leads to rhythmic mistakes. For most rock performances this effect is minimized by increasing the strength of the initial signal so that it can be distinguished from the overly confusing reverberation of a large, hard-surfaced interior.

This is not to say that acoustic reflection is an undesirable quality in a room. Quite to the contrary, the ability to "listen as the audience listens" depends on the *liveness* of a room. It is just that the ear of the musician is trained by experience with recordings and the performance of other groups to distinguish a reverberation effect which is precisely controllable and is neither *flat* (as in the outdoor case) nor *muddled* (as is the case in large, hard-surfaced interiors). The existence of surfaces which are acoustically absorbent, such as wood and cloth, is often involved in accounts of good rooms.

HSB: Have you ever played a gig in a gym that sounded good?

L: It depends on the place. Some of the older ones are really good because they're wood walls and ceilings. Usually they're smaller, too, and so that means fewer people can fill them up.

HSB: Why does that make any difference?

L: People are even better than wood, man. They soak up just the right amount of sound. [*Guitar player*]

Both the parameters of sound absorption and sound reflection have upper and lower thresholds of acceptability, and are known by even the most inexperienced musicians to be related to the size, shape, and building materials of the performance site. It is irrelevant that many of a local musician's explanations of what makes a good room are logically and scientifically unacceptable, for it is only the perceptions which his ears are providing for him which matter. The beginning group's mutually established assessments of good places to play may conflict with other groups' accounts, and may ultimately be reversed. This is a necessary part of a sense training process which is accomplished through group experience. Whether or not a beginner can sense the fine differentiations in the sound of a room that more experienced musicians claim can be heard, there is an immediate awareness of the environments which make that difference, since local musicians are inevitably put in the position of making music under the most diverse conditions imaginable.

For local groups a stage may not be available, and when one is provided it often proves inadequate. However, a stage is only found to be absolutely necessary when audience contact becomes physical and not musical.

One of the roughest things about fraternity parties is that they usually don't have a stage. People are always crowding up really close to the bandstand just to watch, and then there's always some drunk son-of-a-bitch that tries to grab the mike and be a rock and roll star for his buddies. One time I can remember this guy knocked the mike into my teeth really hard. I was so pissed off, I almost hit him . . . it really hurt. At least when you play bars you get some protection. [*Singer/ band leader*]

Sometimes when a stage is provided it is more of a liability than an asset to the sound of the group.

Like this one bar we played at had a stage about the size of a postage stamp—the drums just barely fit on the thing and I couldn't use my other bass drum. It was really shitty for the sound too, 'cause the drums went right into the mikes, and the asshole manager wouldn't let us put the speakers far enough away from the mikes to keep the P.A. from feeding back. It reminded me of those predictions for the year 2000 where everybody's got about a square foot of operating room. [*Drummer*]

An ideal room would include a good stage, properly placed in the room and large enough to accommodate instruments and equipment in the way they were designed to be used.

In actual performance a group's environment also includes the bodily presence of the audience. The audience places constraints on good sound by virtue of the fact that it is a sound-producing entity in itself. In a crowded room the sound of conversation and bodily movement produces an ambient noise level which the group must take as the performance's definition of silence. A rock event is thus very different from a classical music concert where it is conventional for the audience to enforce its own silence, and therefore produce an artificially low ambient noise level.

> One of the things that always gets me about these acoustic groups is that they expect their audiences to shut up while they play. That's just ridiculous, though . . . because most of the people that come to a concert or a party these days are used to a steady background of music while they're talking. In a way it's a kind of honest statement—musicians have known for a long time that the audience doesn't listen to their music . . . they clap at the wrong time and tap their feet out of time and that kind of thing. Now the audiences have loosened up to the point where they don't pretend to listen too hard. The kind of music that works in that kind of situation has to be *loud*, man . . . just to get through to them. If you want undivided attention you've got to play so loud nobody can possibly hear anything *but* the music. [*Guitar player*]

The initial constraint on good sound from the audience's presence is the definition of a minimal ambient noise level in the performance space, but this is immediately *turned up*, because the electric performance produces a louder sound than the audience's, and the audience in turn engages in voice-raising, and ultimately in yelling and screaming. Perhaps a single human voice cannot compete with a two-hundred-watt amplifier at close range, but thousands of human voices, hands, and feet can provide an amazingly

high level of environmental sound, especially if one is at the back
of the room.

As a local rock performer hears the good sounds of performances,
the timing of audience sound-making is crucial.

> Man, the thing I just can't stand is a tight crowd.... You know, when
> you finish this dynamite number and there's a complete silence, and
> you wait and you wait and nothing. I don't mean they should be
> clapping for you or anything—that makes me nervous anyway—
> but when they're not moving, or dancing, or making noise you feel
> like you might as well go home. . . . I mean when you stop play-
> ing there should be the music of the audience for *you* to listen to.
> [*Drummer*]

Instead of the formalized response of other musical forms, rock
events are founded on the informal freedom of sound-making and
action on the part of the audience. It is absolutely impossible for the
crowd to compete with the extra-human scale of a rock group's sound
control, anyway, and so most any audience action that respects the
musicians' staging area is permitted. It is, in fact, the lack of audience
sound and movement that is the conventionalized audience response
of musical disinterest and rejection. For musicians this can only be
sampled aurally at the time when they are not playing, and so there
comes to be a cyclic expectation on the part of the performers of the
ambient audience noise they assume to be masked by the sounds they
themselves are making. Therefore, the good sound of a performance
(to the ears of the group) is not wholly dependent on sounds which
the group makes.

Analogous to this aural expectation is the visual manifestation of
the same kind of audience response.

HSB: Is there any way to know whether you're getting through to the
     audience?

L: Oh sure, you can just feel the vibes when it's right.

HSB: What happens then?

L: Maybe they'll start dancing, or even just sort of moving while they're standing there, or if it's a song they know they'll sing along and you can see because their lips move right in time with it.

HSB: You can't hear them when you're playing. . . .

L: No, but you can see. If only a few people are moving you're not really there, and if you've got a lot of movement that isn't in time then that's not much better, but when you've really got 'em they're all moving in time with the music and they sorta *sway*. . . . It's hard to describe. You just can't help but see that whatever they're doing, they're doing it together, and it's because you're doing what you're doing.

HSB: Do you think you control the crowd?

L: I didn't say that. It doesn't have to be some magical power or anything. It's just that when it works, you—even you—can see it . . . everybody's doing the same thing at the same time. [*Bass player*]

The sometimes hollow phrases for the audience/musician interaction which are put forth by musicians (such as "good vibrations," "getting it on with the audience," and the like) are often based on the connection of visual sensation from the audience with the rhythmic temporality of the musicians' own internal time consciousness. When these two are simultaneously sensed, the *feeling of a good room* is established. When the audience is observed to act in a manner that is "out of synchronization" with the group's time consciousness there is an assessment of the event, the audience, and therefore the place, as a bad room.

HSB: What's the worst place you've ever played?

G: There's a lot of worst places.

HSB: What are they like?

G: They're like morgues, man. Nobody moves, nobody makes any attempt to groove with the music . . . they're all off on their separate trips. . . . Like I can remember this concert we played in Vail for these teenyboppers—they just sat on their asses, except for this one kid that came up to us and told us we were outasight but he had to get out of there because the place was just too weird.

HSB: Would you play there again?

G: I guess I'd play anywhere for money, man, but that's really a crap-ass place to play.

HSB: How were the acoustics?

G: It was a good building, but it was a terrible room to play. . . . Can you dig it? [*Singer*]

A final aspect of the audience presence is the likelihood that other rock musicians will be in the audience.

You can always tell when you're getting checked out because they'll stand up front in little bunches of four and five and they've got their eyes glued to your fingers. Every time you make a mistake they'll sort of smirk a little, and they keep pointing and talking among themselves . . . and you can usually count on 'em coming up and asking if they can play a number if they think they can cut you . . . if you're smart, you'll say no. [*Guitar player*]

That musicians have a category for performances that include "them" (other musicians) is an engaging discovery. Not only is a musician's attention focussed on what is being played, the movements of the crowd, and so forth, but also on the recognition of those who are in the "same" state of musical awareness: Those who will likely apprehend mistakes, and who might in fact be able to play "better" themselves. In my estimation, local rock events are not sufficiently defined unless there are rock musicians present *as audience members*.

HSB: Have you ever played a gig where there were guys from other groups in the audience?

G: Oh, sure man, it happens all the time. I can't think of when it doesn't happen. . . . Like last week in Greeley—I don't know anybody in Greeley—these guys came up after the first set and started talking, and sure enough they were in a group and sure enough they wanted to play a number or two. Wherever there's a band there's got to be extra musicians.

HSB: Do you ever go to hear other groups?

G: Every chance I get. You've got to find out what's going on out-side of your own music or you don't get new ideas.

HSB: Do you mean you steal ideas?

G: [*Smiles.*] You don't have to steal 'em; you give them away every time you play.

HSB: Would you ask someone if you could sit in with them?

G: No. If they were cats I know, they might ask me. Then it would be O.K. [*Guitar player*]

The presence of other musicians means that there is not the gulf of understanding between rock musicians (even at the local level) and their audience which is often thought to exist for other kinds of musicians. If, for some reason, a musician feels that it is impossible to play to the entire audience, at least there is confidence that the musicians or aspiring musicians in the audience will listen to what is played with an admiration for its technical virtuosity. Sometimes, too, musicians feel a lack of confidence when they do not turn in a virtuoso performance for another musician's ears.

Another constraint of the performance reality is pressure from the entrepreneur of the event.

It's really a drag to play at ———, because of Chuck [the *manager*]. He's always running around like he owns the place and everybody in it, and he's really a hassler. He comes back to the green room and chews you out for not being at the stage and ready to go on ten minutes before you're supposed to go on—I mean he talks to you shitty: "Get your ass in gear," "Let's get started on time *tonight*," "Let's go now," it's like being in the fucking army, man. . . . So then you're ready to go and he spends fifteen minutes of the first show running off at the mouth. By the time you get on down there you're down, man, really down. [*Guitar player*]

As I have pointed out, *getting up for the gig* is a very delicate part of the group's ceremonial invocation of unity. The hours and minutes before going on are carefully negotiated between members to exclude from attention any issues of conflict and tension that might actually exist between them, and, in particular, the moments before a performance are spent in close physical proximity to one another with alcohol, dope, or simply in-group conversation as the ceremonial sacrament.

> After we're all set up we always try to get together some place and sort of get our heads together. . . . You go out in the car and smoke a joint and relax. . . . It's like taking a deep breath before you dive into the pool. [*Drummer*]

When an entrepreneur enters this ceremony he disrupts the group's sense of control over its own musical performance in the sense that he disallows the group's own specification of their *readiness* by his superordinate demands. The entrepreneur/musician conflict is inevitably couched in terms of the entrepreneur's economic sense of the musical product which is rationally producible, and the musician's musical sense of performing as an episode which must be properly invoked to be produced.

Instrument and equipment failure can also add devastating constraints to performance situations.

HSB: Have you ever had any equipment hassles at a gig?

B: Are you kidding me? All the time *something* is going wrong. Like usually it's just a guitar cord that comes unglued for the zillionth time, which is a pain in the ass, but fixable. . . .

HSB: Anything more serious?

B: Like an amp not working? That happened to us the last time we played. We tried everything—fuses, wires to the speakers, hooking it up to other speakers, using those speakers with different amplifiers—and it was the amp . . . there was nothing we could do. So I end up playing the entire gig through the bass amp with

Ron, and it sounds like shit, really flat . . . no punch . . . and the bass sounded shitty, too. The whole thing was a disaster. [*Guitar player*]

The performance sound is a precisely expected phenomenon to musicians, and the absence of a piece of equipment removes the ability to control sound in an expectable way. If performing music is *playing* (as I maintain), then the failure of an instrument or a piece of equipment limits the playground and subsequently narrows the possibilities for staying in the *play* state of consciousness. A minimal definition of a good room must include the working presence of the group's equipment.

The most elusive constraint on a performance reality is the collective awareness of the music-makers themselves. If any member is chemically, socially, or physically isolated from the rest of the group, the performance can be disrupted.

You just can't get into drugs too heavy, man, it makes you a goddamned vegetable. It's like Mike; he used to come to gigs so strung out on speed you thought his eyes were coming out of his fucking head. And you couldn't talk to him, you couldn't *say* anything about it, and he couldn't remember any of the songs or the changes or anything, he'd just play what sounded like random notes, you know? . . . Finally we just had to get rid of him. It doesn't make any difference to me what kind of dope somebody does, but when you're inoperable that's just not fair to the rest of the group . . . you're really not in the group any more. [*Drummer*]

Equivalent in effect to the intractable presence of drunk or doped personnel is the socially constructed isolation of interpersonal relationships.

They were getting along pretty well with this new guy on congas . . . doing the same old material, but it was good. Then he started fucking the guitar player's old lady—ain't this a classic?—and things got really hot between them, and then finally the guitar player just didn't show up one night and they were fucked over bad. What do you do in a situation like that? [*Bass player*]

Interpersonal conflicts sometimes result in group separation at the performance.

I got into my first money-making group because the drummer walked out one night. They had been playing at this bowling alley with a bar—it was a pretty "in" place to go at that time—and they were making good bread and everything. The leader was a real asshole, though, and everybody just tolerated him because the gig was so good. One night in the middle of a set he got down really hard on the drummer and I guess that was the straw that broke the camel's back; he just stopped playing and started packing . . . stopped the whole thing right there. So the leader gets on the phone to my brother, who is his age, and asks if he knows any other drummers, and he tells him about me. So the kid brother drives over and sets up and in about an hour the band's back in business. I played with those guys for about six months before I couldn't stand it either and quit. [*Drummer*]

Perhaps the ultimate constraint on the performance reality is the expectation that the musicians will be bodily present and in reasonable operating condition. Since that reality definition is so well known to any musician, one's personal power can be shown by one's absence. There is a special sense in which rock groups are especially vulnerable to the absence of a member, since getting a replacement is not simply a question of finding another person with the standardized skills of the last, as is possible in a factory or a symphony.

It's no problem if you want to get some guys together and jam, you can always do that, but if you really want to have a good group and do really far-out material, you've got to practice a lot and just play together for a long time. Just when my last group was getting good, we broke up, and we'd been playing together for more than four years—four years is a long time, to be just beginning, but that's how long it takes if you want to be really good. [*Drummer*]

As the time investment in a group grows, the importance of each individual increases considerably. In the example above, the fact that one person out of five quit was sufficient to disintegrate the group, since "it just wouldn't be the same thing after all we'd been through together."

Many of the constraints which are interwoven with performance realities—the size of the room, its architectural characteristics, its stage or lack thereof, the presence of the audience, equipment and instrument failure, the inability to correct mistakes—are not problematic in the production of recorded music. For the most part this difference is due to the potential for editing in the recording medium, although it is also inherent in the knowledge available through recording personnel, and in the physical and electronic environment of the studio—something which is more predictable and therefore less likely to impede the flow of music than a performing musician's next site. This is not to overlook the extremes of social and economic pressure under which studio musicians work,[1] but to point out that, in contrast to live performances, studio technical problems are more likely to be under control, less likely to stop the music, and therefore less likely to be a source of pressure on the performers. As the techniques of live performance continue to develop they isolate and emulate studio techniques. Certainly the designers and producers of electronic devices have not ignored the live performance market, nor have they failed to perceive what I call the recording consciousness as its guide. The idea of a copy group, then, has a double meaning. Not only do local musicians copy The Music, they copy the means of production of The Music as well.

PERFORMING WITH THE RECORDING CONSCIOUSNESS

The sound control possibilities of a live rock performance are intricately intertwined with the resources which the group has available. Although the availability of electric instruments and electronic devices is surely the technological precedent for the live medium of rock, the phenomenon is neither adequately nor interestingly described unless the manner in which these technological innovations are converted into musical innovation is accounted for. A key issue in the sociology of innovation is the question of multiple discovery: Is change of technique the simultaneous inspiration of a number of individuals, or the singular inspiration of one person, which is then diffused within a society? In local rock groups the formulation of discoveries and rediscoveries on the part of many unconnected individuals is surely the case. The career of each group shows the acquisition of resources as the only socially reified part of the enterprise. What to do with the resources once they are acquired is not as specific. I have emphasized the imitation of recorded music as the essential interactive element in the process of becoming a rock musician, and delineated the institution of the copy group as its inevitable sociological result, and although this accounts for compositional and notational input to the performance situation, actual playing techniques appear as spontaneous discoveries. My analysis of these techniques shows that each musician discovers relatively unique ways of playing, and that groups develop unique ways of playing *together*. What is of sociological significance, then, is not the uniqueness of each individual's playing techniques, but the recently defined sound control possibilities which have allowed those techniques to be discovered. It is therefore important to have some grasp of the way in which electronic devices are selected and used in performance if the resultant innovations in musical technique are to be understood.

The polyphonic possibilities of studio sound control are only partially evident in performance. For one thing, amazing polyphonic controls exist in the studio by virtue of re-recording processes, and the one-shot nature of a live performance cannot compete with voicings that are not achieved in real time in the studio. Secondly, the tape medium preserves its voices in spatially (and therefore musically) separate tracks, where the air medium of the performance provides no such separability. The polyphonics of performed rock are ultimately dependent on multiple microphones, amplifiers, and speakers to simulate the separation and independent voice control which is an element of the recording consciousness. The most common mode of operation is that each voice has its own electronic circuitry and its own mechanical input (a speaker system) to the air in the room. The ear distinguishes separate voices in performance because each voice is connected to a distinct air-moving mechanism. A more elaborate (and costly) way of operating is to mike *everything* through a single sound system. In this sense the sound system is only one voice for the purposes of air-movement, while its multiple microphones and mixing apparatus simulate the polyvocality of the studio configuration. However, physical separation of the microphones is practically impossible in the small, uncompartmentalized space of the performance's stage area, and *leakage* of unintended signals into adjacent microphones is prevalent. A sound system tends to be an effective polyvocal device only for vocalists and other human-scaled instruments which can get into close physical proximity to the microphone, allowing for mixing in the same manner as in the studio, but a separately tracked polyvocal sound does not tend to carry over into the air space of a performance. Even with elaborate sound systems and expert operators, it often comes to pass that some voices dominate others, or that all voices devolve into a muddy conglomerate of sounds.

Dynamics exist in performance primarily as an electronic phenomenon. Although amplification devices contain elaborate volume and equalization control circuitry, practical performance dynamics are most often controlled from the instrument itself. The fact that electric guitars, basses, pianos, organs, and so forth are equipped with level controls gives the electric musician an instantaneous dynamic control which is essentially identical to the musically sequenced dial-twisting which produces studio dynamics. The difference is that in performance each musician is separately responsible for level changes, and no one person can exclusively regulate dynamics. Of course, where all sound sources are reinforced by a single sound system, the sound mixer can take dynamic control out of the musicians' hands.

Dynamics also exist in the traditional technique of exerting more muscular force on the vibrating object. In an electric instrument this makes the input signal to the amplification device stronger, and, as expected, a louder sound results. However, electronics provide a (practically) stable gain to the entire range of human-scaled dynamics control, and although the effect of the instrument's non-electronic dynamic possibilities remains unchanged, the absolute loudness of those effects may be greatly increased. For example, an electric guitar may be played with the fingers of the left hand without picking the strings[2]—something which would be inaudible on an acoustic instrument.

The greatly increased intensity of the bass frequencies, which is the predominant perceptual experience of equalized recordings, is achieved in performance by using high-powered amplification devices and specially designed bass speakers and enclosures. An inspection of the Fletcher-Munson loudness contours (see appendix) shows that the bass frequencies must be boosted several orders of magnitude to be *perceptually equal* in loudness to simultaneously performed mid-range frequencies. In the transformation of the recorded sound to the performance event the bass boost must become an experience of tremendous air-movement generated by the bass amplification/speaker system if it is to *fill* the performance site with *equalized* bass sound. The rapid recognition of the musician's need for "more bass" can be seen in the example of equipment catalogs. In the early 1960s, devices which were sold as bass amplifiers typically consisted of electronics which could deliver no more than fifty watts (rms),[3] and a system of two ordinary twelve-inch speakers. There is no way to estimate the attempts at custom designing and constructing amplifiers which would deliver "more bass" than these "top of the line" production models in the years that ensued. In the 1980s there are many devices sold as bass amplifiers which deliver two hundred to four hundred watts (RMS)—and more—to specially designed fifteen- and eighteen-inch speakers in a variety of bass-enhancing enclosures. Further, most equipment manufacturers have provided for the addition of modular amplifier/speaker systems in what has been advertised as an "end-less chain of power," allowing only economics to determine the amount of air one can choose to move with a bass instrument.

The control of frequency contour (or *timbre*) in electric instruments takes place primarily in elaborate equalization circuitry prior to final amplification. Equalization devices are selected for particular wave form control possibilities, and are usually pre-set and then left unchanged during performances. Virtually all electric instruments are equipped with *tone* control circuitry as an integral part of the instrument, providing for limited but instantaneous sound quality changes at the instrument during performance. This promotes qualitative as well as quantitative voicing possibilities, since each musician has some independent wave form *and* dynamic sound control *at the instrument*.

In addition to these conventional electronic wave form controls, there are hundreds of special effects devices (and now specialized synthesizers) which operate on an electric instrument's signal after it leaves the instrument. This approach originated in the 1950s with the innovation of the foot pedal volume control, which was then used almost exclusively in electric country and western music. The next logical modification was to combine the volume and tone controls in a foot pedal, an item which was available at least ten years before it came into popular use in rock groups in the form of the *wah-wah pedal*. This is exemplary of the general form of the connection between technological and musical innovation in popular music. Even though they existed, devices which could produce the wah-wah effect did not become a widespread influence on performed music until electric musicians reconceptualized their electronic sound controls as interactive rather than static, i.e., until they realized that electronic controls could be played in the same sense (and at the same time) that the instrument is played.

Other special effects wave form controls include the archetypical electronic feedback device known as *fuzz tone*, which intentionally distorts the instrument's signal, and which, with the aid of mixing circuitry, combines the unaltered signal with the distorted signal to provide certain effects. Wave form controls somewhat similar to the fuzz device in conceptualization (often generically referred to as *effects boxes*) but differing in circuit configuration and complexity allow an electric musician choices of gain, sustain, compression, distortion, filtration, phasing, flanging, and so forth *ad infinitum*.

If polyphonies define the primary trait of studio sound control, signal-to-noise ratio is the defining trait of sound control in performance. Most performance situations are constrained by an extremely high noise level which, from the musician's viewpoint, is sound that is not generated by the group. Audience sound, outside environmental sound, electronic system noise, destructive interference promoted by architectural constraints, sound absorption by objects, and dissipation in large air volumes affect the signal-to-noise ratio at any point in the performance site. Increasing the signal-to-noise ratio in performance to satisfy the expectations of the recording consciousness can follow two courses of action: decreasing noise or increasing signal. The environmental design and operating techniques of the studio are geared to noise reduction (hence the Dolby and dbx systems, or tape rolling at thirty-inches-per-second), just as the conventions of audience behavior at classical music concerts increase the musician's signal-to-noise ratio by decreasing competitive sounds. The single most important connection between electronic innovations and rock events is that amplification devices which produce sound intensities at many times human scale allow increased signal-to-noise ratios not by constraining competitive sound but by drastically increasing the signal. What has resulted is a dynamic range which begins (i.e., at its lowest loudness) above the loudness of the competitive sound which can be expected from the performance reality. The recording consciousness considers a signal-to-noise ratio of 60 to 80 dB good. Assuming that average performance site noise can reach 70 dB (and more, with intense clapping, foot stomping, whistling, and shouting), studio quality signal-to-noise ratios cannot even be approximated until the 100 dB level is surpassed. Estimates of the ear's pain and damage threshold begin at 120 dB, although in recent years less biased investigations have revised these experimentally derived assessments upwards to 130 dB or more. In any case, rock events are *loud* acoustical phenomena, louder than most sounds that exist in everyday American life, possibly damaging to hearing, and sufficiently louder than traditional musical forms to elicit bitter and venomous condemnations from outsiders that rock is "not music."

The attempt at reproducing studio-quality signal-to-noise ratios in performance has surely led to new conventions in the musician/audience relationship. At such sound levels ordinary vocal communication is impossible—even close-range shouting is inaudible. The members of an audience have no choice but to listen to the musicians; but, in turn, they can choose to make as much sound and movement as they desire without disrupting the performance. This redefinition of audience and musician expectations is an essential characteristic of rock events. There is no way that performed rock music can be considered background music for the socializing of the audience, but neither does it command the stoic illusion of attentiveness inherent in the definition of the classical concert event. When one is in the room with live rock, one is immersed in an aura of music, and the magnitude of that immersion is unique in the history of musical performances. One striking image of this is that some musicians wear earplugs while "filling the room with sound."

Electronically produced resonance effects are made in the same way in the studio and in performance. The operating principle is to delay the instrument's signal and then mix it in variable proportions with the unaltered signal. The highest quality (best s/n) delay is produced by purely electronic devices which use digital circuitry. Before the 1970s, delay effects relied on tape recording devices which played back a sound a moment after it was recorded. To the extent that such devices have been made portable, studio and performance delay controls are identical. However, a studio's "big room" reverberation effect is unavailable in performance. If a performance site has good reverberation, such an effect will be automatic, while a bad room can override all electronic attempts to bring the resonance parameter in line with studio-defined expectations. Devices known as reverberation units simulate the studio's "big room" resonance effects to some extent, and their inclusion in performance equipment is typical; however, their design is often considered too noisy for studio applications—the reverb units themselves produce a noise level which is insignificant in performance, but disturbing enough to be noticeable in the more sensitive studio atmosphere. The delay is achieved by changing an electronic signal into mechanical energy, which sets up wave motion in a metal spring, simulating the resonance of a large enclosure. The mechanical energy is then converted back into electronic signal and mixed with unaltered signal. Reverberation (i.e., a spring) is the cheapest and most common resonance device and is integral to many commercial instrument amplifiers and sound systems.

The *spatial* effects of contemporary recordings (stereo, for example) would seem unnecessary to transfer to performances, since they rely on stereophonic or quadrophonic speaker systems strategically placed in a room, and on purely synthetic rerecording practices in the studio. To play a room in this manner one could set up at least two spatially distinct speaker systems with separate electronics, and then provide a control for shifting (or *panning*) signals back and forth between them. The fact that most large sound systems are supplied with this stereo capability—two distinct channels of sound after mixing—attests to the pattern of deriving live performance sound controls from studio configurations. To some extent it is possible to replicate studio spatial effects in live settings by differential placement of voices in multiple channels. Whether in the studio or on stage, though, this spatialism is a synthetic effect which does not replicate the actual physical arrangement of the musicians and their instruments. Recorded stereophonic sound is itself a recent historical entity, but since it has become an expectable studio sound control possibility, the appearance of equipment so obviously intended to copy that control in performance is both a theoretical and practical next step. (See figure 5.)

Type of control	Studio performance	Live performance
Poly-vocality	Mixing board/multiple microphones	Mixing board/multiple microphones
Dynamics	Electronic signal control at mixing board at instrument Mechanical signal control at instrument	Electronic signal control at instrument at mixing board Mechanical signal control at instrument
Equalization	EQ: at mixing board channel, at instrument, at amplifier loudness contours Overall graphic and para-metric EQ Effects boxes and synthesizers	EQ: at instrument, at amplifier, at mixing board channel Overall graphic and para-metric EQ Effects boxes and synthesizers
Resonance and delay	Digital, tape, and mechanical Architectural (now rare)	Digital, tape, and mechanical Architectural (often problem-matic), e.g., feedback
Signal-to-noise ratio	Fast tape speeds (15 or 30 I.P.S.) Dolby or DBX noise reduction Noise gates Studio architecture	High original signal level Ambient noise (e.g., audience) Noise gates
Spatial effects	Pan pots (placing sound between right and left stereo channels)	Pan pots (effect is hard to achieve)
Editing	Overdubbing Splicing tape	

Figure 5 Studio and live performance sound control possibilities in contemporary popular music.

The editing possibilities which exist in the studio, by sequencing various takes, are obviously unavailable in performance. What is available is the practiced set, which takes the album format's uninterrupted sequence of music as the program of the performance event, and in many cases collapses an album's silent grooves (between selections) into a medley of continuous music. Of course, musicians programmed their selections long before the recording medium was a reality, but the example of the long-playing record album has provided a benchmark for the format of rock events. The standard rock group's set includes as many selections per hour as would be reproduced in that same amount of time by the recordings of the day—a *selection density* of around fifteen songs per hour. A shorthand comparison of the studio sound control possibilities and performance sound control possibilities which have been discussed is provided in figure 5.

9

"Other People's Music"

INNOVATIONS IN PLAYING TECHNIQUE

Up to this point I have shown the aesthetic career of becoming a rock musician as a sequence of imitative episodes: the acquisition of resources which are manufactured and specified by others, the accommodation to aesthetics which are produced and reproduced by the manipulation of electronic sound control parameters, and the transformation of studio sound controls into the "real space" of the performance reality. Another set of seemingly imitative episodes—learning playing techniques—is the individual contribution to the collective development of copy groups. For a local beginner, pedagogical episodes of demonstration, copying, and correction are rare, and when they do exist—in the song-teaching and song-learning of group practice—they pair musicians of essentially identical skills. The question, then, remains: Where do local beginners learn the techniques which are passed on to contemporaries? The interactional form of "the blind leading the blind" appears most plausible.

An imitative explanation establishes the derivative aspects of a local rock musician's enterprise: that is, things and ideas are imported intact from *outside* social realities. It is not, however, a sufficient explanation for establishing the connection between outside resources and the muscular movements which are the experiential necessity of performing music. Local rock musicians, by a series of

economic exchanges and social negotiations, assemble the resources
of a rock band, learn the aesthetics of The Music, and even learn
to translate those aesthetics to the performance reality, independently of attaining the ability to play music within those industrially
defined physical and ideational boundaries. After all, it is possible
for nearly *anyone* to learn the resource-skills of rock music, including definitions of what sounds good on record and in performance.
Many disc jockeys, record store employees, managers, agents, producers, sound mixers, electronics repair people, and, for that matter,
ordinary people who listen to popular music successfully manage to
assimilate these skills. Be that as it may, what separates rock musicians from others with a knowledge of their medium is the ability to
play with it.

Earlier I outlined my view of *play* as a sociological concept. It is
sufficient here to note that chief among the insights available from
my observations is the principle that playing techniques need not be
products of formal institutional socialization, and therefore, that a
player cannot be expected to provide a formalized account of play
activity. The special awareness of a playing episode means that a
player is not in a position to *objectively* analyze what is being done in
order to do it.

HSB: What do you think about when you're playing?

K: Man, I know this sounds really mystical and everything, but
       when I play I'm not really thinking about what I'm doing. I'm
       just *playing.* It's like this tape we just made. . . . We've been taping
       our practices . . . and I hear things I didn't even know I played.
       A riff will come along and . . . wait a minute, is that me? I don't
       remember doing that. Really weird.

HSB: Don't you remember *any* of it?

K: Oh sure. The first time I listened to that tape I knew exactly
       where every fuck-up was going to be. [*Bass player*]

Playing music means entering an episode which lacks an analytic
awareness, and which, therefore, renders the typical account of a

performance an account of a lack of an account. Whatever theoretical explanations might be offered for this aspect of playing, its actual occurrence presents a logical anomaly. The disciplined imitative career which leads a local beginner to the brink of a performance event is at that moment *not* imitation, for although the performance may consciously be a copy, it is experientially original: it comes into being at that moment only through the musician's mind and musculature. This is, after all, what rock musicians are lured to do: to reproduce "by hand" what is produced and reproduced by machine. Were one to render sounds in performance that were truly *identical* to the aural experience of The Music, it would be hard to imagine a demand for those services. No matter how imitative the consciousness of The Music while *preparing* to play, a rock performer *originates the techniques* which transform that consciousness of recordings into sonic experience. Inevitably, the transformation is a version, analogous to but not identical with the recording. And it is the empirical result of the quest for an account of such transformational playing that it cannot be accounted for.

Sociological insight into the specific process of learning playing techniques is blocked at this stage of analysis precisely because musicians refrain from categorizing that process themselves. Instead of frustration at this state of affairs, however, there is room for insight: There is really no need to have a socially reified course of action for transforming the music of the imagination into music of the moment. Once the socially and culturally facilitated steps I have already described have been accomplished, any method that succeeds is sufficient—and it is evident that there are a multiplicity of playing techniques.

An interesting reformulation of the sociological problem of playing techniques can be derived from these insights. What is of sociological significance, that is, what is extra-individual in nature, is that playing techniques are guided and limited by instrument design. For example, there may be as many ways to play guitar as there are guitar players, but the design of the guitar itself places limits on the sound control which is possible with that instrument, and creates a unity which is common to all guitar music. The attempt to attain the amount and complexity of an electronic studio's sound control outside of the studio environment has generated new musical instruments, and those instruments have, in turn, created new playing techniques by changing the boundaries within which a musician can play. Further, the past few decades have seen musicians' studio-based *images* of sound control possibilities become actual performance possibilities—either through custom-designed, custom-made equipment or, more importantly, continued innovation on the part of commercial equipment manufacturers. Just as a new way of categorizing (i.e., noting) sound experiences has led to nontraditional music-making careers, re-designed sound control possibilities (new instruments) have allowed actual nontraditional music-making.

In order to illustrate this I will describe in some detail an example which connects innovations in instrument design to innovations in playing techniques: the electrification of the Spanish guitar. For one thing, electrification has displaced the generation of air movement from the locus immediately surrounding the vibrating string to the locus surrounding the paper cone of a loudspeaker, which is mounted in a cabinet some distance away from the guitar.

> I started playing guitar as a folk singer . . . you know, the usual coffeehouse Kingston Trio trip. It wasn't until about three years had passed that I picked up on electric guitar. I can still remember that sensation because I was expecting the sound to come out of the *guitar* instead of way across the room some place. . . . [*Guitar player*]

It does not suffice to play only the *strings* of an electric guitar, for it is a loud speaker that moves the air which reaches the ears of the audience. It is not surprising, therefore, that loudspeaker design and selection has become part of an electric guitarist's interactions with fellow musicians.

HSB: What kind of speakers do you have?

D: The amp came with two twelve-inch Fender speakers. . . . I don't know who makes them, but I decided they sounded terrible after about three months, so then I got my two twelve-inch JBLS. I really like the way they sound—plenty of punch, but you can still get a mellow sound out of them. . . . [*Guitar player*]

To hear talk about the sonorous qualities of speakers is to recognize that electric musicians have established electronic and magnetic devices as component parts of their instruments. The situation is similar for amplifiers.

HSB: What kind of amp is that?

T: That's a pre-amp a friend of mine made for me. Those five levers are five distinct tone controls for different frequencies. Right now I'm playing it through this Bandmaster amp into the two SROS in this cabinet I made. Eventually there'll be another cabinet with two more SROS, and a power amp for each one of them.

HSB: Will your friend build those too?

T: Sure . . . when I get the money together. [*Guitar player*]

Exemplary of a playing technique which has its precedent in guitar electrification is the *light touch*.

D: . . . like Hendrix, man, he was the master of the light touch.

HSB: What's *light touch*?

D: It's the way really outasight cats like Hendrix play . . . really smooth and effortless. . . . You just barely touch the strings. [*Guitar player*]

For a traditional acoustic guitar the light touch is an impossibility when performing before large audiences. The instrument is capable of producing sounds with little string excursion, but their intensity is so small that they are audible only to a few people who are immediately adjacent to the performer. The acoustic performer's choices are to pick the instrument with a great deal of force and produce loud sounds mechanically, or to somehow *electrify* the instrument with a sound system. The former specifically prohibits the qualities inherent in a light touch, and the latter is involved with electronics—something which is not so different from an electric guitar with built-in pick-ups. To play any kind of guitar with a light touch for more than a handful of people involves some method of electrification.

For the player who starts with an electric instrument, the light touch is an immediate possibility. By adjusting the amplifier to a high setting even the most miniscule string sounds may be amplified to a level where they may be heard by thousands of people. The aural experience of this technique is a greatly enhanced sustain, or staying power, of the string's sound.

> Clapton's really good at the touch, especially when he's playing straight blues—like on that Howlin' Wolf album. Some of those notes hang on *forever*, man. . . . It just flows on, one note blending into the next, without any hard picking to chop it up. . . . Smooth and clean. . . . [*Guitar player*]

It is apparent that in the process of electrification a new sound control possibility was made available to guitarists. When a string is struck or picked with the *right* amount of force it resonates in a linear mode and without the destructive interference which comes with *too much* force. Since it starts off as a soft sound, the duration of that resonance can be many seconds without noticeable decay. The traditional trade-off for long resonance, then, has been low sound intensity, yet the electrified instrument allows the string a linear vibrational mode *and* enough loudness to be heard in performance.

This leads to the contribution of signal-processing devices to the light-touch technique. By itself the addition of a magnetic pick-up to a traditional guitar design allows the small-scale, long-sustaining sound of a string to be amplified to any desired volume.

However, since this ultimately depends upon the string's purely acoustic (mechanical) energy, the sound tends to decay. By electronically modifying the signal from the pick-up, a very long sustain can be produced. One obvious example of this is a device known as a *compressor*, which tends to maintain a constant undistorted output signal from a preamplifier by turning it down when a large input signal is received, and turning it up when a small input signal is received (something like the AVC, or automatic volume control, circuit found in car radios). The result is that an electric guitar player can hold a tone for at least as long as a vocalist or a wind-instrument player. Before the advent of electronics, string musicians achieved continuous tones by various innovations that actually added *mechanical* energy to the string (consider the prevailing style of mandolin playing or the bowing of a violin, both of which involve continuous contact between pick or bow and string), but now the same general result can be achieved *without* added energy. All of this means that electric guitars can be played long and loud with relatively minute physical contributions from the musician.

Learning to play with a light touch, although it requires manual dexterity, is ultimately dependent upon the musician's choice of a definition of "the way electric guitars work."

HSB: Where'd you learn to play with that touch?

B: It was only a few months ago, really. Before that I picked everything really hard without much sustain. Then I started getting turned on to what an electric guitar really is.

HSB: Say some more.

B: Have you ever fucked around with a fuzz-tone?

HSB: Sure.

B: Well, it's like that. . . . If you hit the string too hard everything gets distorted and the fuzz doesn't work right, but if you hit it just right, the thing just keeps on going and going by itself. It's the same thing without the fuzz too, it's just more obvious because the fuzz-tone makes anything have a really long sustain.

HSB: What does that mean about electric guitars?

B: It means you've got something that doesn't need a lot of muscle
       to make sounds. You can just lay back and play with as soft a
       touch as you want and the amp will make it loud. Once you fig-
       ure that out, you realize you can relax because what you're doing
       doesn't need to take much energy at all. [*Guitar player*]

This doesn't mean that the light touch is the only way to play electric
guitar—it is simply one playing technique. It does mean that amplification has given guitar players a new way to define an approach to
the instrument, as compared to the acoustic version, since loudness
is virtually independent of human musculature. The elements of this
new definition are clear in comparisons of the two instruments.

       A lot of people will try to tell you that playing electric guitar is
       harder than acoustic, but that's bullshit. They're just *different*,
       that's all. . . . Playing acoustic is a lot of chords and harmonies—
       and rhythms, too, because you've got to keep hitting something
       to be heard. . . . Playing electric is more single notes and melodies,
       because one note can sound as full as a chord through an amp.
       [*Guitar player*]

The coincidence of instrument definitions and playing techniques is
unmistakable. When musicians are asked the difference between two
instruments, the reply will likely refer to the different ways of playing each one. In the particular case of the electric guitar, a recurrent
definition is its potential for a playing technique variously described
as *light*, *soft*, and *sustained*.

One of the results of the light-touch technique is an increase in
the speed of single-note playing.

       If you've got the touch down, man, you can really play fast. You
       don't even need to pick every note, because you just put your finger
       down and the guitar plays itself. That means you can play two or
       three times as many notes as you can pick . . . and you can learn to
       pick plenty fast. [*Guitar player*]

Speed is a common parameter of perceived expertise between electric guitar players.

> We used to have these speed contests to see who was the best guitar player. . . . Oh shit, that was ridiculous. All the guitar players in town would get together and smoke horrendous amounts of dope and then try to "put each other down." They called it jamming. [*Guitar player*]

The outcome of the electric guitar's provision of light-touch possibilities is also the capacity for faster and more complex melodic performances. In this case, a connection between instrument design and musical aesthetics is clear, and the conventionalized playing techniques that result tend to pattern musician/musician interactions.

Other aspects of electric guitar design which are only indirectly connected to its amplification enhance the light-touch technique. One is the recent availability of light-gauge strings. By light-gauge I mean sets of strings in which the high E string could be as small as nine, eight, or even seven thousandths of an inch in diameter. They require little pressure to be brought into contact with the fingerboard, and they are easy to displace laterally, promoting the string-bending that is usually associated with contemporary guitar playing. Therefore one result of light-gauge guitar strings is continuous frequency control, which complexifies pitch possibilities, as opposed to the fixed frequency control originally designed into fretted instruments. That there is a market for light-gauge guitar strings is evidence of the existence of the light-touch rock playing style.

The light-touch technique is also grounded in the quality of the guitar's design: especially of its neck, fingerboard, nut, and bridge. In the twentieth century, construction techniques have been refined to the point where very thin, narrow guitar necks may be obtained without warpage. For the most part this is due to innovative tool technology and the design of necks with steel reinforcing and tensioning rods which resist warpage and allow for adjustment. A small neck thickness means that less muscular force is needed for beginners to hold and finger the guitar. In addition, the strings are closer together than in the classical guitar design, and the bridge height is typically adjustable. All these design innovations result in string-to-fingerboard distances which are small enough to be measured in sixty-fourths of an inch. These design details in a good electric guitar make it conducive to light-touch playing in a way that traditional acoustic guitars cannot match.

The light-touch playing technique is also evident in the case of the electric bass. To most people the electric bass instrument is considered a guitar—it looks like, plays like, and is even tuned like a guitar. To the beginning bass player, especially one who previously played guitar, the use of a pick is logical.

HSB: Why do you use a pick when you play bass?

K: I don't know . . . it's different, I guess. I'm really into a distinctive style, so when you hear me playing bass you know it's me, because of my riffs and stuff.

HSB: Does that have anything to do with using a pick?

K: Oh sure, it's all different what you can do with a pick. Most bass players play a Fender Jazz bass with their fingers and they all sound the same to me.

HSB: How's that?

K: It's just a real clean electric bass sound.

HSB: And you don't want that?

K: No. Well, I want to be versatile. I guess I'll learn how to play with my fingers sometime. . . .

HSB: Did you play guitar before you played bass?

K: Yes.

HSB: Did you learn to play bass from someone who played himself?

K: Nope . . . picked it up by myself. [*Bass player*]

To many *acoustic bass* players who switch to the electric instrument, playing with a pick is unheard of. And to just as many musicians who began their bass-playing careers on the electric bass, the fingering technique is the "only way."

> You've got to decide whether you're playing bass or guitar. The only advantage I can see in using a pick to play bass is that you can play faster . . . at least until you learn how to be pretty quick with your fingers. But who the hell wants to hear a bass part with a lot of notes? Playing bass isn't being fast, it's being tasty . . . having a subtle sense of rhythm that ties the whole group together. One thing's for sure, I've never seen a good bass player that used a pick. [*Bass player*]

The point I want to make here is analogous to that of the light-touch approach to guitar playing, in that the bass/amplifier/speaker instrument provides the opportunity for relatively little physical energy exerted on the instrument to produce extremely loud bass sound. As I have pointed out in examining the origins of the recording consciousness, *loud* means an intensity which at least equals the bass equalization inherent in recordings. Since bass loudness can now be electronically produced, the musculature of the performer need not be concerned with its production, and can combine *rhythmic control*, from the jazz style of fingering an acoustic bass, with the *linearity* ("clean sound") and *sustain* of the light-touch technique.

An unobtrusive measure also supports the existence of loud, long-sustained bass-playing technique. The electric musician "equalizes" a performance simply by adjusting the volume control on the bass amplifier to the point where the bass *sounds* as loud as the other instruments. The sheer power which this acoustically determined adjustment demands is evident in the bass player's relationship to his equipment, which sometimes is not equal to the strain.

> I finally did it last night—blew both speakers all to hell. What I got now is a full-time fuzz-tone bass amp. [*Bass player*]

Bass amplifiers and *blown speakers* are often found together. Their coincidence provides an understanding of how an electric bass player's aesthetic expectations often outstrip the abilities of available amplifiers, and how the prevailing playing technique is *legato* and not *staccato*. It is comparatively easy to design electronics which will supply the high power and frequency response which the electric bass requires, but the speakers to handle this output are just now being perfected. The shoddiness of equipment is a recurrent topic of conversation, but special attention is reserved for the deficiencies of bass amplifiers.

HSB: What kind of amp would you get if you could buy any one you wanted?

G: I don't think they make one that really does it for you. I guess I'd have to get somebody I trusted to build one for me.

HSB: What would that be like?

G: It'd probably have to have sixteen fifteen-inch speakers and eight one-hundred-watt amplifiers, but when you turned it up there wouldn't be *any* distortion. Of course, then I'd be rich enough to hire somebody to carry it around. [*Bass player*]

The hyperbole of this example is only indicative of the electric bass player's search for an undistorted but loud bass sound. In the process, existing equipment has been pushed to its limits, and sometimes beyond. Speaker pathology therefore reveals a great deal about the way bass players are using their equipment.

One common bass speaker malady is the separation of the speaker's paper cone from the moving piece of the voice-coil assembly, indicating the excursion of the cone past its maximum design-point: evidence of "the big note." A more gradual speaker death is evident at the outer edges of the cone which is attached to the speaker frame, where hairline cracks develop around the cone's entire perimeter. At first these simply distort the sound, but finally open up into major mechanical damage and inoperability. A third kind of speaker damage is the over-heating (burn-out) of the speaker's voice-coil itself, a condition which can only come about through *continuous* overloading and consequent heat build-up. Momentary (transient) overloading of electromagnetic coils is an expected phenomenon, and most speaker coils are designed to take momentary overloads and dissipate the resultant heat before a burn-out condition is possible. Aside from cases of defective workmanship and improper use (the application of power supply current to the voice-coil, for example) burned-out bass speaker voice-coils are evidence of a playing style where there is an extremely large DC component (continuous or sustained output) from the instrument, and consequently not enough time between overloading conditions to dissipate excess heat. This condition or the gradual deterioration of the speaker cone are typically not the results of catastrophic failure, but indicate a continuous overloading condition resulting from a more or less continuous signal from the instrument. An exception is when the bass player's touch is heavy instead of light. With powerful equipment this overloading and nonlinear input signal can destroy all but the most meticulously overdesigned amplifiers and speakers. Of late, speaker designers have responded to this situation with both an awareness of the problem, and a willingness to overdesign until the problem has been solved. Needless to say, this is one source of the escalation in the weight and costs of such equipment. Attempts to boost the effective radiated power of the bass speaker's sound in air have also resulted in new enclosure designs, such as the rear-loaded folded-horn enclosure. The point is that the particulars of bass amplifier design innovations are direct results of changes in playing techniques among bass players.

Percussion instruments also demonstrate the relationship between design changes and modified playing techniques. Drummers now obtain high sound levels by using drum shells made with many laminated layers of hardwoods, all-metal snare drums, other all-metal drums (such as tymbales) and strong plastic drum heads which can be hit hard with heavyweight drum sticks. Many rock players remove one of the traditional two heads on tom-toms and bass drums, to provide an intense but fast-decaying percussive sound. Other changes, such as the use of two bass drums and newly designed quick-response foot pedals with which to activate them, signal musical changes which seek *coordinated independence* in drumming. This means that all four limbs may be used to produce independent rhythmic patterns where no limb need be more important than another. In terms of mind and musculature, this separation and equalization of rhythm voices requires concentrated practice to master. Often it accompanies ambidextrous playing techniques where right and left hand stick positioning is symmetrical, and cymbals (including the high-hat) can be played with either hand.

Drumming is incorporated into The Music by isolating the sound of each type of drum and cymbal with closely spaced microphones and sound absorbent baffles. Often each of these separated ear-points is given a distinct track on the recording tape, and the result is mixed and re-mixed to produce a clarity and distinguishability for each percussive sound which would be impossible to control during a non-electrified performance. Of course, when this "impossible" sound is heard on a recording, it provides an expectation for live performances. The result is that performing drummers now tend to use multiple microphones and player-controlled equalization and mixing devices, whose signals are fed to the mixing console of the group's sound system. Going beyond this is the innovation of *electric drums*: physically compact single drum heads directly connected to pressure sensitive transducers, that create an electronic signal without a microphone. Typically, the equalization of each voice of an electric drum set can be controlled at the instrument, and when this is coupled with other signal-processing devices (such as a synthesizer, or simply a delay device) the kind of polyrhythmic sound control which is available in the studio can be reproduced (or even surpassed) in actual performances. Here is another clear example of how electronic sound control possibilities have revolutionized live playing techniques. The aspect of the recording consciousness that I have called polyvocality has allowed previously inaudible features of popular percussion playing to be sorted out. Now that each voice can be distinguished, drummers are concerned with tuning drums to particular pitches, and manufacturers are supplying a large variety of drum sizes (both electric and non-electric) which can be tuned to an even larger variety of pitches (including those that may be re-tuned while being played). All of this could be described as "Africanism" although it is obvious that electronic possibilities and studio aesthetics are also involved. The best thing to notice in this

regard is how well polyrhythm and electric sound control complement one another.

Perhaps electronic design changes are most notable in keyboard
instruments, and it is certainly true that popular keyboardists now
share the limelight with vocalists and guitarists, yet actual playing techniques have changed only in certain limited ways. This is
because keyboards are, for the most part, switching devices which
can only indirectly be responsible for producing vibrations, and
so even in the situation where a complex synthesizer is being controlled a player's fingers approach the keys in much the same fashion as they might approach a traditional keyboard instrument.
State-of-the-art electronic keyboards are made so that the keys are
velocity-sensitive, and allow direct control of dynamics by the player's hands and fingers—something similar to the *feel* of an acoustic
piano. Otherwise, the bulk of the innovative controls available to an
electronic keyboardist involve connecting or disconnecting various
signal-processing circuits that take effect *after* an oscillator is acti-
vated from the keyboard. In this sense, electronic keyboard playing
technique is as much involved in a technical understanding of how
to program signal-processing possibilities as it is in actually manipulating the keys. One significant exception to this is the provision of a
continuous pitch control (*portamento*) which allows contemporary
keyboardists to *slide* from pitch to pitch and, therefore, to deviate
at will from the fixed temperament to which keyboard instruments
have traditionally been bound. The voice-like expressiveness of this
capacity is similar to the string-bending and sliding possible on
electric guitars equipped with light-gauge strings, and, in fact, it is
sometimes difficult to distinguish an electric guitar solo from an
electric keyboard solo.

As digital control and memory circuits come to the forefront
of electronic signal-processing, the complexity of understanding
required to program keyboard devices will expand enormously.
Already synthesizers with digital storage allow musical sequences to
be pre-programmed and retrieved at the push of a button during performance. Digital delay devices (which are somewhat similar) have

made immediate inroads in all phases of electronic music-making where springs and tape delay devices previously held sway. Ultimately, the analog (or hardware-type) devices I have described will be integrated with (or replaced by) digital devices that *build* a complex sound on command, rather than modifying simple sounds (like sine waves) to make them more complex. Digital devices, then, process signals *before* they are created (using software) rather than after they are created, and tend toward making the techniques of electronic music studios available to live performers. In this way, even the *editing* feature of the recording consciousness is finding a place in real-time sound control. It has, of course, always been possible to play back a recording during a performance and play along with it. Contemporary devices that can store portions of a performance and then immediately play them back (often used by soloists to bewilder or overwhelm an audience) are simply refinements of existing techniques. Pre-programmable digital circuitry, though, allows hundreds of tremendously complex sounds (which have been worked out in advance) to be selected at will from one source during a performance. In contrast to this, analog devices require an actual (wired-in) circuit for each kind of sound that is desired in performance. The large number of added-on oscillator modules for synthesizers, or the huge stack of specialized keyboard instruments behind which players often hide, or the large number of effects boxes on the floor in front of a guitar player attest to this situation. It is evidence of the effort and expense that contemporary performers will undertake to approach a studio sound control aesthetic. It is also evident that the performance aesthetic resembles the recording aesthetic as closely as possible within the boundaries posed by the inherent limitations of the performance event.

In respect to the elements of polyvocality, dynamics, equalization, signal-to-noise ratio, and delay, electronic innovations have allowed musicians to impart studio sound control to performance events. Where these controls are lacking in some respect it is due to financial limitations or aesthetic choices, and not technical impossibility. In respect to editing, however, the performance event and the recording studio will always represent separate ways of making music. To speak or act or dance or sing or play music has always meant facing the real time of vivid presentation. Even if the show does not go on, time consciousness goes on and mistakes can never be "edited out" of real time performances, nor can extra material ever be "edited in." A studio represents unreal time, synthetic time, that can be started, stopped, and spliced at will. It typically takes more than a hundred minutes of real time in-the-studio to make one minute of synthetic time on-the-record. As with films and video tape and printed matter, the time consciousness in which such recordings are created is isolated from the time consciousness in which an audience hears them. This "literary" aspect of recordings makes them impossibly superhuman and flawless. To the extent that they have become the standards by which others judge the efforts of live musicians, recordings have pressured performers to pursue the impossible. In the same way that John Henry is said to have challenged the steam hammer, beginning rock musicians challenge machine-made music. Sometimes it is even possible to "win" the contest—for a moment—with lots of equipment and players, but when that isolated event is over untold millions of radios, juke boxes, home stereos, and car tape players will continue to standardize the experience of The Music for the audience. Because it is part of their taken-for-granted aural environment, the audience cannot be expected to do other than confound the synthetically produced time consciousness of recordings with the actual time consciousness of living musicians. Synthetic events inevitably dominate their perceptions. And, since they are so readily available, these synthetic events become intimately associated with the actual life events for which they provide a sonic backdrop. In the long run, machine-made music dominates the relationships that performers can possibly have with their audiences and this is the very reason that contemporary popular performances are so blatantly derived from the recording consciousness. However, in the sense that no live performers will ever be able to edit life itself, performances will retain some absolutely unique qualities that defy synthetic time.

A beginning rock musician's identity is marked by an uninspected acceptance of The Music as a standard of performance and as a standard for learning purposes. By learning to analyze sound in the way that is necessary to get reproducible musical ideas from recordings, a recording consciousness is constructed. Once the recording consciousness has enabled the beginner to hear recordings as a medium of musical idea transmission, that consciousness can provide criteria for the performed version of the same idea. For the limited case of the copy group, the recording aesthetic (the particular pattern of studio sound controls evident in a recording's electronic manipulation) is transformed into a performance aesthetic (the particular pattern of spatial sound controls evident in the rock event) through the socially negotiated conduct of the group. The fact that these transformations are recognizable to audiences and provide the beginning musician with a first market reveals that the combination of The Music and the recording consciousness is a *music distribution system*. The result for the performance event, however, is a subtle reversal of the original relationship between resources and aesthetics.

By recognizing the impossibility of copying all aspects of a recording in performance, a beginning musician starts to deemphasize the standards which recordings have set up, and places more and more importance on his or her own standards of performance. This marks the end of an initiatory musician identity and the beginning of a more self-conscious identity, in which multiple musical aesthetics may be conceptualized.

THE ROCK AESTHETIC

As time goes by the contradictions which are built into a local rock musician's identity come to the surface. Countervailing cultural forces make themselves felt at the individual level as limitations on what, where, when, and how to play. As might be expected, this produces personal stress. By the steps they take to reduce such stress musicians mark their exits from the beginning phase of popular musicianship.

Some simply quit playing music. Others more or less passively accept the constraints of their cultural context, suppress stress, and continue in their singular style of playing until a market for it ceases to exist. The former decision accounts for the large number of former musicians in the world. If it does not simply end in natural death, the latter decision accounts for the rather unnatural life that aging musicians choose by chasing their similarly aging audiences through the rolling terrain of geographic and economic mobility. Consequently, yesterday's famous (and, for the most part, not-so-famous) popular musicians can often be found doing yesterday's songs in motel lounges. Similarly, vacation entertainment is often intentionally matched to the musical period which is known to characterize an audience's adolescent years (Las Vegas, Nevada, is a case to consider). The musicians who neither evacuate nor accommodate tend to express their feelings strongly when they realize that limitations have somehow been placed on their creativity.

> Man, I tell you I'm sick and tired of being a fucking juke box. . . . That's all this goddamned group is anyway . . . one big juke box, and you know it. If you want to keep on playing this commercial bullshit then you're gonna have to do it without me. . . . Who wants to play other people's music, man, I want to play *my* music. [*Angry guitar player*]

For a musician to distinguish *my music* from *other people's music* is to arrive at a critical point in conceptualizing the way in which musical identity is constituted. This could be construed as an identity crisis, but for those who continue identifying themselves as musicians, I see it as more of an identity breakthrough. Prior to this, beginning musicians uncritically accept The Music as the appropriate context for their musical conduct, and, although they may denounce some commercial sources and identify strongly with others, they do not view *themselves* as legitimate sources of music. On the other hand, those who try out the role of composer or arranger for the first time become involved in some degree of debunking of commercial sources in general, or, what amounts to the same thing, some degree of equilibrating their own abilities with those heard on commercial recordings. After all, the more successful one is at copying someone else's performances, the less will those other performances be perceived as unattainable standards of excellence. As beginners close the gap between their skills and the skills heard on recordings, they acquire the ability to evaluate their own abilities without reference to a recording. The criterion of personal satisfaction is invoked for the first time:

> I guess everybody tries to write songs—even from the very beginning, but it doesn't really mean anything until you do something you like. I wrote four of the songs I do now in about a week, and that was the first time I'd ever been satisfied with any of my own music. . . . That same week was the week when we [*band*] broke up too. All kinds of changes, all at once. . . . [*Guitar player*]

After the beginner identity is left behind a musician may continue to play in copy groups, although he or she will typically seek a group in which at least some of the members have undergone similar identity transformations. A group of this sort tends toward experimentation rather than routine copying of the recorded material that happens to get radio airplay. This could take the form of selecting old or obscure material and arranging it before it is performed, but it most likely includes the performance of original material which is written by some member of the group. Groups which have pretensions to a contract from a recording company may even attempt a policy of all original material. Although the performance of a fairly large repertoire (say twenty or thirty songs) of previously unrecorded material could be just the item that a record producer might appreciate at an audition, the local audience, geared as it is to the standard of The Music, is likely *not* to appreciate the absence of current hit songs from the repertoire. Most groups of this sort who want to make money have learned to distinguish two repertoires: one for themselves and one for the crowd. In the event that selections from the group's own resources fail to invigorate an audience, some "sure-fire" hit tunes can be offered up to appease the gods of familiarity.

Whether they have grandiose dreams of becoming rock stars or more modest expectations of continued local success, players who have passed the beginning phase go on to develop multiple abilities: many repertoires, many styles of playing, and many audiences. The most flexible musicians achieve the greatest financial success (by being able to work for a variety of employers), and also accumulate the highest esteem from their colleagues. Actually two main types of multiple talent tend to be recognized: that of the musician who accents performances and is said to be able to *play* "anything," and that of the musician who accents compositions and arrangements and is said to be able to *write* "anything." Either way, a sustained identity as musician in the popular music world is a multiple identity: multiple in the sense that new material can always be learned and incorporated, multiple in the sense of presenting an appropriate performance identity to various audiences, and multiple in the sense that a variety of ways to communicate with other musicians is possible. One of the secrets behind multiple abilities is that notation systems can be generalized; that is, notational accounts (or perceptual partitions) can be created for more than one kind of music. Also, notation systems set the possibilities of *composing* music by allowing musical events to be memorable. Whatever methods of partitioning sound they might emphasize, notation systems become a musician's medium for externalizing and artifactualizing musical passages which are eventually built-up into compositions. A person who has learned a method of taking musical notes, who is equipped with the skills of attending to sounds so that they can be remembered and reproduced, and who is able to analyze the organization of musical passages (and perhaps teach others to make such analyses) is a musician in the unqualified sense of the word.

Upon closer investigation it turns out that the skills of flexible musicians are rooted not only in the internalization and generalization of a notation system, but that more than one *kind* of musical notation is being used. Versatile contemporary musicians can demonstrate music and learn by demonstration; they know and use various ways of talking about music; they use various systems of making and reading written marks that institute musical parameters (only one of which is the five-line system); and they can learn music from recordings or show music to someone else by using the conventional parameters of the recording consciousness. Interestingly, these levels of individual notational ability parallel historical and cultural patterns of notational elaboration. As an aid to understanding this idea, my developmental analysis of notation systems is condensed into the form of figure 6.

I call the most fundamental way of taking note of music the *phenomenal* system. It relies only on the presence of a teacher and a learner and the sounds of their music-making. The phenomenon of music itself is the medium of communication. It would be reasonable to question the difference between this situation and that of a performance; and, therefore, how a phenomenal system could possibly be isolated as a form of notation. The distinction between the sound of music in performance and the sound of music as notation lies in the feature of *continuity*. A live performance in its culturally appropriate setting is continuous in musical time. It includes repetition as a part of a composition, but not otherwise; it does not stop until its conventionally anticipated ending actually arrives. A live learning event in its culturally appropriate setting is discontinuous in musical time. Passages are repeated to produce attentional focus and to demonstrate conventional patterns of partitioning for the learner; playing is stopped whenever and wherever convenient to the teacher's method

Type of notation	Medium of notation
Phenomenal	Sound
Spoken nominal	Sound
Written nominal	Sight
Symbolic	Sight
Synthetic phenomenal	Sound

Figure 6 Developmental types of music notation systems.

of communication. In this sense the playing of a piece "all the way through" for an audience is likely to be considered music, even if the player is not outstanding. On the other hand, the didactic demonstration of a piece—even by an outstanding player—would not be considered music. The phenomenal system is ultimately limited by the quality and quantity of human contacts that a skilled musician can make, and is emblematic of small, traditional social settings.

Language adds another dimension to the phenomenal system since whatever can be isolated for special attention can be given a name. It is hard to imagine a situation in which a *spoken nominal* system is not used in conjunction with a phenomenal system, but it is also important to see the distinction between them. The distinct perception of a musical quality in sound precedes the coining of a name for it, and, in fact, most musical vocabularies are borrowed from an existing language which was not particularly designed to refer to sound. However, if a name is successfully associated with a particular sound event, mentioning it can call forth the previously demonstrated focus, and conventionalized talk between musicians can ensue. Most languages, though, may also be written, and in their written form words about music constitute a *written nominal* system of notation. Marks on paper can somewhat replace the presence of a musical communicator, and in this way a sort of efficiency may be woven into the transmission of music; however, visual markings require communicators to learn extra cognitive linkages between the media of sound and sight—and then from sight back to sound again. Nevertheless writing lends stability to the formal specifics of compositions by acting as a single shareable standard for their performance; while at the same time writing documents musical work in a way that detaches it from its composer and allows it to be transported over great distances.

A *symbolic* notation system—the most notable example of which is the Western European system—uses visual markings *other than names* to cue the performance of musical sound. By attempting to perfect a purely symbolic way to picture both pitch and time value with the same mark (a so-called note) monks of the Roman church started a long historical process which began before the eighth century with the modification of ancient Greek and Oriental symbols used to display accents in spoken words, reached a period of peak innovative activity around 1300 (e.g., *Ars Nova*), and, with the application of some finishing touches (like black notes and bar lines), settled down to the presently accepted system around 1600.[4] In their attempt to standardize and regulate the music of religious ceremonies the monastic orders promoted the unintended consequence of standardizing the techniques of composition, transmission, and performance of secular art music. According to many academic musicologists European music is the most refined in the world because of its primarily symbolic notation system. The expansionist tradition of European culture has become an international art music culture in which this one form of symbolic notation has reigned as the world standard for the literary approach to music.

A *synthetic phenomenal* notation system—the only notable example of which is electronically produced sound recordings—returns to the purely sonic medium used by traditional musicians. Since sound is mechanically and not humanly produced, however, a learner can unilaterally interrupt the time sense of the performance for purposes of analysis. Also, the polyvocal possibilities of studio sound control provide for clear focussing on the numerous parts which make up the whole piece (as does the European system). Electronic control has instituted a new notation system which, unlike the hundreds of alternate written systems which have been conceived (and left in obscurity) in the last four hundred years or so, has done away with the complexities of sight-to-sound linkages and has, in one sense, been widely distributed. I have qualified the idea that the synthetic phenomenal system is truly widespread because most people listen to recordings as if they were music, and not as forms of communication about music. From this standpoint recordings have yet to be fully explored or utilized as systems of notation.

It should be pointed out that my use of the term notation breaks with its rather strict usage in the world of academic music, where it would have to imply something written, and usually implies the idea of a common mark for pitch and duration of sound. Not surprisingly, this narrow definition conforms with the much-heralded qualities of the Western European system; weeding out anything unwritten while relegating written nominal systems to a lesser, undeveloped status. Such conventional academic assumptions not only indicate myopic ethnocentrism and crusty aristocratic impression management, but they reveal an incomplete understanding of what music notation is and how it works. I will hold back on the temptation of giving a lengthy technical, sociological, and philosophical analysis of what is missing in the strict definition of notation. It will suffice to point out that *all* music notation systems have a phenomenal component; that the direct apprehension of sound as it is made by humans conventionalizes the way in which names, or markings (or even recordings) come to be interpreted in performance. Clearly this is the case with the European symbolic system where an identical set of marks might be rendered into sound in dissimilar ways depending on the taken-for-granted style assumptions which are deemed appropriate to a particular historical period or composer. Direct human-to-human transmission of performance conventions—what is often referred to as pedagogy in academic music—is the foundation upon which the more developed systems stand (or fall). To speak of the cultural context in which new musicians learn to play is to recognize that the perception of sound can be altered (or shaped, or, as I have said before, partitioned) through the interactive presence of others. By sharing other musicians' patterns of attention some aspects of sound are evoked as remarkably important while others are deemphasized. Eventually perceptual sets are embedded, and the sound of things is wrapped in anticipation. Without a way to connect unspoken and unwritten (and therefore deeply embedded) structurings of sound to a piece of music a performer would be left with a code (the mere artifact of a notation system) that could not be cracked to reveal the message (musical sound). In its expanded sociological sense, then, a music notation system refers not merely to words or marks on paper but to living, breathing people, and the specially sensitized consciousness of sound that they have acquired. Very simply, a notation system is a *noticing* system—a patterned way of paying attention to sound.

The implication is that people actually use notation systems in multiples, and shuttle back and forth between them in the course of musical communication. From this standpoint it can be seen that individual patterns of consciousness recapitulate patterns of historical and cultural development. A crucial aspect of becoming any kind of musician (or, in general, artist) is assimilating culturally provided patternings of attention, but the particular kind of musician one does become depends on which patterns are accessible and which are not accessible. This statement cries out for concreteness. Without even trying to fully expand the typologies it anticipates I have presented in figure 7 three cases which are relevant to the world of contemporary music. Column I represents a beginning rock musician who can copy some songs from records and is experimenting with words for various aspects of music. The main problem this machine-oriented beginner faces in developing musical skills is a privatized musical identity

Notation system	Music culture	"Popular"		"Classical"	"Flexible"
		I	II	III	IV
Phenomenal	Western European			▪	▪
	American popular	☐	▪		▪
Spoken nominal	Western European		☐	▪	▪
	American popular	☐	▪		▪
Written nominal	Western European (defective)			▪	▪
	American popular		☐		▪
Symbolic	Western European			▪	▪
Synthetic phenomenal	American popular	☐	▪		▪

▪ = notational proficiency
☐ = only partial notational proficiency

Figure 7 Three types of contemporary musician identities and related notational skills.

which inhibits direct contact with more experienced musicians and, therefore, the grounding of his or her synthetically derived copying skills in a phenomenal form of notation. Column II represents a rock musician who has had sufficient contact with other musicians to solidify the experiential and language resources which underlie the expertise of being able to copy "anything" from commercial recordings. Such a person is typically somewhat familiar with the written nominal popular system (letters for chords and the like which are actually based on European music concepts) as well as having at least a partial understanding of the European music vocabulary. Column III represents an academically trained musician. Column IV represents a versatile contemporary musician. The point is that more than one route—more than one aesthetic career—leads to the situation of full musical versatility. The rock musicians I studied who made it through the identity breakthrough phase tended to stand in awe of those who were academically trained, and many were planning to obtain or were actually involved in gaining so-called classical skills. Similarly there are some academically trained musicians who passionately seek the ability to play by ear, to improvise, and to communicate with popular musicians. Those who stay within the economic envelope of colleges, universities, or orchestras are less inclined in this regard than those who seek an alternate economic and social identity as versatile freelance musicians. Whatever else may be said about all this it points out that a newly flexible kind of musician is among us.

By delving into the lives of American popular musicians and the technical world that surrounds them as they take their first musical steps, a pattern of domination of their creative abilities and cultural interests has emerged. Like most people they depend on what controls them. To some this is a bleak finding; to others it is deeply disturbing. But when the sociological aspects of music and musicians are considered it is in no way unusual. A comparison of commercial and classical music worlds shows similarly organized patterns of domination. The focus on stars and outstanding individual talent in either of these walks of musical life tends to take attention away from the pattern of collective conduct that brings music into existence. That there is a high degree of specialization in modern musical work means that an individual's contributions are tempered by specialists of organization—the directors, producers, composers, and impresarios who view performers as recipients of musical orders. The cultural and political identities of those who are perched toward the top of musical stratification systems show a strong nonmusical component. Which is to say that the appropriateness of any musical activity is managed; that there is a certain closeness of fit between audiences and performers which is the result of negotiations and alliances reaching far beyond the technical and aesthetic concerns of the musicians themselves, but which, at the same time, place limits on the abilities of performers to shape their own presentations. Music, in short, is useful to non-musicians.

The owners and operators of popular culture[5] depend on elaborate knowledge of their products; they know how many of what kind of units are sold in what regions during what time periods. The production and distribution of cultural products, analyzed largely through these same industry-provided accounting techniques (sales charts, for example), has been the main focus of the few sociological studies which have attempted to explain the organization of popular culture.[6] These processes—concerned with products and their markets—are the ones I call *primary* processes. For as much as the owners and operators of popular culture (and the academic analysts, for that matter) know about primary popular culture processes, they are notoriously unknowledgeable about the meanings which their clients attach to mass-distributed culture objects. Through survey data they may know that people of a certain age who live in a certain area who tend to own certain other culture objects tended to buy a certain recording. But they don't really know *why* such a pattern emerges (when it does). Even more unknown is how new cultural workers come into existence. Nevertheless a healthy supply of personnel—like musicians, technicians, producers, sales people, amateur music experts, and dedicated listeners—keep popular culture economically viable. At the most basic level cultural workers are actually being recruited from the general audience. They are assimilating cultural products into their lives and changing their social and personal identities as a result of that assimilation. These processes—concerned with people and their identities—are the ones I call *secondary* processes. To the extent that there is a labor market for industrial culture it is based upon secondary popular culture processes. It should now be obvious that the local musicians I studied are specific examples of this general secondary process.

Hopefully this provides a way of conceptualizing the workings of popular culture in a new way. I offer a general model of this conceptualization in figure 8. The attempt here is to go beyond the ideas

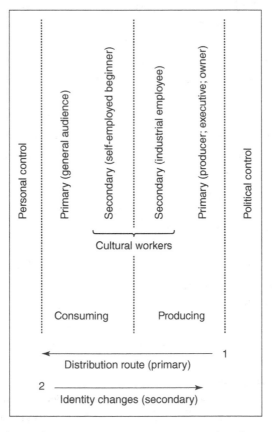

Figure 8 Identity change processes in contemporary popular culture.

used by previous analysts of the organization of popular culture who have not reckoned the *product market* with the *labor market* (which I take to mean the market for *work*) in the culture industry, and have therefore ignored the effects that one can have on the other. The right hand side of the diagram stands for those who control the production of popular culture, including the possibility of political control. The left hand side of the diagram stands for those who control the consumption of popular culture, including the possibility of personal choices. Arrow one (1) represents the direction in which products travel to get to consumers—the primary process which conventional understandings of popular culture assume. Arrow two (2) represents the direction in which people (and their ways of identifying themselves) travel to get more directly involved in production—the secondary process to which I am now drawing attention. As objects are distributed their perceivers assimilate them into new insights and new ways of acting, and the experience of popular culture is actually a mix of identification and production. There is a supply characteristic and a demand characteristic to each side of the model: the general audience consumes cultural objects and supplies cultural workers, while the central producers make and distribute cultural objects and consume the identities of their employees. The most basic—but most numerous—kind of cultural worker is "simply" an audience member; an individual who subscribes to popular culture services as they become appropriate to maintaining a particular identity.[7]

This brings out an aspect of domination in people's lives that has remained virtually unconceptualized in the literature of social thought.[8] For the general process of constituting one's personal and social identities, as well as the more specific process of training cultural workers, certain perceptual experiences—cultural events—are made available. Sights and sounds and other clusters of sense experience are organized at a level which is both beneath and beyond the organization of abstract ideas or legitimations. In the case of music some kinds of sounds are made easy to encounter, while others are ignored or even suppressed. There seems to be no more effective way of accomplishing this patterning of the sound environment than by promoting music distribution through a specific notation system. Notation systems, then, are the technical means by which human organization becomes possible in music, not merely by providing a medium of communication among musicians, but by defining an imperative—an expectation as to who may legitimately send and who may legitimately receive communications in that medium. To the extent that they are trained to a particular notation system musicians accept the differential statuses of sender and receiver without considering the possibility that the two could be merged; or, to put it another way, that the one-way imperatives of notation serve to keep the two separated. Wherever and whenever musicians have learned to distinguish between *my music* and *other people's music* they have discovered the imperative feature of notation systems, and the attention-organizing aspect which is built into every world of music.

Afterword

This book is based on sociological fieldwork—interviews, observations and participations—with American popular musicians. They rehearsed, jammed, socialized, and performed in 1970, 1971, and 1972. That's so last century!

What has changed in the nearly half century since then? Based on the breathless post-post-modern accounts of change to which twenty-first-century citizens have become accustomed: nearly everything. Based on the kind of sociological imagination my original fieldwork sparked: not nearly that much.

One gradual change is that there is now a more widely distributed and inclusive sociological sensibility. So called popular culture is somehow a more appropriate topic. Why? One aspect is that sociology is still extending its scope. After about two hundred years in Europe and a few decades more than one hundred years on the North American continent, sociological analysis is the most innovative way of understanding the human condition. Yet it is still short on coherent theories that manage to account for collective experiences as lived by actual people.[1] Even considering its shortcomings, twenty-first-century sociological thinking is undergoing reorientation. The wide-ranging ideas expressed in this book—once the province, for example, of elitist criticism or aesthetic philosophy, cultural anthropology, ethnomusicology, acoustics, neurophysiology, communications, or semiotics—are now at least plausible ingredients in sociological recipes.

When the book was first published in 1980, some reviewers saw it as yet another "old school" piece of Chicago-style "occupations and professions" fieldwork. Other reviewers took it more as a hip, "off-beat" experiment than serious sociology. They found my comparative analysis of music notation systems as integral to the interactional experiences involved in learning to be a musician, however, to be a bit *too* serious. Perhaps too "phenomenological." Maybe even arcane, since I extended this idea to include recordings as notation systems. Using commercially distributed recordings as musical notation, the young and relatively unschooled musicians I studied managed, on their own, to achieve the skills and recognition sufficient to perform—musically and economically—as self-producing local bands. This provided at least a partial and contemporary answer to the question: How do people "learn how" if they don't go to school? I saw this—and still see this—as a worthwhile sociological question.

I caution readers not to read a great deal into the use of *rock* in the book's title. As with any other category name for popular music, the main reason to claim that compositions and musicians belong in one "genre" or another is commerce. The actual sounds and actual playing skills involved do not sort out so neatly. Consider the gamut of performances and musicians inducted into the Rock and Roll Hall of Fame in Cleveland, Ohio. In the book I developed a way of referring to whatever commercially promoted and distributed recorded music was "in the air" at any moment as The Music. *Rock* music can be understood as coded speech meaning The Music.

The idea in this book most cited by other writers[2] is what I called *recording consciousness*. I encourage readers to consider the "impossible" theme embedded in the idea of recording consciousness. Twentieth-century recordings achieved the impossible using analog technologies. They are still in use. Yet twenty-first century citizens are predominantly conditioned by differently achieved impossible audio experiences—ones that rely on hardware and software that embeds *digital* signal processing technology. For example, anyone who, like me, now uses a DAW (digital audio workstation) can make entire recordings in which *every* sound a listener hears is impossible to create by live musicians in live performance. Much is made of such impossible possibilities in reports about the technical feats of electronic and computer-facilitated music.

My viewpoint adds a sociological emphasis. How are interactions between musicians, between composers and publishers and musicians, or between musicians and audiences affected? It turns out that this putatively new state of sonic affairs has a history, since composers in centuries past have used (or abused) notation systems to concoct written scores that were intended to be impossible for human musicians to play. In response, performers took the resulting John Henry–style challenge "past the limit" and did it anyway.[3] A similar impossibility can happen in a technically different way when twenty-first-century "amateurs with computers"[4] act like composers by using (or abusing) notation software to print out scores displaying an embarrassment of notes that actually are impossible for humans to play.

Recording consciousness, then, stems from a kind of human collective action that responds to innovations in the material means of production. In this way, digital recordings are sociologically similar to old analog recordings—ones based on magnetism or grooves in engravable materials—since they are ways that changes in signal processing technology have been brought into the play of creating and distributing music. The original insights in this book came grounded in actual experiences of popular musicians whose musical, performance, and audience interaction skills were (in Marshall McLuhan's wonderful turn of phrase[5]) taking a "hot bath" in recordings. There are ambiguities to unravel in this enigmatic process—perhaps by approaching the topic as a kind of magic.[6]

Even as technical changes manifest themselves, and the sonic details of recordings familiar to widespread populations change, the sociological relevance of ways that recordings interact with music, musicians, and their audiences is a recognizable pattern. Once the audience for recorded music has heard a piece, they become a pool of people from which live audiences for that piece may be recruited.

Live audiences subsequently communicate with live performers—mostly by showing up, then responding to what they "like" and "don't like." What they think they want to hear, though, is conditioned by what they've previously heard on recordings. And what can be created in a recording studio is not what is possible to create during live performances.

These circumstances set up aesthetic expectations between artist and audience based on a *dimension*—from uniquely presented "version" through "just like the record." How this dimensionality gets handled cuts across decades, locations, venues, music genres, and ways of identifying audiences. There is a technical aspect to it—a perennial quest to *reproduce* "live" sound as it was recorded in a studio. However quixotic that mission may be, it is made materially obvious when studio-style equipment affects a performance's aural presence.

In the twenty-first century, such equipment can be a minor presence—like a pedalboard, which integrates an individual guitarist's custom collection of effects devices. But studio-style equipment often dominates performances—it can be as elaborate as a whole group's front-of-house sound and on-stage monitor sound, mixed live as multiple channels from multiple signal sources by an audio engineer using effects, pitch-correction, and synchronization devices. Not only does such studio-like equipment shape the sensorial experiences available at popular music concerts, it is also working within performances of Broadway musicals, operas, and classical concerts. This even includes prepared sonic material played back "as if live" during "live" performances—with or without revelation to the "live" audience.[7] The local musicians I studied in the 1970s used less advanced technology to produce themselves, but the technically facilitated aesthetic quest to integrate "studio quality" into live performance sound was the same.

Twenty-first century recordings, distributed using multiple forms of electronic media, can contribute to the soundscape anywhere on Earth, with collectively recognized aural results. "Earworms" or "stuck-song syndrome" are slang for one way such sonic consequences are discovered "in the wild." Beyond considering material technologies, this book argued that collectively human phenomena can infuse performances with a consciousness of recordings. I wrote:

> As long as the copy group delivers its services, the collective memory of the audience seems to fill in the gaps between the sound of the group and the sound of the recording. When a copy group has fulfilled the expectations of its contractors it has played what it cannot play, and the audience has heard what it cannot hear.[8]

The ideas I proposed lead to a still-relevant line of questioning about what happens during live performances: How does it make sense to describe twenty-first-century audience-musician interactions? Can our ears be "fooled" in some way? Are they? If so, how does this work? Is a kind of "careless" or "mindless" sonic attention possible? Have we developed sonic habits in response to a liminal "radio" or "background" muzak/mood-media sensibility? How focused are collective events of hearing and listening? Is there an ability of human sense-brain circuits to "fill-in" what is not actually presented, or what is indeterminate or undetailed? If so, where does such "fill-in" material come from?

I don't pretend to have the deep knowledge required to provide well-grounded answers to all these questions. I do understand that even while copresent in the same performance space, there is a skill difference (something learned) between the experiences of most audience-listeners as compared to most musician-listeners. Live musical performers discover that their audiences respond in different ways and to different sound events than they do. Locally expressed sonic responses, as well as the timing of those responses, show performers that general audiences are not reliable perceivers of quality. On some nights the muse visits less experienced players, while virtuosity routinely emanates from players whose preparation and skill level is high, but audiences often can't tell who's merely "showing off" or who is "not playing well tonight"—or even distinguish "good" from "average." What is it, then, that audiences deem worthy of attention? What is it about a performance that renders it aesthetically valuable? And are these two questions—or one?

This book encourages contemporary readers to wonder about the extent to which its ideas can be generalized. Obviously there are other kinds of recording and distribution. Virtually all of twenty-first century collective life is electronically mediated, initiated as productions for specific media forms and ritualized through repetition into a virtual commonwealth of sense memories.

Merged audio-video, for example, is ubiquitous. Text—in either audio or visual form—becomes a ripe subject for this line of sociological inquiry. Consider the rise of "internet memes" and "fake news." To be a citizen is now an everyday experiment in parsing what's possible, what's impossible, and what cannot be so easily distinguished. Each day's mediated playout and playback events lead people to consider the authenticity of what they experience. In response, the aesthetic skills—like how to see or how to imagine or how to hear—commonly associated with the arts merge with the aesthetic skills needed to negotiate everyday life. Sociological insights into how these skills are acquired and how they are used by performers and audiences alike endure in this "old" book.

December 2016
Peaceful Valley, Colorado

Appendix

Loudness and Equalization

In a series of experiments conducted in the early 1930s at the Bell Telephone Laboratories by Harvey Fletcher and W. A. Munson the concept of *loudness* was developed. Loudness demonstrates that human hearing is differentially sensitive to the intensity of sounds as frequency changes. Loudness, then, is a sound's psychophysical or perceived magnitude which does not exactly correspond to its magnitude when measured by non-human equipment. Consider the Fletcher and Munson curves shown in figure 9. At very low frequencies a sound level (SL) of, say, 50 decibels is virtually inaudible, while at a frequency of 1000 Hz. a 50-decibel sound level is clearly audible (corresponding to *p* or *piano*). At frequencies around 3000 Hz. ear sensitivity is greatest and sounds are heard as slightly louder than a non-human device would measure them. This effect has to do with the size and shape of the auditory canal (outer ear) which, like any other cavity, exhibits a *resonant frequency* (that is, it builds up standing waves at a certain frequency). The 3000 Hz. bulge in the curves is also determined by certain physical properties of the small bones in the middle ear. As a sound's frequency passes 5000 Hz. hearing sensitivity again diminishes. This phenomenon increases dramatically with age, and it is often impossible for old people to hear high harmonies and overtones—a condition which is referred to as *presbycousis*. Notice that the curves have been (arbitrarily) standardized to the 1000 Hz. reference frequency.

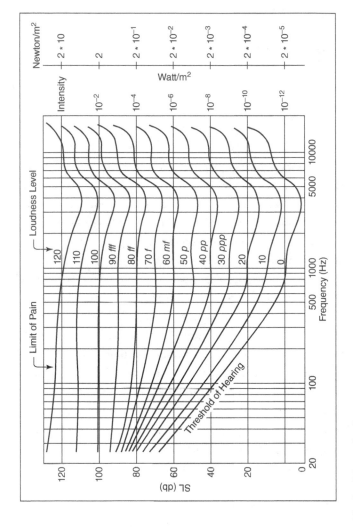

Figure 9 The Fletcher-Munson loudness contours.
Reprinted from H. Fletcher and W. Munson, "Loudness: Its Definition, Measurement, and Calculation," *Journal of the Acoustical Society of America*, No. 5, 1933. (Used with permission.)

What can be derived from an inspection of these curves is that for the lowest tones of the bass instrument (say 40 Hz.) the actual intensity of the sound must approach 70 decibels (a fairly loud sound at higher frequencies) simply to be audible. Under actual playing conditions the bass instrument's sound might have to be as much as 100,000 times as intense as a middle-range frequency (say 500 Hz.) to be heard at an equal loudness. Traditional (that is, acoustic) musical performances have no way of compensating for this loudness contour and the expectation of a listener at a symphonic concert is that the bass instruments will be barely audible, save for the occasional very quiet passage. This is why many bass instruments are played in unison in an orchestra, yet it would take *ten* instruments playing together to make a sound which would be perceived to be only *twice* as loud as one instrument playing alone.

The original innovative instrument design for increased intensity at low frequencies was the cathedral pipe organ, and the excitement which this instrument caused in the world of music was to some extent due to its control of frequencies so low that they were previously unavailable to the ears of a listener. The increased audible frequency range created a whole new part or *line* in the polyphonic music which was written for the instrument, and an understanding of the technical possibilities of low-frequency sound is essential to any discussion of the change in aesthetics—not to mention ear-shattering awe—which accompanied the appearance of organ music in church.

Since the experiments of Fletcher and Munson all commercial recordings have been adjusted according to some kind of loudness contours. In America those set forth by the Recording Industry Association of America (RIAA) are most pervasive, and people who listen to such recordings have become accustomed to sound experiences in which very low and very high frequencies are boosted for them.

This original *equalization* of the overall loudness of a recording sparked the elaborate techniques of manipulating the intensity of sound at particular frequencies which have become essential to contemporary recordings. The term *equalization* as it is commonly used today is actually a misnomer when it is applied to situations where a certain frequency is purposely enhanced or suppressed as a basic means of sound control without necessarily attempting to "equal" the Fletcher and Munson curves.

Because of the primacy of recorded sound most people expect that frequency-manipulated sound will be provided in live performances. In keeping with the pattern I have demonstrated throughout this book, live performance technology has closed the gap on sound possibilities which were previously available only on recordings. High-powered sound reinforcement systems with elaborate filtering devices attest to this fact. Similarly the electric bass instrument with its amplification equipment produces low-frequency sound at an intensity unknown in the history of music. In contradistinction to its forerunner—the pipe organ—an electric bass (or keyboard equivalent) is portable, and therefore more easily encountered by audiences. Both instruments share the role of a technical turning point in the performance of music. They share, as well, the use of the building materials of a structure as a musical medium. Reports that a rock group was "shaking" or "rocking" the place can often be taken literally.

Notes

PREFACE

1. Among other methodological strategies, I subscribe to the practice of seeking out negative cases; occurrences that would be impossible if my analysis is correct. Discovering several of these has changed my way of constructing analytic statements. Statements which will, in the wake of Karl Popper, never be proven, but which have not yet been *disproven*.

2. For an excellent introduction to this way of understanding sound and a development of the idea of *soundscapes*, see Murray Schafer's *The Tuning of the World* (Knopf, 1978).

3. See John Cage's *Silence* (M.I.T. Press, 1966), which contains his *The Future of Music: Credo* from 1937.

I. GROUP DYNAMICS

1. Consider, for example, the *Guitar Institute of Technology*, 5858 Hollywood Boulevard, Hollywood, California, 90028; or *The Rhythm Section Lab*, 130 West 42nd Street, Suite 948, New York, New York, 10036.

2. This is a famous phrase in sociological circles. It was contributed by W. I. Thomas in his *The Child in America: Behavior Problems and Programs*, (Knopf, 1928).

3. This is also W. I. Thomas talk. It is a preliminary statement of the "reality constructionist" approach to social life—to which I certainly subscribe. The standard introduction to this point of view is *The Social Construction of Reality* by Peter Berger and Thomas Luckmann (Doubleday, 1966).

4. For surveys of this type of philosophizing see Monroe Beardsley's *Aesthetics: From Classical Greece to Present* (Macmillan, 1966); or George Dickie's *Aesthetics: An Introduction* (Irvington Press, 1971).

5. See William Weber's *Music and the Middle Class* (Holmes and Meter, 1975).

6. This is from Howard S. Becker's *Art Worlds* (University of California Press, 1980).

7. This is from Kurt Wolff's translations in *The Sociology of Georg Simmel* (Free Press, 1950), p. 40.

8. Ibid., p. 41.

9. Ibid., p. 41.

10. Ibid., p. 42.

11. From my original idea about the relationship of play, anxiety, and boredom (see "An Exploratory Model of Play," by Mihaly Csikzentmihalyi and H. Stith Bennett, *American Anthropologist* 73:1 [1971]). Mihaly Csikzentmihalyi has developed his own concept of *flowing* (see page 49 and after in his *Beyond Boredom and Anxiety* [Jossey-Bass, San Francisco, 1975]). Actually play, or flowing, or unfolding action, or creation, or even "peak experience" seem very close in meaning. The important thing to me about all these terms is that they define a way in which individual and collective experiences meet, a way in which context may be seen to affect people's conduct. Csikzentmihalyi (and others, I'm sure) might maintain that the flaw in this model is the wide variability in people's awarenesses of what options are available (ibid., p. 50). Due to this he seeks to typify the "flowing" or "playful" *personality*. As far as I am concerned the idea is intended to illuminate changes in awareness—the "ins" and "outs" of humorous episodes— that anyone having any personality can experience. Part of my original intention was to admit the assumption that people can and will control what is perceived. Now I would identify the ability to focus perceptual abilities as an essential motive of all cultures; of all artifactualizations; of all *arts* in the expanded sense of the term. There may be spiritual or political or technical reasons for directing, attracting, and even diverting attention, but the process itself works (when it works) because it is playful; because it alters perceptual possibilities and therefore defines new ways to conduct oneself.

12. See Thorstein Veblen's *Theory of the Leisure Class* (Augustus M. Kelley, 1899 [reprint]).

13. Georg Simmel, *The Sociology of Georg Simmel* (Free Press, 1950), p. 37.

14. See, for example, Barney Glazer and Anselm Strauss, *Status Passage: A Formal Theory* (Aldine, 1971).

15. See "Conditions of Successful Status Degradation Ceremonies," by Harold Garfinkel, *American Journal of Sociology*, Vol. 61 (March, 1956).

16. There may be a telephone number to call and a registry of names, or various players' groups might publish a directory of members.

17. Undoubtedly the slang which is advanced to describe the goodness of popular music making marks its user's cultural identity and musical age. To *swing* or to *cook* or to *rock* or to *blow* or to be *far out*, however, all imply changes in state.

18. There may be religious overtones to the state of consciousness of a musician at play. See Rudolf Otto's *The Idea of the Holy*, translated by John W. Harvey (Oxford University Press, 1950).

II. ROCK ECOLOGY

1. Often abbreviated as S/N, a signal-to-noise ratio is conventionally expressed in decibels of sound intensity for both signal (desired sound focus) and noise (competing sound). A "good" signal-to-noise ratio—where competing sound can be completely masked by the desired sound—might be 60 dB., which means that the intensity of the signal is one million times greater than the intensity of the noise.

2. The kind of material used to make the body greatly influences its sound (whether amplified or not). This "new" instrument design is not without ancient precedent: the Chinese *Ch'in* comes to mind, as does the practice of placing the *Ch'in* on a table to increase its audibility.

3. Wave form refers to the "shape" of a complex sound; to the fact that it may be composed of a number of frequencies, and that those frequencies may be present at different intensities. In European art music terms, wave form might be understood as *timbre*.

4. The live performance approach should be distinguished from wholly synthesized and recorded electronic compositions made by the many thousands of "serious" electronic composers who work in hundreds of permanent electronic music studios—usually located at colleges and universities—throughout the United States.

5. MXR Innovations, Inc., 247N. Goodman Street, Rochester, New York, 14607.

6. Georg Simmel, *The Sociology of Georg Simmel* (Free Press, 1950), p. 114.

7. This means a bar which is licensed to sell alcoholic beverages which contain no more than 3.2 percent alcohol. In the state of Colorado eighteen-year-olds may purchase such alcoholic beverages (typically beer) while full-strength booze is legally available only to those who are twenty-one or older.

8. The "Islamic" instrument was most likely a *rabab* (the Arabic name for an extended family of wooden string instruments which were most often actuated with a bow). Known in a multitude of ways throughout Europe (often as a *rebec*) it was a street instrument in France when the use of the violin was prohibited to itinerant musicians. In German *geige* (from the Old German *gige*) means violin. It seems plausible to me that sixteenth-century English folk dances (jigs) were based on a popular way of playing music and making instruments which shows its "Islamic" features, the so-called modal quality being an obvious example. Since English, Scottish, and Irish music is implicated in the origins of American popular music, and since aspects of certain instrument designs, compositional

techniques, broad humor, social comment, and community events with spirited social dancing can be found to this day in America, the thread of an ancient and multicultural popular music tradition can be understood to exist. If we look in the other direction to consider the origins of instruments of the *rabab* family, we might find an ancient Indo-European music culture (paralleling the ancient Indo-European language), especially if we consider another instrument type—the *free-reed* instruments like the harmonica, or concertina, or bagpipes. Certainly European music has not been immune to influences from a variety of music cultures. From an ethnocentric viewpoint even upperclass foreign music might be considered "popular," and, in any event, popular music would be less insulated from outside change than academic music. I should point out that my speculative historical ethnomusicology is a dangerous business which is filled with pit-falls. On the other hand it is my firm belief that music and instruments come from *somewhere*, and that no matter what the relationship (if any) between, say, banjos and Afghan *rohabs*, their structural similarities are worth mentioning.

9. See Everett C. Hughes, *Men and Their Work* (Free Press, 1958).

III. MASTERING THE TECHNOLOGICAL COMPONENT

1. See Paul Oliver's *Savannah Synchopators: African Retentions in the Blues* (Stein and Day, 1970).

2. This is the well-known set of characteristics contributed by Richard A. Waterman, "African Influences on the Music of the Americans," in *Acculturation in the Americas*, edited by Sol Tax (University of Chicago Press, 1952).

3. It should be noted that since the song form dominates the world's folk music, people with an entirely popular orientation tend to call *any* piece of music a "song." Although this is technically a mistake, it is an understandable one.

4. Could this have anything to do with the interest many black Americans express in Islamic religions?

5. Of course there were many highly developed Native American music cultures, but it is enlightening to note how completely they have been excluded from American popular music.

6. See, respectively, Mantle Hood's *The Ethnomusicologist* (McGraw-Hill, 1971); and Ronald Byrnside's "The Formation of a Musical Style: Early Rock" in *Contemporary Music and Music Cultures*, by Charles Hamm, Bruno Nettl, and Ronald Byrnside (Prentice-Hall, 1975).

7. See William Weber's "Mass Culture and the Reshaping of European Musical Taste, 1770–1870," *International Review of the Aesthetics and Sociology of Music* 8:1 (June 1977).

8. See, for one example of this, the earlier work of Serge Denisoff like *Folk Consciousness: The People's Music and American Communism* (University of Illinois Press, 1971); or *Sing a Song of Social Significance* (Bowling Green University Popular Press, 1972).

9. See my "Secondary Popular Culture," *Symbolic Interaction* 2:1 (Spring 1979).

10. It should be noted that the English language lacks terms (and idioms) which express the mental processing of sound. There is no aural counterpart for the visual process of seeing images—that is, *imagining*. When speaking of sound it might be possible to use hearing as a counterpart to *imagining*, but this confuses the category of external phenomena with the internal process of "hearing in the head."

11. This was quoted in Paul Henry Lang's edited volume based on The Princeton Seminar in Advanced Musical Studies, *Problems of Modern Music* (W. W. Norton, 1960).

12. I am using the familiar term *consciousness* even though it brings some danger of misinterpretation with it. This is because in contemporary American conversation and media language consciousness tends to refer to abstract ideas; perhaps to *false* consciousness or ideology. This is not the sense in which I mean it. Here, consciousness refers to the process of coming to one's senses, of "becoming conscious," of inquiring as to whether someone is conscious or not. *Awareness* might be a better word, but it has its own alternate implications. Whatever word is used my intention is to emphasize the purely perceptual realm of meaning, and to deemphasize the purely cognitive realm.

13. This is taken from P. B. Laxton, "A Gilbertese Song," *Journal of the Polynesian Society*, 62 (1953).

14. See Alfred Schutz, "Making Music Together," in his *Collected Papers Volume II* (Martinus Nijhoff, 1964).

15. See Nelson Goodman's *Language of Art: An Approach to the Theory of Symbols* (Bobbs-Merrill, 1968), especially sections 2, 4, 5, and 6; and Hugo Cole's *Sound and Signs: Aspects of Musical Notation* (Oxford University Press, 1974). In this regard there is, of course, the standard work by Willi Apel, *The Notation of Polyphonic Music*, 900–1600 (Medieval Academy of America, 1942).

16. See Alfred North Whitehead's *Science and the Modern World* (Free Press, 1967).

17. See Thomas S. Kuhn's *The Structure of Scientific Revolutions*, second edition (University of Chicago Press, 1970).

IV. PERFORMANCE

1. See Robert Faulkner's *Hollywood Studio Musicians* (Aldine, 1971).

2. For this example I'm assuming that the guitar and the guitar player are right handed.

3. RMS means root mean square, a more conservative way to rate audio power than *peak* power ratings.

4. There are many more notation systems in the world than there are notation systems in use. There are, for example, hundreds and hundreds of alternate written music notation systems—many of which eliminate the quirks and ambiguities of the five-line mensural system, but none of which have made a dent in the hegemony of the European art music tradition. (On the other hand it is somewhat fashionable for modern academic composers to provide unique notational formats for particular pieces—many of Karlheinz Stockhausen's works exemplify this.) Beyond music, however, there are other instances of this phenomenon of notational monopoly. Consider the language *Esperanto* which combines aspects of many Germanic languages and has *no* grammatical irregularities, but which has not exactly caught fire as the international language it was intended to be. Or, consider the example of the Dvorak typewriter keyboard design which requires only *5 percent* of the finger movement required by the familiar Sholes keyboard (which, amazingly enough, was intentionally designed to impede a typist's speed), but which remains unused. These examples attest not only to the arbitrariness of notation systems, but to the organized human interests which surround them and maintain programs for training new personnel to them. Controlling a notation system is a fundamental form of cultural control.

5. For sound recordings five large corporations—CBS, Warner Communications, American Broadcasting Companies, MCA, and RCA—account for more than 90 percent of all the owning and operating that goes on. Wholesale grosses in the recording industry top two billion dollars annually.

6. For examples pertaining to the recording industry see Paul Hirsch's "Processing Fads and Fashions: An Organization Set Analysis of Cultural Industry Systems," *American Journal of Sociology* 77:1 (1972) or any of his other work.

7. See Stanley Aronowitz, *False Promises* (McGraw-Hill, 1973), which includes the concept of *colonized leisure.*

8. A parallel observation for the case of language can be found in Walter J. Ong's "Literacy and Orality in Our Times," in *Profession 79,* (Modern Language Association, 1979). In my terms the *phenomenal* system of music notation (Ong's *primary orality* for language) has been usurped by the *symbolic* system (simply *literacy* to Ong).

AFTERWORD

1. Test this proposition by comparing several introductory sociology textbooks. Even the most astutely researched and well-edited of them are more lists of topic areas than an integrated way of knowing that makes sense from first to last page.

2. See, for example, Richard Middleton's *Studying Popular Music* (Open University Press, 1990); Francois Ribac's *L'Avaleur de Rock*: La Dispute (L'imprimerie Sagim-Canale, 2004); Greg Milner's *Perfecting Sound Forever: An Aural History of Recorded Music* (Farrar, Straus and Giroux, 2009); David Byrne's *How Music Works* (McSweeney's, 2012); or Babette Babich's *The Hallelujah Effect: Philosophical Reflections on Music, Performance Practice, and Technology* (Routledge Ashgate Series, 2013).

3. The *18 Études for Piano* by György Ligeti are infamous examples, as are pianists Pierre-Laurent Aimard and Jeremy Denk who managed to perform them.

4. I've stolen this turn of phrase from master statistician J. Stuart Hunter who it used to describe the dangers of statistical software packages when applied at the push of a button by those with "a little knowledge" (a dangerous thing!). Every day, people who consume findings based on statistical data analysis (e.g. in the news, in professional and scientific reporting) are faced with a mix of competent authors and fools "rushing in where angels fear to tread." Even for experts, it can be both difficult and time-consuming to sort out the difference.

5. "People don't actually read newspapers. They step into them every morning like a hot bath." Marshall McLuhan, in his *Understanding Media: The Extensions of Man* (New York: McGraw-Hill, 1964).

6. "Any sufficiently advanced technology is indistinguishable from magic." Attributed to science fiction writer Arthur C. Clarke by Neil McAleer, Clarke's biographer.

7. Consider the August 12, 2012 performance billed as *Il Divo and the Atlanta Symphony Orchestra*: "The ASO played live during the entire performance with live microphones hanging overhead. Nevertheless, the ASO was not in the mix piped to the audience through the sound system." . . . "Instead, it heard prerecorded audio tracks by an entirely different orchestra. The tracks included instruments that were not present on stage, such as a synthesized bass guitar." . . . "The Il Divo singers were live, but the orchestra was relegated to the role of visual window dressing." See Mark Gresham, "Silenced: ASO Used as Musical 'Prop,' Audience Hears Recorded Music at Il Divo Concert," *Arts ATL*, August 14, 2012, http://www.artsatl.com/atlanta-symphony-forced-pantomime-pre-recorded-tracks-sunday%E2%80%99s-il-divo-concert/ and http://www.trumpetherald.com/forum/viewtopic.php?t=117057&start=0&postdays=0&postorder=asc&highlight=.

8. Last words of part 3, "Mastering The Technological Component."

Bibliography

Adorno, Theodor W.

1976   *Introduction to the Sociology of Music* (translated by E. B. Ashton), New York: Seabury Press. (Originally published as: *Einleitung in Die Musiksoziologie*, Frankfurt: S. Fischer.)

1973   (1949) *Philosophy of Modern Music* (translated by Anne G. Mitchell and Wesley V. Blaustar), New York: Seabury Press.

1941   "On Radio Music," *Studies in Philosophy and Social Science* 9, p. 17, New York: Institute for Social Research.

Albrecht, Milton C.

1973   *The Arts in Market Systems*, paper read at the American Sociological Association Meetings.

1970   *The Sociology of Art and Literature*, New York: Praeger.

1968   "Art as an Institution," *American Sociological Review* 33.

Allen, Warren Dwight

1962   (1939) *Philosophies of Music History: A Study of General Histories of Music 1600–1960*, New York: Dover.

Ansermet, Ernest

1961   *Les Fondments de la Musique dans la Conscience Humaine*, Neuchatel (Suisse): Editions de la Baconniere.

Apel, Willi

1968a   (1944) *Harvard Dictionary of Music*, second edition, Cambridge: The Belknap Press of Harvard University Press.

1942   *The Notation of Polyphonic Music, 900–1600*, Cambridge: Mediaeval Academy of America.

Arian, Edward

1971   *Bach, Beethoven, and Bureaucracy: The Case of the Philadelphia Orchestra*, University, AL: University of Alabama Press.

Arnheim, Rudolf

1969   *Visual Thinking*, Berkeley: University of California Press.

Aronowitz, Stanley

1973   *False Promises*, New York: McGraw-Hill.

Ayars, Christine Merrick

1937   *Contributions to the Art of Music in America by the Music Industries of Boston 1640–1936*, New York: Wilson.

Backus, John

1969   *The Acoustical Foundations of Music*, New York: W. W. Norton.

Baldwin, James

1960   "Mass Culture and the Creative Artist: Some Personal Ideas," *Daedalus* 89, pp. 373 ff.

Barnauw, Erik

   A *History of Broadcasting in the United States*, New York: Oxford University Press.

1970   Volume Three: *The Image Empire*

1968   Volume Two: *The Golden Web*

1966   Volume One: *A Tower of Babel*

Basirico, Lawrence A.

1974   "Stickin' Together: The Cohesiveness of Rock Groups," unpublished master's Thesis, Stony Brook: State University of New York.

Beardsley, Monroe C.

1966   *Aesthetics: From Classical Greece to the Present (A Short History)*, New York: Macmillan.

Becker, Howard S.

1980   *Art Worlds*, Los Angeles: University of California Press.

1955   "Careers in a Deviant Occupational Group," *Social Problems* 3 (July).

1953   "Some Contingencies of the Professional Dance Musician's Career," *Human Organization* 12 (Spring).

1952   "The Professional Dance Musician and His Audience," *American Journal of Sociology* 57 (July–May, 1951–1952).

Bekker, Paul

1916   *Das Deutsche Musikleben*, Berlin.

Belz, Carl

1969   *The Story of Rock*, New York: Oxford University Press.

Bensman, Joseph

1967   "Classical Music and the Status Game," *Trans-Action* 4 (9), pp. 54 ff.

Berger, Morroe

1947   "Jazz: Resistance to the Diffusion of a Culture Pattern," *Journal of Negro History* 32 (October).

Berger, Peter L., and Thomas Luckmann

1966   *The Social Construction of Reality*, New York: Doubleday.

Berk, Lee Eliot

1977   *Legal Protection for the Creative Musician*, Boston: Berklee Press.

Blacking, John

1973   *How Musical Is Man?*, Seattle: University of Washington Press.

Blaukopf, Kurt

1950   *Musiksoziologie*, St. Gallen: Zollikopfer.

Blesh, Rudi, and Harriet Janis

1971   *They All Played Ragtime*, New York: Oak.

Boorstin, Daniel

1964   *The Image: A Guide to Pseudo-Events in America*, New York: Harper and Row.

Braun, D. Duane

1969   *Toward a Theory of Popular Culture: The Sociology of American Music and Dance, 1920–1968*, Ann Arbor: Ann Arbor Publishers.

Briggs, Asa

1963, 1965, 1970   *The History of Broadcasting in the United Kingdom* (3 volumes), London: Oxford University Press.

Brown, R. L.

1968   "The Creative Process in the Popular Arts," *International Journal of Social Science* 20 (4), p. 613.

Brunswick, Ann

1962   "Popular Taste in Music as Reflected by Behavior with Regard to Phonograph Records," Chicago: National Opinion Research Center.

Buecher, Karl

1896   *Abeit und Rhythmus*, Leipzig.

Burns, Joan Simpson

1975   *The Awkward Embrace*, New York: Alfred Knopf.

Cameron, William B.

1954   "Sociological Notes on the Jam Session," *Social Forces* 33 (December).

Cantrick, Robert P.

1965   "The Blind Men and the Elephant: Scholars on Popular Music," *Ethnomusicology* 9 (2), p. 100.

Carey, James T.

1969a   "Changing Courtship Patterns in the Popular Song," *American Journal of Sociology* 74, pp. 720 *ff.*

1969b   "The Ideology of Autonomy in Popular Lyrics: A Content Analysis," *Psychiatry* 32, pp. 150 *ff.*

Carlino, Angelo

1975   *The Evils of Music Management: An Exposé*, New York: LeCar.

Cattell, Raymond B., and David R. Saunders

1954   "Musical Preferences and Personality Diagnosis: A Factorization of 120 Cases," *Journal of Social Psychology* 39.

Chapple, Steve, and Reebee Garafalo

1977   *Rock and Roll Is Here to Pay*, Chicago: Nelson Hall.

Charters, Samuel

1968   *The Bluesmen*, New York: Oak.

1959   *The Country Blues*, New York: Holt, Rinehart, and Winston.

Clark, Sharon Leigh

1973   *Rock Dance in the United States: Its Origins, Forms and Patterns*, PhD dissertation in Anthropology, New York: New York University.

Cohen, Norman

1970   "Urban vs. Rural Values in Country and Pop Songs: A Review Essay," *John Edwards Memorial Foundation Quarterly* 6, p. 62.

Coker, Wilson

1972   *Music and Meaning*, New York: Free Press.

Cole, Hugo

1974   *Sounds and Signs: Aspects of Musical Notation*, New York: Oxford University Press.

Collingwood, R. G.

1958   *The Principles of Art*, New York: Oxford University Press.

Conyers, James E.

1963   "An Exploratory Study of Musical Tastes and Interests of College Students," *Sociological Inquiry* 33(1) (Winter), p. 58.

Cooper, Grosvenor, and Leonard B. Meyer

1960   *The Rhythmic Structure of Music*, Chicago: The University of Chicago Press.

Copland, Aaron

1939   *What to Listen for in Music*, New York: McGraw-Hill.

Corry, Catherine S.

1965   *The Phonograph Record Industry: An Economic Study*, Washington: Library of Congress, Legislative Reference Service.

Courlander, Harold

1963   *Negro Folk Music, U.S.A.*, New York: Columbia University Press.

Csikszentmihalyi, Mihaly, and Stith Bennett

1971   "An Exploratory Model of Play," *American Anthropologist* 73 (1) (February).

Davis, Clive

1975   *Clive: Inside the Record Business*, New York: William Morrow.

Denisoff, Serge

1975   *Solid Gold*, New Brunswick: Transaction Books.

1973a   "The Evolution of Pop Music Broadcasting: 1920–1972," *Popular Music and Society* 2, pp. 202 ff.

1973b *The Sounds of Social Change: Studies in Pop Culture*, Chicago: Rand McNally (with Richard A. Peterson, eds.).

1972 *Sing a Song of Social Significance*, Bowling Green: University Popular Press.

1971 *Folk Consciousness: The People's Music and American Communism*, Urbana: University of Illinois Press.

Denzin, Norman K.

1970 "Problems in Analyzing Elements of Mass Culture: Notes on the Popular Song and Other Artistic Productions," *American Journal of Sociology* 75 (6) (May).

Dewey, John

1934 *Art as Experience*, New York: Capricorn Books.

Dickie, George

1964 *Aesthetics: An Introduction*, New York: St. Martin's.

1962 "Is Psychology Relevant to Aesthetics?" *Philosophical Review* 71, pp. 285 *ff.*

Dilthey, Wilhelm

1933 *Von Deutscher Dichtung und Musik: Aus Studien zur Geschichte des Deutschen Geistes.* Leipzig.

Dixon, R. M., and John Godrich

1970 *Recording the Blues*, New York: Stein and Day.

Doelle, Leslie L.

1965 *Acoustics in Architectural Design (An Annotated Bibliography)*, Ottawa: NRC of Canada Division of Building Research Publication.

Drinker, Sophie

1948 *Music and Women*, New York: Howard McCann.

Dufrenne, Mikel

1973 *The Phenomenology of Aesthetic Experience* (translated by Edward S. Casey, et. al.), Evanston: Northwestern University Press. (Actually a combination of two volumes: (1) The Phenomenology of the Aesthetic Object, (2) The Phenomenology of Aesthetic Perception.)

1964 "The Aesthetic Object and the Technical Object," *Journal of Aesthetics and Art Criticism* 23 (Fall), pp. 113 *ff.*

Duncan, Hugh Dalziel

1968 (1962) *Communication and Social Order*, New York: Oxford University Press.

Eisen, Jonathan, ed.

1970 *The Age of Rock, vol. 2*, New York: Vintage.

1969 *The Age of Rock*, New York: Vintage.

Ellis, Alexander J.

1885 "On the Musical Scales of Various Nations," *Journal of the Society for Arts*, 33

Embridge, David M.

1976 "Down Home with the Band: Country-Western Music and Rock," *Ethnomusicology* 10 (3).

1973   *A Dialog of Energy: Rock Music and Cultural Changes*, PhD dissertation in music, Minneapolis: University of Minnesota.

Etzkorn, K. Peter

1976   "Manufacturing Music," *Society* (November/December).

1973   "On Music, Social Structure, and Sociology," *International Review of the Aesthetics and Sociology of Music* 5(1).

1973a   "On the Sphere of Social Validity in African Art: Sociological Reflections on Ethnographic Data," in Warren L. D'Azevedo, *The Traditional Artist in African Societies*, Bloomington: Indiana University Press.

1973b   *Music and Society: The Later Writings of Paul Honigsheim*, New York: John Wiley and Sons.

1966   "On Esthetic Standards and Reference Groups of Popular Songwriters," *Sociological Inquiry* 36(1) (Winter).

1964a   "Georg Simmel and the Sociology of Music," *Social Forces* 43 (1) (October).

1964b   "The Relationship Between Musical and Social Patterns in American Popular Music," *Journal of Research in Music Education* 12 (4) (Winter).

1963   "Social Context of Songwriting in the United States," *Ethnomusicology* 7 (2) (May).

Ewen, David

1968   *The World of Twentieth Century Music*, Englewood Cliffs: Prentice-Hall.

1966   *Popular American Composers from the Revolution to the Present*.

1964   *The Rise and Fall of Tin Pan Alley*, New York: Funk and Wagnalls.

Faulkner, Robert R.

1975   "Hollywood Film Composers and Their Clients: Some Contingencies of Cooperation in Commercial Work." Unpublished manuscript, Department of Sociology, University of Massachusetts, Amherst.

1974   *Coming of Age in Organizations: Some Contingencies of Mobility and Career Socialization in Symphony Orchestras and Professional Hockey.* Unpublished manuscript, Department of Sociology, University of Massachusetts, Amherst.

1971   *Studio Musicians: Their Work and Career Contingencies in the Hollywood Film Industry*, Chicago: Aldine.

Felixson, Nancy, et. al.

1975   *Women in American Music*, Aptos, Calif.: Written Word Collective.

Finkelstein, Sidney

1960   *Composer and Nation*, New York: International Publishers.

Fisher, Ernst

1963   *The Necessity of Art*, Baltimore: Penguin Books. (Note Chapter Three.)

Fisher, Renee

1973   *Musical Prodigies: Masters at an Early Age*, New York: Association Press.

Fletcher, Harvey

1935   "Newer Concepts of Pitch, Loudness, and Timbre of Musical Tones," *Journal of the Franklin Institute*, no. 220.

1933   "Loudness: Its Definition, Measurement, and Calculation," *Journal of the Acoustical Society of America* (with W. Munson).

Forbes

1973   "The Rockers Are Rolling It In," April 15, pp. 28 *ff.*

Freedman, Alex S.

1969   "The Sociology of Country Music," *Southern Humanities Review* 3 (4), p. 358.

Furlong, William Barry

1974   *Season with Solti*, New York: Macmillan.

Gans, Herbert L.

1966   "Popular Culture in America: Social Problem in a Mass Society or Social Asset in a Pluralistic Society?" in H. S. Becker, ed., *Social Problems: A Modern Approach*, New York: John Wiley.

Gelatt, Roland

1966   *The Fabulous Phonograph: From Edison to Stereo*, New York: Appleton-Century-Crofts.

Gentry, Linnal

1964   *Encyclopedia of Country, Western, and Gospel Music*, Murfeesboro, Tenn: University Press.

Gilford, C. L.

1972   *Acoustics for Radio and Television Studios*, London: P. Peregrinus (an I.E.E. Monograph).

Gillett, Charlie

1974   *Making Tracks: The Growth of a Multi-Billion Dollar Industry*, New York: E. P. Dutton.

1970   *The Sound of the City: The Rise of Rock and Roll*, New York: Dell.

Goldberg, Isaac

1930   *Tin Pan Alley: The American Popular Music Racket*, New York: Day.

Goldin, Milton

1969   *The Music Merchants*, Toronto: Macmillan.

Goldstein, Richard

1970   *Goldstein's Greatest Hits*, New York: Prentice-Hall.

1968   *The Poetry of Rock*, New York: Bantam.

Goodman, Nelson

1968   *Languages of Art: An Approach to a Theory of Symbols*, Indianapolis: Bobbs-Merrill. (Especially sections II, IV, V and VI.)

Grana, Cesar

1971   *Fact and Symbol*, New York: Oxford University Press.

Greene, Bob

1974   *The Billion Dollar Baby*, New York: Signet.

Griff, Mason

1960   "The Commercial Artist: A Study of Changing and Consistent Identities," in Maurice R. Stein, et. al., eds., *Identity and Anxiety*, New York: Free Press.

Hall, James B., and Barry Ulanov

1967   *Modern Culture and the Arts*, New York: McGraw-Hill.

Hamill, Katherine

1961   "The Record Business, It's Murder," *Fortune* (May), pp. 149 *ff.*

Hamm, Charles, with Bruno Nettl and Ronald Byrnside

1975   *Contemporary Music and Music Cultures*, Englewood Cliffs: Prentice-Hall.

Hanslick, Eduard

1854   *The Beautiful in Music*. (Reprint of a later edition available, New York: Da Capo.)

Harris, Paul

1968   *When Pirates Ruled the Waves*, London: Impulse Press.

Harrison, Frank L.

1973   *Time, Place and Music: An Anthology of Ethnomusicological Observations c. 1550 to c. 1800*, Amsterdam: Frits Knuf.

1963   *Musicology* (with Mantle Hood and Claude V. Palisca), Englewood Cliffs: Prentice-Hall.

Hart, Philip

1973   *Orpheus in the New World*, New York: Norton.

Harvey, Edward

1967   "Social Change and the Jazz Musician," *Social Forces* 46 (1), p. 34.

Hatch, D. J., and D. R. Watson

1974   "Hearing the Blues—An Essay in the Sociology of Music," *Acta Sociologica* (Copenhagen) 17 (2).

Hauser, Arnold

1951   *The Social History of Art* (3 volumes, translated by Stanley Godman), New York: Vintage.

Hayakawa, S. I.

1955   "Popular Songs vs. the Facts of Life," *A General Review of Semantics* 12 (Winter), pp. 83 *ff.*

Heifetz, M.

1977   *An Empirical Examination of Music Listening as an Autotelic Activity*, PhD dissertation, Chicago: University of Chicago.

Heinsheimer, Hans W.

1969   "Music from the Conglomerates," *Saturday Review* (February 22).

Henry, Jules

1973   *On Sham, Vulnerability and Other Forms of Self-destruction*, London: Allen Lane.

1963   *Culture Against Man*, New York: Random House.

Hesbacher, Peter

1975   "Record Roulette: What Makes It Spin?" (with Robert Downing and David G. Berger), *Journal of Communications*.

1974   "Sound Exposure in Radio: The Misleading Nature of the Playlist," *Popular Music and Society* 3 (Spring), pp. 189 ff.

1973   "Contemporary Popular Music: Directions for Further Research," *Popular Music and Society* 2 (Summer), pp. 297 ff.

Hirsch, Paul

1973   *The Organization of Consumption*, PhD dissertation, Ann Arbor: University of Michigan.

1972   "Processing Fads and Fashions: An Organization Set Analysis of Cultural Industry Systems," *American Journal of Sociology* 77 (January), pp. 639 ff.

1971   "Sociological Approaches to the Pop Music Phenomenon," *American Behavioral Scientist*, pp. 371 ff.

1970   "A Progress Report on an Exploratory Study of Youth Culture and the Popular Music Industry," Ann Arbor: Survey Research Center, University of Michigan.

1969   *The Structure of the Popular Music Industry*, Ann Arbor: Survey Research Center, University of Michigan.

Hodeir, André

1962   *Toward Jazz*, New York: Grove Press.

1956   *Jazz: Its Evolution and Essence*, New York: Grove Press.

Hodges, T. A.

1944   *Wilhelm Dilthey: An Introduction*, London.

Honigsheim, Paul

1973   *Music and Society*, edited by Peter Etzkorn, New York: John Wiley.

Hood, Mantle

1971   *The Ethnomusicologist*, New York: McGraw-Hill.

Horkheimer, Max, and Theodor W. Adorno

1972   (1956) *Aspects of Sociology* (byline reads: The Frankfort Institute for Social Research), Boston: Beacon Press.

Horowitz, Irving Louis

1971   "Rock on the Rocks or Bubblegum Anybody?" *Psychology Today* (January).

Horton, Donald

1957   "The Dialog of Courtship in Popular Songs," *American Journal of Sociology* 63 (May), pp. 569 ff.

Huizinga, Johan

1950   *Homo Ludens*, Boston: Beacon Press.

Hurst, Walter E., and William Storm Hale

1974   *Record Industry Book: Stories, Text, Forms, Contracts*, Hollywood: Seven Arts Press.

Hutchinson, Ann

1961   (1954) *Labanotation*, New York: New Directions.

Jahn, Mike

1976   *How to Make a Hit Record*, Scarsdale: Bradbury Press.

Johnstone, J., and E. Katz

1957   "Youth and Popular Music: A Study in the Sociology of Taste," *American Journal of Sociology* 62 (May).

Kadushin, Charles

1969   "The Professional Self-Concept of Music Students," *American Journal of Sociology* 75 (3), pp. 389 *ff.*

Kaeppler, Adrienne L.

1975   "Polynesian Dance as Airport Art," manuscript in progress, Honolulu: University of Hawaii.

Kamin, Jonathen

1975   "Parallels in the Social Reactions to Jazz and Rock," *The Black Perspective in Music* 3 (3) (Fall).

Kaplan, Max

1955   "Teleopractice: A Symphony Orchestra as It Prepares for a Concert," *Social Forces* 33 (4), p. 352.

Karshner, Roger

1971   *The Music Machine*, Los Angeles: Nash.

Kartomi, Margaret J.

1973   "Music and Trance in Central Java," *Ethnomusicology* 17 (2).

Kaufman, Donald L.

1974   "Woodstock: The Color of Sound," *Journal of Ethnic Studies* 2 (3) (Fall).

Kaufman, Walter

1965   "Rasa, Raga, Ala and Performance Times in North Indian Ragas," *Ethnomusicology* 9 (3), pp. 289 *ff.*

Kavolis, Vytautas

1972   *History on Art's Side: Social Dynamics in Artistic Efflorescences*, Ithaca: Cornell University Press.

1968   *Artistic Expression—A Sociological Analysis*, Ithaca: Cornell University Press.

Kealy, Edward

1974   *The Real Rock Revolution: Sound Mixers, Social Inequality, and the Aesthetics of Popular Music Production*, PhD dissertation in sociology, Evanston: Northwestern University.

Keesing, Hugo A.

1974 "The Pop Message: A Trend Analysis of the Psychological Content of Two Decades of Music," paper presented to Eastern Psychological Society Meetings, Philadelphia.

Keil, Charles

1978 *Tiv Song*, Chicago: University of Chicago Press.

1966 *Urban Blues*, Chicago: University of Chicago Press.

Kooper, Al

1977 *Backstage Passes*, New York: Stein and Day.

Kryter, Karl K.

1970 *The Effects of Noise on Man*, New York: Academic Press.

Kunst, Jaap

1960 *Ethnomusicology*, third edition, The Hague: Martinus Nijhoff. (Includes large bibliography.)

Lastrucci, Carlo L.

1941 "The Professional Dance Musician," *Journal of Musicology* 3 (Winter).

Lawrence, Vera B.

1975 *Music for Patriots, Politicians, and Presidents: Harmonies and Discords of the First 100 Years*, New York: Macmillan.

Laxton, P. B.

1953 "A Gilbertese Song," *Journal of the Polynesian Society* 62.

Leichtentritt, Hugo

1947 *Music, History and Ideas*, Cambridge: Harvard University Press.

Leiter, R. D.

1953 *The Musicians and Petrillo*, New York: Bookman.

Leonard, Neil

1962 *Jazz and the White Americans: The Acceptance of a New Art Form*, Chicago: University of Chicago Press.

Lesure, Francois

1968 *Music and Art in Society*, University Park: Pennsylvania State University Press.

Levine, Faye

1976 *The Culture Barons*, New York: Crowell.

Lippincott, Bruce

1958 "Aspects of the Jam Session," in Ralph Gleason, ed., *Jam Session*, New York: G. P. Putnam's Sons.

Lomax, Alan

1968 *A Staff Report on Cantometrics* (ed.), Washington, D.C.: American Association for the Advancement of Science.

1962 "Song Structure and Social Structure," *Ethnology* 1 (4).

1959 "Folk Song Style," *American Anthropologist* 61 (6).

Mabey, Richard

1969   *The Pop Process*, London: Hutchinson Educational Publications.

Marcus, Greil

1976   *Mystery Train: Images of America in Rock'n'Roll Music*, New York: Dutton.

1969   *Rock Will Stand* (ed.), Boston: Beacon.

Marcuse, Sibyl

1975   *Musical Instruments: A Comprehensive Dictionary*, New York: Norton.

Marks, E. B.

1934   *They All Sang: From Tony Pastor to Rudy Vallee*, New York: Viking.

McPhee, William N.

1966   "When Culture Becomes a Business," in Joseph Berger, Morris Zelditch, Jr., and Bo Anderson, eds., *Sociological Theories in Progress*, New York: Houghton-Mifflin.

Mendolsohn, Harold

1966   *Mass Entertainment*, New Haven: College and University Press.

Merriam, Alan

1964   *The Anthropology of Music*, Evanston: Northwestern University Press.

1960   "The Jazz Community" (with Raymond W. Mack), *Social Forces* 38 (3) (March).

Meyer, Leonard B.

1967   *Music, The Arts, and Ideas*, Chicago: University of Chicago Press.

1958   *Emotion and Meaning in Music*, Chicago: University of Chicago Press.

Meyerson, Rolf, and Elihu Katz

1957   "Notes on a Natural History of Fads," *American Journal of Sociology* 62 (6).

Meyerson, Rolf, William McPhee, and Philip Ennis

1953   *The Disc Jockey: A Study of the Emergence of a New Occupation and Its Influence on Popular Music in America*, New York: Bureau of Applied Social Research, Columbia University.

Monaco, James

1978   *Media Culture* (ed.), New York: Delta.

Montagu, Jeremy, and John Berton

1971   "A Proposed New Classification System for Musical Instruments," *Ethnomusicology* 15 (1).

Mueller, John H.

1951   *The American Symphony Orchestra: A Social History of Musical Taste*, Bloomington: Indiana University Press.

Nanry, Charles

1972   *American Music: From Storyville to Woodstock* (ed.), New Brunswick: Trans-Action.

Nash, Dennison

1957   "The Socialization of an Artist: The American Composer," *Social Forces* 35 (4), p. 307.

1954   *The American Composer: A Study in Social Psychology*, PhD dissertation, Philadelphia: University of Pennsylvania.

Nattiez, Jean Jacques

1975   *Fondements d'une Semiologie de la Musique*, Paris: Union Generale d'Editions.

Nettl, Bruno

1965   *Folk and Traditional Music of the Western Continents*, Englewood Cliffs: Prentice-Hall.

1964   *Theory and Method in Ethnomusicology*, New York: Free Press.

Netzer, Dick

1978   *The Subsidized Muse: Public Support for the Arts in the United States*, New York: Cambridge University Press.

Noebel, David A.

1966a   *Rhythm, Riots and Revolution: An Analysis of the Communist Use of Music—The Communist Master Music Plan*, Tulsa: Christian Crusade Publications.

1966b   *Communism, Hypnotism and the Beatles*, Tulsa: Christian Crusade Publications.

Oliver, Paul

1970   *Savannah Synchopators: African Retentions in the Blues*, New York: Stein and Day.

1969   *The Story of the Blues*, London: Cresset.

1964   *Screening the Blues*, London: Cassell.

1968   *Conversation with the Blues*, London: Cassell.

1963   *The Meaning of the Blues*, New York: Collier Books. (*Blues Fell This Morning*.)

Olsen, Dale A.

1975   "Music-Induced Altered States of Consciousness Among Warao Shamans," *Journal of Latin American Lore* 1 (1).

Ortega y Gasset, José

1968   *The Dehumanization of Art, and Other Essays on Art, Culture, and Literature*, Princeton: Princeton University Press.

Palmer, Tony

1976   *All You Need Is Love*, New York: Viking.

Parrish, Carl

1959   *The Notation of Medieval Music*, New York: W. W. Norton.

Passman, Arnold

1971   *The Deejays*, New York: Macmillan.

Peterson, Richard A.

1973   "The Unnatural History of Rock Festivals: An Instance of Media Facilitation," *Popular Music and Society* 2 (Winter), pp. 1ff.

1972a   "Three Eras in the Manufacture of Popular Song Lyrics," in R. Serge Denisoff and Richard A. Peterson, eds., *The Sounds of Social Change*, Chicago: Rand McNally.

1972b   "A Process Model of the Folk, Pop, and Fine Art Stages of Jazz," in Charles Nanry, ed., *American Music: From Storyville to Woodstock*, New Brunswick: Trans-Action.

1971   "Entrepreneurship in Organizations: Evidence from the Popular Music Industry," (with David G. Berger), *Administrative Science Quarterly* 16 (March), pp. 97 *ff.*

—— and Paul DiMaggio

1975   "From Region to Class: A Test of the Massification Hypothesis," *Social Forces.*

Raynor, Henry

1976   *Music and Society Since 1815*, New York: Schocken.

1972   *A Social History of Music*, New York: Schocken.

Read, Oliver, and Walter L. Welch

1959   *From Tin Foil to Stereo*, Indianapolis: Bobbs-Merrill.

Rich, Alan

1964   *Careers and Opportunities in Music*, New York: Dutton.

Ridgeway, Cecelia, and John M. Roberts

1976   "Urban Popular Music and Interaction: A Semantic Relationship," *Ethnomusicology* 20 (2).

Riesman, David

1950   "Listening to Popular Music," *American Quarterly* 2 (Fall), pp. 359 *ff.*

Roederer, Juan G.

1973   *Introduction to the Physics and Psychophysics of Music*, New York: Springer-Verlag.

Rosenberg, B., and D. M. White

1957   *Mass Culture: The Popular Arts in America* (eds.) Glencoe: Free Press.

Roth, Ernest

1969   *The Business of Music: Reflections of a Music Publisher*, New York: Oxford University Press.

Rumbelow, Allen S.

1969   *Music and Social Groups: An Interactionist Approach to the Sociology of Music*, PhD dissertation, Minneapolis: University of Minnesota.

Sablosky, Irving L.

1969   *American Music*, Chicago: University of Chicago Press.

Sachs, Curt

1965   *The Wellspring of Music*, edited by Jaap Kunst, New York: McGraw-Hill.

1943   *The Rise of Music in the Ancient World, East and West*, New York: W. W. Norton.

1940   *The History of Musical Instruments*, New York: W. W. Norton.

Salem, Mahmoud

1976   *Organizational Survival in the Performing Arts: The Marketing of the Seattle Opera*, New York: Praeger.

Sanders, Clinton R.

1974   "Psyching Out the Crowd: Folk Performers and Their Audiences," *Urban Life and Culture* 3 (3) (October).

Schafer, R. Murray

1977   *The Tuning of the World*, New York: Knopf.

Schueller, Gunther

1968   *The History of Jazz*, New York: Oxford University Press.

Schuessler, Karl F.

1948   "Social Background and Musical Taste," *American Sociological Review* 13 (3), p. 330.

Schutz, Alfred

1964   "Making Music Together: A Study in Social Relationship," *Studies in Social Theory* (volume 2 of *Collected Papers*), The Hague: Martinus Nijhoff.

Seashore, Carl E.

1967   (1938) *Psychology of Music*, New York: Dover.

Seeger, Charles

1957   "Music and Class Structure in the United States," *American Quarterly* 9 (3), p. 281.

Shankman, Ned, and Larry Thompson

1975   *How to Make a Record Deal and Have Your Song Recorded*, Los Angeles: Hasting House.

Shemel, Sidney, and M. William Krasilovsky

1977   *This Business of Music*, revised and enlarged second edition, edited by Paul Ackerman, New York: Billboard.

Silbermann, Alphons

1974   *Art and Society in Comparative Perspective* (ed.), New Brunswick: Trans-Action.

1963   *The Sociology of Music* (translated by Corbet Stewart), London: Routledge and Kegan Paul. (An edition of the International Library of Sociology and Social Reconstruction, founded by Karl Mannheim.)

Simmel, Georg

1955   *Conflict and The Web of Group Affiliations* (translated by Reinhard Bendix), New York: Free Press.

1950   *The Sociology of Georg Simmel* (translated by Kurt Wolff), New York: Free Press.

Slotkin, J. S.

1943   "Jazz and Its Forerunners as an Example of Acculturation," *American Sociological Review* 8 (5) (October).

Southern, Eileen

1971   *Music of Black Americans*, New York: W. W. Norton.

Spiegel, Irwin O., and Jay L. Cooper

1972   *Record and Music Publishing Forms of Agreement in Current Use*, New York: Law Arts.

Spitz, Robert S.

1978   *The Making of a Superstar: Artists and Executives of the Rock Music World*, New York: Anchor.

Stambler, Irwin, and Grelun Landon

1969   *Encyclopedia of Folk, Country, and Western Music*, New York: St. Martin's Press.

Stebbins, R.

1966   "Class, Status, and Power Among Jazz and Commercial Musicians," *Sociological Quarterly* (Spring).

Stokes, Geoffrey

1976   *Star-Making Machinery: The Odyssey of an Album,* Indianapolis: Bobbs-Merrill.

Strunk, Oliver

1950   *Source Readings in Music History: From Classical Antiquity through the Romantic Era*, New York: W. W. Norton.

Supici, Ivo, et. al.

1970   "Sociology in Music: Results and Perspectives of Current Research," in *Report of the Tenth Congress of the International Musicological Society*, University of Ljubljana, p. 405.

Swoboda, Henry

1967   *The American Symphony Orchestra* (ed.), New York: Basic Books.

Taylor, A. J.

1966   "Beatlemania—A Study of Adolescent Enthusiasm," *British Journal of Social and Clinical Psychology* 5 (September), pp. 81 *ff.*

Toffler, Alvin

1973   *The Culture Consumers*, New York: Random House.

Von Hornbostel, Erich M., and Curt Sachs

1914   "Classification of Musical Instruments," *Zeitschrift fur Ethnologie*, Jahrg, Heft 4 u. 5. [Berlin].

Wassen, R. G., et. al.

1914   *Maria Sabina and her Mazatee Mushroom Velada*, New York: Harcourt, Brace, Jovanovich.

Weber, Max

1968   *Economy and Society: An Outline of Interpretive Sociology*, edited by Guenther Roth and Claus Wittich. New York: Bedminster Press.

1958   *The Rational and Social Foundations of Music* (translated and edited by Don Martindale, Johannes Riedel, Gertrude Neuwirth), Carbondale: Southern Illinois Press.

Weber, William

1975   *Music and the Middle Class*, New York: Holmes and Meter.

Weissman, Dick

1979   *The Music Business: Career Opportunities and Self-Defense*, New York: Crown.

Whitcomb, Ian

1972   *After the Ball*, Baltimore: Penguin.

Wilder, Alec

1972   *American Popular Song: The Great Innovators, 1900–1950*, New York: Oxford University Press.

Wilhelm, Sidney, and Gideon Sjobert

1958   "The Social Characteristics of Entertainers," *Social Forces* 37 (1) (October).

Wolf, Johannes

1904   *Geschichte der Mensuralnotation* (3 volumes), Leipzizg: Brietkopf and Gaertel.

Wolfe, Tom

1967   "The First Tycoon of Teen," in *The Kandy-Kolored Tangerine Flake Streamline Baby*, New York: Farrar, Straus, and Giroux.

Yasser, J. A.

1932   *A Theory of Evolving Tonality*, New York: American Library of Musicology.

Index